PRAISE FOR *NANCY WAKE*

'Russell Braddon has written the story of this indomitable woman with skill and understanding, played up the friendship, love, laughter and adventure; and played down the tragedy, the horror, the vulgarity of war.'

— *The Observer*

NANCY WAKE

NANCY WAKE

World War Two's Most Rebellious Spy

RUSSELL BRADDON

Previously published in 1956 by Cassell.

Published by Little A, New York

www.apub.com

Amazon, the Amazon logo, and Little A are trademarks of Amazon.com, Inc.,
or its affiliates.

ISBN-13: 9781542021661
ISBN-10: 1542021669

Cover design by: @blacksheep-uk.com

Printed in the United States of America

NANCY WAKE

AUTHOR'S NOTE

The story that follows is Nancy Wake's and because of that I have asked her to write the next and only important sentence on this page.

'I dedicate this book to everyone in France who helped us, even if it was only by refraining from helping the enemy, for that in itself required courage, but especially I dedicate it to my comrades in the Maquis d'Auvergne.'

PART ONE: NANCY'S WAR BEGINS

1 THE ENEMY ARRIVE

A rebel, always laughing and very, very feminine – that's the best way to describe Nancy Wake. Although one could add that she had the disconcertingly direct stare of an infant child – candid, unhurried and perceptive – and a child's serene brow. Her eyes were hazel ordinarily, but they went green when she cried and blue when she walked outside on a fine day.

As a twelve-year-old she was a brilliant pupil in an Australian high school. Even then she cooked the household meals and often had to clean the house and she didn't like these tasks at all. She ran away from home twice.

At eighteen she was a nurse, cheerful and popular with the inmates, in a country mental hospital.

In her early twenties she began a world tour, supporting herself by freelance journalism, her sales stemming from good looks and personality as much as from an adequate literary talent. She earned enough to live and to keep moving.

When she was twenty-two she took a flat in Paris and, with her first wage packet, bought two wire-haired terriers – one a dog, one a bitch – and these she promptly named Picon and Grenadine, as a compliment to France's drinking habits. She always loved Picon most and it was he who was to live right through the next fantastic seven years of her own life, so that when he died after the War, she wept for days. Friends asked her why. After all, he was only a dog. And she replied, 'If you love dogs you'll know part of the reason. The other part is that when Picon died, the last of my youth died too.' By then, of course, she had spent almost the entire War fighting the Nazis in France; she had become a distinguished Resistance leader; she had earned more decorations than any other British servicewoman; and she had lost her husband to the Gestapo torturers in Marseille. Picon had lived through it all and now he was dead and she felt that the last link with her life as a girl had vanished. So she wept.

But we run ahead of time. When she was twenty-three she was a considerable beauty and had the dubious compliment paid her one evening of being strenuously pursued round and round the Cannes Palm Beach Casino by a wealthy sheik or pasha, she wasn't sure which. Eventually she cooled his ardour by introducing him to her fiancé, Henri Fiocca, a Marseille steel industrialist who was equally as wealthy as the sheik or pasha, whichever he was.

She had first met Henri Fiocca at a party. He was fourteen years older than she, and his partner, on that occasion, was an incredibly beautiful young woman. The next evening, he contrived to be at the same restaurant as Nancy and her friends and his companion was another beautiful woman. Nancy's group moved on to a nightclub and later Fiocca turned up again – this time with a third beautiful woman.

'For heaven's sake,' Nancy exploded, 'how does he do it?'

'He has great charm,' one of her companions pointed out.

'I'm not saying he hasn't,' she replied. 'But all those gorgeous-looking girls. How does he do it?'

Her partner shrugged. 'Henri has many more girls than you have seen,' he assured her.

For weeks it went on. Finally, Nancy, who could not bear not to understand, tackled Fiocca bluntly on the subject.

'How do you get on to so many beautiful girls?'

'They ring me up.'

'They ring you up?'

'Yes,' he sighed. 'Every girl, except the one I want, rings me up.' He looked at her quizzically as he spoke and she, understanding at once what he meant, stared at him very straightly in reply.

'If you want to speak to me on the phone, Fiocca,' she announced finally, '*you* will ring *me* up!'

He did.

He courted her and wooed her and a little while later – despite his enraged family's objections – he announced his engagement to her. Nancy had never known that any man could be so charming and so amusing, or that anyone could mean so much to her. It was early 1939 and they planned to marry in 1940.

Now her life was transformed. From being one of the least affluent journalists in the world, Nancy had become the fiancée of one of the wealthiest men in Marseille. Money had never been of any importance to her, but now she realised that lots of it is more pleasantly unimportant than none.

'Get us an apartment and furnish it,' Fiocca ordered. By June she had obtained the lease of a huge flat in a luxury block on the hill that overlooks all of Marseille and its harbour. The apartment had a bathroom window that looked out over the Old Port. She had even ordered lavish drapes and Persian rugs and a bar for the drawing room. Together, she and Henri chose a huge table and the best monogrammed Sèvres china and crystal glasses for the dining room. Nancy employed servants to look after them when, in the New Year, she would be married. Purring with contentment, she decided that now, at last, the harsh memories of her childhood housekeeping were to be expunged forever. Never again, she thought, need she go without anything.

Meantime, Henri made her life a constant joy. He taught her the best places to eat and thought nothing of driving 150 miles to find the meal he desired for her. That was customary in the wealthy society of those days, but in those matters Fiocca was an expert and a fanatic.

He often took her to Cannes at weekends, where she stayed with a Madame Digard and her daughter Micheline. They swam during the day (this was something she did better than Henri, which pleased her) and went to the casino in the evening.

Although it is only five minutes' walk from the Martinez, where Henri had his suite, to the casino, they always drove the short distance. Henri loathed walking and had a passion for cars, which he drove at appalling speed.

At the casino Nancy found she had no desire to gamble. 'Just not interested,' she told Henri, when he offered her chips and pointed to the green-topped tables with their fringe of fanatical players who plotted every fall of the numbers and then worked out their infallible theories. 'I'd much rather talk to Miracca.'

And so, for hours, she would sip brandy in the bar and talk with Miracca. He was an immaculately dressed *hôtelier*, a director-manager of the Palm Beach Hotel in which the casino was housed. The friend of royalty, of the aristocracy, of the rich and the famous, he had an endless fund of anecdotes which fascinated the journalist in Nancy.

He told her how his wife had once run a fashionable millinery shop in London's Bond Street and sold a dozen hats to a Scottish girl who was then about to be married to the Duke of York – and who later became, as she was at that very moment, Queen Elizabeth of England.

He told her how once he had been assistant manager at the Café Royal in London, after working there for twenty years, starting as a child under Madame Nicol and going each evening to night school. Then he had become manager of Prince's in Piccadilly. He remembered the girl who was later to become George VI's queen coming to Prince's every week. He remembered his bandmaster, Fortoni, composing a special song for her. He remembered the three royal princes coming in regularly for a seven-and-six dinner before the theatre. And he always wondered why the Prince of Wales once called him over and said, 'Miracca. Be a good fellow and put a couple of lemons in my coat pocket, will you? I'm going to the theatre.'

'He still comes *here*,' Nancy had protested. 'Why don't you ask him?'

'No,' said Miracca emphatically, 'I cannot do that.'

Doubtless he was right, Nancy decided, but she knew that if ever she met the Duke of Windsor she would have to ask. Then she wondered why it would be wrong to question a royal duke about the lemons he had once requested to be put in his coat pocket before he went to the theatre. She was a fanatical royalist but she liked to know these things.

'Please,' she urged, 'ask him some time.' The powerfully built Italian, stocky, good-humoured and perfectly groomed, glared at her with stern brown eyes.

'Never,' he replied. Fiocca walked across to them at the bar. 'Your fiancée,' Miracca told him, 'is probably the most beautiful girl here, but she asks me the most difficult questions. How can I do what she asks? It is quite impossible.'

'Of course it is,' Fiocca agreed amiably. 'What do you want him to do?' he asked Nancy. Briefly she told him; briefly her Henri answered her.

'Miracca is a *Grand Ufficiale* of the Italian Crown and a friend of all the kings and queens, and ex-kings and ex-queens, of Europe. He knows best. So now, my dear, shall we drive home?'

As they left, Miracca's eyes followed them good-humouredly. 'A beautiful girl,' he murmured. 'The most beautiful. And he is a wonderful man for her. A most serious businessman. Very rich.' To Miracca there were no higher compliments!

◆　◆　◆

Her future home was now quite ready for occupation, and Nancy found that she had time to spare and nothing much to do in it except listen to the endless café talk of whether or not there would be a war. At night she and Henri could dance or go to the cinema or an occasional concert – though Marseille was not much of a town for concerts – but for the rest of the day it was just society women and talk of the coming war.

Suddenly she conceived a fierce desire to see England again before she married. It was then considered highly fashionable to go to England, to Tring, there to take a three-week slimming course. All the chic Frenchwomen were doing it. So Nancy asked Fiocca would he mind if she went slimming for three weeks. He looked her up and down, found nothing wrong with her figure and then assured her that he didn't mind at all. She left for London in August of 1939.

When she arrived there she found that her booking for the Tring 'cure' had been somehow bungled and that she could not immediately take it. A quick look at the newspapers made her decision simple.

'The war's definitely coming,' she told herself in her cheap back room at the Strand Palace Hotel (she had refused Henri's money for the trip), 'and when war comes we'll all starve anyway, so why start off with three weeks of it at Tring?'

Promptly she wrote and cancelled her course. Equally promptly war broke out and Nancy prepared to return to France. First, though, realising that Fiocca would inevitably be called up into the French army, and anxious to do something to help the Allied war effort herself, she offered her services to the British. In return they could only suggest that she might work in a NAAFI: Navy, Army and Air Force Institutes, an organisation that ran canteens for British service personnel.

'Not at all my cup of tea, thank you,' she replied, abandoning her notions of military service.

Then came a letter from Cannes asking her please, when she returned, would she bring Mme Digard's daughter Micheline back with her? Micheline was a pupil at the convent of St Maur in Weybridge.

Nancy rushed off to Weybridge and found that the Mother Superior was, quite properly, utterly unwilling to allow Micheline to leave for France with anyone until she had direct authority so to do from the girl's parents. For all the Mother Superior knew, Nancy could have been a Nazi spy or a kidnapper.

Time passed whilst word went down to Cannes and then returned to Weybridge and with it passed the last of Nancy's money and her exit permit, which had expired.

Then the Mother Superior received the authority she required from Mme Digard and Nancy received fifty pounds from Fiocca. Now all that was needed were the necessary permits from the British and French passport offices.

At this time thousands of people had the same idea as Nancy – to get out of England and back to France. The queue at the permit office stretched for hundreds of yards, an undisciplined queue of impatient Frenchmen. Each day they received queue numbers so that they could take up their correct positions next morning, and each morning they tried desperately but unavailingly to cheat. Nancy queued for seven days outside the British office and then for three days outside the French office. This done, she collected

Micheline, packed her bags and stumbled gratefully out of her hotel into London's blackout.

The streets were chaotic, with lurching pedestrians and groping cars, and Nancy's trip to the boat-train strained even her sense of humour. Then there was no proper boat for the boat-train – only a car ferry – and before she could get on board even this unpromising craft she had to run the gauntlet of a dozen gloomy officials questioning her sanity, attempting to prevent her departure.

'You really sure you want to go, Miss? You, an Australian girl, to France?'

'You'll be sorry, you know.'

'If you go, you'll never come back. You understand that, don't you?'

'Can't even guarantee you won't be sunk halfway across the Channel.'

'Quite sure you want to go?'

'You'll never get back.'

To that chorus she clambered aboard with Micheline. The Channel crossing was hell. They were completely blacked-out, no one was allowed to smoke, there were numerous submarine alarms – all false – and the whole atmosphere on the car ferry was fraught with the direst fears and restrictions of total war.

And then their blacked-out, zigzagging craft entered the harbour of Boulogne. There, before them, lay war-ridden Europe – every light ablaze, no security whatsoever, the traffic racing briskly! Nancy and Micheline gazed at it a moment, aghast, and then shrieked with laughter.

'Ah,' announced Micheline gravely, when they had controlled their mirth, 'now I know I'm home in France!'

Nancy and Henri married on 30 November 1939 – the Fiocca family still far from reconciled to the advent of an Australian, Protestant daughter-in-law. Then the newly-weds set out to enjoy themselves as much as possible before Henri should be called up to fight.

Fiocca would leave their flat early each morning for work after the maid had brought them tea. Nancy would then remain luxuriously in bed till ten, reading the papers, gossiping with her maid and discussing what they would have for lunch when Henri got home at noon.

'Shall I bring in Picon and Grenadine?' the maid would ask.

'Have they been for their walk?'

'Yes, Madame.'

'And have they . . . ?'

'Yes, Madame, they have!'

'Then bring them in.'

The two dogs would curl up on her bed with her and watch her eat her *pétit dejeuner*. Halfway through this light breakfast she would retire to her bath, boiling hot and quite full. There she would lie, with her big toe against the hot tap, ever ready to increase the temperature, a glass of champagne in one hand, a book in the other and a small slice of toast and caviar by her side. This, not so much because she was addicted to champagne and caviar, as that she was endlessly delighted at being suddenly able to afford them.

Thus, nibbling her toast, sipping from her glass, reading her novel, pausing occasionally to glance out of the bathroom window and gaze upon Marseille – sometimes idly wondering whether any of the Old Port could see her as clearly as she could see it – a pleasant hour passed.

Then she would dress quickly and lunch with Henri. After that, drive into town, where the afternoons were always full. Full with visits to the dress salons, the beauty salons, the hair salons, to restaurants and to cinemas. Buy something, order something, have

11

an egg-pack facial here or a hair wave there; eat cream cakes at the Marquise de Sévigné or drink aperitifs at Basso's or the Hôtel du Louvre.

These were her afternoons each week, every week. Hers was a frivolous, extravagant life. And, as each week passed, it became even more frivolous because every night there were parties – parties to farewell yet another husband off to the Front. Without any compunction Nancy thoroughly enjoyed every minute of it. A more useless woman there cannot have been in the whole of France, she thought.

'It will be my turn soon,' Henri announced cheerfully one night, as they said goodbye to yet another newly drafted warrior.

'Worry about that when it comes,' Nancy declared. 'And when it does, I want to go too.'

'My dear Nanny, what as?'

'An ambulance driver.'

'But you can't drive.'

'You must have me taught.'

'But you have no ambulance. And France has no ambulances either.'

'I know. You must give me one of the firm's trucks. Convert it for me. Then I'll drive it to the Front.'

'But, Nanny, why?'

'Because I want to help.'

'You can help here.'

'Don't be stupid, Henri. Here we help no one.'

'But why do you want to help? War isn't for women.' He paused a moment and then finished lightly. 'How often have I told you how I won the last war for France?' He had served in the First World War for a few months as a boy in 1918. 'Now I will win it again. Have you no confidence in me?'

'Certainly,' she assured him. 'That's why I want to go to the war myself. I'm sick of hearing how *you* won the last one! This one *I* shall win!' Then they both rocked with laughter at her ludicrous notion and Henri felt in such good humour that he promised her a truck and lessons to drive it. When, a little later, he was called up as a second-class soldier and sent to Belfort to fight the Germans, he thought it rather unreasonable of his wife to hold him to his crazy promise, but hold him she did.

A nerve-racked mechanic gave Nancy all her driving lessons in one day. Thereafter, boldly and noisily, she set off for the Rhine. It was January 1940.

It was fashionable at this time for wealthy women to adopt a *filleul de guerre* – a poor soldier to whom food parcels and cigarettes might be sent. Nancy wrote to Henri and asked him to nominate her a *filleul de guerre*. He sent her the names of three fellow privates and from them she chose an ex-tram conductor called Ficetole. She chose Ficetole because he came from Marseille. After that, she regularly sent both Ficetole and his wife and children food parcels.

To drive one's own ambulance was also fashionable in those days of a France that had cheerfully omitted to prepare for the inevitable war by providing enough government ambulances. Nancy's driving, however, was not at all fashionable.

Driving on the right-hand side of the road never came naturally to her. Time after time, as traffic approached, she swerved smartly and instinctively to the left and so pinned the oncoming vehicle to any hedge, fence or wall that happened to be nearby. Passengers in her ambulance (mere civilians, but in the phony war ambulances acted as buses, because all the buses seemed to have been requisitioned and sent elsewhere as ambulances) would protest loudly; the driver of the other vehicle would shriek with rage; pedestrians would hurl in their own fierce denunciations. Placidly Madame Nancy Fiocca would wait for silence. Then she would announce, '*Je*

suis Australienne. En Australie on fait comme ça!' Which statement
the French invariably found so perplexing that the discussion ended
then and there. With a crash of gears, she would lurch off, leaving
a heap of wreckage behind her.

In February the French government decided that the department in which she worked must be evacuated. It was winter and
there was chaos on the roads – a chaos of refugees towards Paris
one way, and of military traffic the other. Nancy made her own
handsome contribution to the chaos by helping with the evacuation. Later she worked, for weeks on end, driving loads of clothing
up to the refugee centres and sorting it out when she had arrived.

Then the Blitz began and with it all semblance of organisation vanished. Nancy just picked up refugees, wounded soldiers,
machine-gunned civilians, anyone at all, and drove them out of
immediate danger. Then she drove back – always ignoring the
police who forbade her to approach the Front any closer – and
loaded up her ambulance again. Her work was made no easier for
her by the facts that blood made her feel sick and death shocked
her profoundly.

Everywhere were dead bodies, bombed-out vehicles, Stukas flying low and machine-gunning – machine-gunning anyone. There
was a bedlam of French refugees, Belgian refugees, Allied soldiers
and fifth columnists disguised as senior French officers and giving
wrong directions . . . Total disorganisation.

Belgium fell, and Nancy realised that she must now get out or
be taken prisoner by the advancing Germans. Taking on a last load
of passengers, she drove off, her face grim and her eyes cold – except
when the bodies of slaughtered children brought tears to them. But
she drove on. This was no fashionable business now. This was a slow,
murderous lurching down roads reeking with the stink of death and
despair, roads hideous with screams and roaring dive-bombers and
machine-guns. This, suddenly, terrifyingly, was defeat.

Nancy was asleep in a small hotel when, on 13 June 1940, Paris fell. Now there was humiliation too. Grief-stricken for France, because at that moment she felt wholly French, she wept all day. Where, she asked herself frantically, was Henri – if he was alive? Heading for Marseille, of course, she realised suddenly. Stupid not to have thought of it before. Into her ambulance again, she headed desperately south.

Twenty kilometres from Nîmes her truck broke down and nothing in her sadly deficient mechanical repertoire would restore it to life. So, without any feeling at all, she abandoned it and started walking. Soon she got a lift, then she walked some more, then another lift. Finally, white-faced and exhausted, she reached Marseille. There she went straight to her father-in-law's home and asked the family for news of Henri. They had no news.

Then France fell and it seemed as if the world must surely end. Again Nancy wept, refusing to leave her room for two days. The shock, the shame, the awful waste of it all – all those helpless bodies dead on the road and at the Front – were too much for her. And still no news of Henri.

But he returned some weeks later and, when he did, he and she retired to their flat. Half of France was now occupied by the Nazis. The other half, the southern half in which they lived, had promised its goodwill and allegiance to the Führer and could be swamped by him at any moment if that promised goodwill should appear to falter. The fleets which the French kept back in their own ports of Toulon and Oran, rather than dispatch to hard-pressed Britain, thus became their last symbol of power and their last weapon for bargaining with Hitler. But not even the continued existence of these superb ships of war could disguise France's humiliation – Germany, the arch enemy, had defeated her. Life seemed completely hopeless and for days on end the Fioccas endured it numbly because the War, for them, was lost and over.

2 THE FIRST STEP

Unoccupied Southern France was now governed from the city of Vichy. The new administration collaborated briskly with the Germans, was hostile towards Britain and was soon to impose its collaborationist policy upon the public by an officious use of its police force, who were to be known, unaffectionately, as the Milice. The Milice were always, thereafter, to be almost as dangerous to any Allied sympathisers as were the Gestapo who supervised them – which supervision was conducted discreetly and unofficially by Nazi commissions who travelled incessantly throughout the southern zone. Rationing, shortages and black marketeering were the other new aspects of life in conquered but Unoccupied France.

Nancy and Henri now set about making the best of a thoroughly bad situation. For Henri life became a case of 'business as usual', and for his wife it became the chore of stocking the house with as many provisions and as much food – tinned or otherwise – as possible. Henri's wealth made this a more feasible operation for her than it was for many other housewives, and by September of 1940 the Fioccas had acquired a hoard of the most varied provisions.

This was not selfishness. The Fioccas spread the net of their generosity wide. Nancy had a flair for talking with anybody and making friends with many of those to whom she talked. All these friends were regularly provided with meals or parcels of food. They ranged from society women to the wife and family of Ficetole, her ex-tram conductor and *filleul de guerre*; from bartenders to Henri's employees.

Every day for months past Nancy had gone black marketeering – buying. In the course of the haggling that always ensued the language thrown at her was often the ripest of Marseille's abuse. Nancy, followed by Picon and Grenadine, with her maid Claire to help carry her purchases, would make her cautious way home and then wait for Henri to return from work. When he did she would repeat a phrase spoken to her while out shopping and ask him the meaning.

Henri would blush a little and then tell her what it meant and also what to reply. She would repeat after him the correct and lurid response in the language of a fishwife, watching him carefully with that child's stare of hers to see that every nasty nuance was exactly right, her brow smooth and serene in spite of the frightful oaths that were ripping from her mouth.

'*Formidable*,' he would comment. Thus she soon held her own in these wordy battles and even grew to be greatly respected by those with whom she traded. Few ladies, so *sympathique* and *bien gentille*, they told one another, could converse with a quarter of her fluency and colour. In short, now that she had added the idiom and bad language of all classes to her already perfect French, she was ready to deal with any situation. It was probably just as well that she did not realise then just how much, later on, she was going to need her knowledge of bad language.

In those summer months of defeat in France and the Blitz in Britain, Nancy amused herself by swimming. Marseille is full of blue-green, rocky swimming holes and to these – now that hairdressers and clothing salons were no longer either fashionable or feasible – she would adjourn for the afternoon, accompanied by Picon and Grenadine.

Picon was Grenadine's faithful husband and Nancy's most loyal friend, but he loathed water in any shape or form. On the other hand, not only did Nancy and Grenadine love swimming but, it must be admitted, Grenadine was not the unswervingly dutiful wife she should have been. So, whilst they lay sunbathing on the rocks, Grenadine would cast shamelessly come-hither looks at other gentlemen dogs in the vicinity, which enraged Picon. And when Nancy swam, Grenadine swam with her. Thereupon, frantic with anxiety, Picon screamed his head off until both his wife and his mistress returned.

In August Grenadine went for a little walk on her own. This was silly of her because meat was short in Marseille and sausage makers were utterly unscrupulous. She vanished and never returned. For a fortnight after she vanished Nancy felt sad for the warm-hearted terrier bitch and Picon fretted inconsolably. For the same period, being a realist, Nancy bought and ate no sausages.

Her birthday came on 30 August and Henri gave her a heavy gold bracelet.

'Henri,' she thanked him, 'it's lovely. And it must weigh at least a quarter of a pound!'

'At least,' he agreed gravely.

She snapped it on to her wrist and went out proudly to shop. Sometime during her morning tour of sources that supplied illicit soap, English cigarettes, toothpaste, salt, fats, sugar and tinned food, a faulty catch on the bracelet broke and her new present was lost. First Grenadine and now her gold bracelet. Fate seemed unkind at that moment.

Glumly she returned to her flat and melted down all the cakes of soap, pouring the fluid into rough moulds, splashing in some of her own perfume to disguise the manufacturer's original scent and then waited for the blocks to set.

'Now let the black-market police try to prove this is illegal soap,' she muttered grimly to herself. That was the kind of deception that became a routine housewifely chore to the women of France. She wandered into her drawing room, poured herself a drink at the bar and called her maid.

'Claire,' she ordered, 'from now on Picon is never to be allowed out alone. Understand?' Claire nodded. 'Now, where,' she continued, 'do you think we can get hold of some meat?' Claire told her of a splendid black-market butcher's shop, so she went to that and eventually became its star customer.

This was to have a dramatic outcome four years later. For the moment, though, the butcher was to be just a good friend and an unfailing source of illegal meat.

And so September 1940 came and passed and October was upon them. By that time their new life had become almost a habit. The Germans, it seemed, really did not mean ever to occupy Southern France, and Britain continued to resist stubbornly in a war the French were certain she must eventually lose. They watched her with mixed emotions – jealousy because she was still free; dislike because they thought she should have done more when France was attacked; vague hopefulness that she might survive and perhaps, a million years hence, even beat the Germans. Mainly, however, they thought only about themselves and how to cope with their altered way of life. The passionate goodwill towards Britain that was felt by both Nancy and Henri was shared by very few others in Marseille. But even Nancy and Henri had slipped into a routine which seemed likely to go on forever and had little bearing on Britain and the battle she fought at that time. They hardly noticed, for example, that Japan had just joined the Axis or that the rich oil wells of Romania had fallen to the Germans.

Nancy had arranged to meet Henri for drinks in the Hotel du Louvre. The main entrance to the Louvre was from Marseille's Canabière, an elaborate marbled porchway which led into a large foyer. Here it was the habit of the Gestapo – thinly disguised as the German commission – to sit and order drinks. They were an arrogant lot and Nancy, preferring never to go near them, always entered the hotel by a back door off the Cours Belsunce. There she would wait for Henri in a small bar behind the foyer, a bar too obscure ever to be used by the haughty Gestapo gentlemen.

On this particular occasion she slipped into the bar as usual, ordered a drink from the waiter, Antoine, and settled down to wait. Only then did she notice that she was not alone. Sitting at the other end of the bar was a good-looking young man, fresh-complexioned and fair. Quickly Nancy glanced at Antoine. He caught her eye, polished a few glasses, replaced a few bottles and then moved casually down to her.

'German?' she whispered.

'I don't know,' he murmured. His doubts made Nancy wonder. Antoine was a Corsican, stocky, dark-haired, broken-nosed. He hated all Germans and seemed infallibly able to sense their presence even before he saw them. Actually, of all the non-French races, Antoine liked only the English. This latter was not entirely altruistic. The English had always been good tourists and his livelihood had depended upon tourism. He had added to his list of hates against the Germans the fact that they had so rudely terminated the English habit of Continental travel.

'He's had a *Boc*,' Antoine told her. 'And he's reading an *English* book!'

'Then he must be a German,' Nancy announced. 'No Englishman would be silly enough to sit here in Marseille, with the lobby full of Germans, and read an English book.'

Antoine nodded, but he did not look convinced. Soon he returned and whispered, 'He hasn't paid for his drink.'

'Do you think he's just waiting to eavesdrop when the place fills up?'

'He would buy another drink while he waited, wouldn't he?'

'Or at least pay for his first,' she agreed. She had a sudden idea. 'Antoine, offer him a drink. I'll pay you for it later.' Antoine spoke to the man, who at once accepted a brandy, raised his glass coolly to the Corsican, drank and then returned his eyes to his novel. At that moment Henri entered.

Drawing him quickly aside Nancy explained the situation. 'He could be a German or he could be a British soldier who's got through from the north,' she concluded. 'Henri, what should we do?'

'I know what you want to do,' he told her, smiling.

'What?'

'Find out,' he replied. 'I'm right, aren't I?'

'Yes,' she admitted. 'If he's a German we should know it, and if he's English then perhaps we can help.'

'All right, my dear,' Henri murmured, 'I shall find out.'

He crossed to the tall, fair stranger and spoke to him. The stranger put down his book and replied calmly. They talked for about five minutes and then Henri returned to Nancy.

'He's a British officer, from Newcastle upon Tyne; he's been interned here in the fortress, along with all the other British stragglers in these parts; he's on parole; he was fed up and he came in here for a drink. Why don't you go and talk to him yourself?'

Delighted to meet a fellow Brit after so many months, Nancy rushed across to him.

'Come on,' she urged, 'let's have a night out.'

They took him to dinner, they laughed, they drank and they had a splendid evening. During the time they spent together Nancy discovered that there were two hundred British officers in the fortress, interned there by the French military authorities. Conditions were poor, food scarce and money non-existent.

'I'll get you a radio,' she promised, 'then you can listen to the BBC. Meet me tomorrow at Basso's,' she proposed, 'and I'll bring you a thousand English cigarettes.' She thought a second and then made the suggestion that was to transform her life.

'We'll go to a shop I know where we can buy food. Can you come out on parole at lunchtime tomorrow?'

'Yes.'

'Then meet me.'

'At Basso's?'

'At Basso's.'

'Till then.' He grinned in farewell and, thanking them profusely, left them. Only when she got home to the flat and talked it all over with Henri did it occur to her that the man could still easily be a German and, if that were the case, that she would then certainly be in trouble. All night long, worried by these doubts, she lay unable to sleep or to decide what to do the next day. But in the morning she made up her mind that, on the chance of the stranger's being English and needing her help, she must take the risk. Armed with a brown-paper package containing a thousand cigarettes, she marched down to Basso's.

'Albert,' she called the barman. He came across to her. 'Put these away for me, will you? I've got a date but it might go wrong. If it does, I don't want a thousand good cigarettes to go with it.' He asked no questions, just stowed her parcel away behind his bar. A few minutes later, Nancy saw her 'date' walking towards the bar from the other side of the road. He was not alone.

With him were two other young men, one of whom sported the largest and silliest moustache Nancy had seen for years. Looking at it she laughed delightedly. 'Give me back my cigarettes, Albert,' she ordered. '*No* German would ever grow a thing like that!'

They came in, introduced themselves, the other two both being fellow officers of her friend's, thanked her profusely for the cigarettes, and then went shopping with her. They bought huge supplies of food and fruit and Nancy paid for all of it. Then they accepted her invitation to come to her flat for dinner that night. And so, casually, unthinkingly, Nancy Fiocca began her career as an active enemy of Hitler and of the Third Reich in Occupied France.

3 DOUBLE LIFE

Nancy shopped heavily that afternoon, buying food for a dinner suitable for three extra guests who were both English and ravenous. Then she walked home, up the long steep hill that led to her flat, cursing the weight of her purchases and petrol rationing and the icy wind which had her teeth chattering and her fingers numb round her parcels.

She let herself into the flat and called Claire.

'We have three guests for dinner,' she explained, pointing at the heap of food on the armchair where she had dropped it. 'Englishmen,' she added casually.

'Pardon, Madame?'

'Englishmen,' Nancy repeated. 'God, this flat's cold. You know, one of the things I find it hardest to forgive the Germans for is no coal for heating. I don't suppose there's any hot water?'

'None, Madame.'

'All right, Claire. You start with the dinner. I'll get into something warmer.'

She went into her room and put on a warmer dress and, over it, a bathrobe. This bathrobe was a lavish affair in blue, yellow and red. On the shapely Madame Fiocca it looked very exotic indeed. Then she returned to the drawing room and poured herself a stiff brandy. She gulped it down in a way that she knew would have horrified her husband but she was nevertheless gratified to feel its warmth creeping through into her hands and feet. She poured herself a second drink and then sat back comfortably to work out just what she was going to do with three interned Englishman for the rest of the War. The doorbell rang, and Claire, appearing miraculously from nowhere, answered it promptly. Nancy's guests had arrived.

As they came into her drawing room and saw her, apparently clad only in a bathrobe and sipping brandy from a large crystal goblet, all three looked anxious. They had been convinced, when first they met her, that she was British. But no Englishwoman would receive male guests dressed only in a negligee. Obviously their hostess was very, very French – and this made them feel like intruders. They grew sheepish and so excessively English that Nancy wondered what on earth was wrong with them.

'Sorry the place is so cold,' she told them. 'No central heating any longer and only one hour's gas for cooking.' They nodded awkwardly and sat around saying very little, waiting for their hostess to make her next move.

'A drink?' she offered. This, they all recognised, was the next move. They accepted her offer and she walked briskly across to the bar, her bathrobe swinging interestingly as she did so.

'Brandy or whisky?' They asked for brandies. Not only must she be French, they decided, she must also be depressingly rich. She passed their drinks across the bar and they drank each other's health. When they had each had two brandies she began to feel warmer. Her guests were then suddenly petrified to observe her in the act of flinging off her negligee – until it was revealed that under her somewhat suggestive gown was an impeccably modest and well-cut dress. They began to laugh.

'What's amusing you?' Nancy demanded, liking nothing better than a joke herself. They gulped heavily and stopped laughing.

'Nothing,' they muttered, embarrassed. Nancy stared at each man in turn; stared thoughtfully and long. She decided that something must be wrong, probably they wanted to go to the lavatory. After all, they had had a long walk in the cold, so she made an excuse to leave them alone.

'I'll get you some coffee,' she announced and walked out to the kitchen. When she returned she found the three men almost crying with laughter.

'Come on,' she ordered them, 'let's have it. What are you all so hysterical about?'

'Well, you see, we thought when we met you that you were British – you know, that we could let you help because you were one of us . . . I mean, all that food and inviting us back here to your flat. But then we saw that bathrobe . . . Well, we thought then you *couldn't* be British. I mean . . .' But they didn't have to finish. By this time Nancy herself was shrieking with laughter.

'We were so glad to see a dress on underneath your dressing gown or whatever it is,' the moustached officer announced. 'Honestly, I mean, you know what French girls are supposed to be like. We didn't even know which one of us you were after!'

'Oh, *all* of you, of course,' Nancy vowed and then they all laughed again. It was not long before Henri returned and, when he did, the joke had to be repeated, so that, for the third time, the flat shook with their mirth. Then they had dinner and got down to the discussion of more serious things.

◆ ◆ ◆

The Englishmen told Nancy that Fort St Jean held two hundred or so officers, all anxious to escape back to England. Naturally, they could not escape whilst actually on parole, but they could organise escape attempts at this time.

For her part Nancy declared that she would be glad to feed and entertain four or five of the two hundred every day of the week, and to provide what food and help she could for the rest who, in the meantime, stayed behind in the fort.

They talked a lot that night, the three Englishmen and Nancy and her husband. Eventually, more than a little drunk, the internees departed – bearing with them the radio Nancy had given them. When they had gone, Nancy noticed that Henri looked worried but he would not tell her what it was that worried him. She decided not to pester him and so they went to bed.

Now it was Henri's turn not to sleep. He was torn by conflicting duties. There was first of all his duty to protect Nancy herself. Although she had a French identity card it revealed, by giving the place of her birth, that she was in fact a British subject in Nazi-conquered Europe, and the Nazis were still very much at war with Britain and the Empire. If Nancy did anything rash she would almost certainly suffer frightful consequences from the Gestapo. On the other hand, precisely because she was British, and even more so because he himself was a passionate admirer of Britain, he felt that he must allow her to do whatever she thought best about the men in Fort St Jean – even if her idea of what she ought to do went as far as he suspected it would.

Next was his duty to his father and mother and family. If Nancy should attract the unwelcome attentions of the Gestapo, he knew very well that those attentions would not be confined to Nancy and himself. The entire Fiocca family and the vast Fiocca business would probably be destroyed.

Finally, as a Frenchman, was it his duty to adopt an attitude of *laissez-faire* towards the Vichy administration (much as he loathed it) since presumably it aimed at protecting France from further horrors at the hands of Germany, or was it his duty to sympathise with any attempt to oppose Vichy and to resume the war in his own country? Whichever way he looked there was some pressing loyalty tugging at his heart to make him look the opposite way. Whatever he did could bring him only recrimination and never any reward. Most painful of all, his strongest instincts pointed the way which his realistic mind told him offered the ghastliest end. The true horror of his situation was finally demonstrated when, in 1943, as he had feared, he fell into the hands of the Gestapo.

This, however, was only the latter end of 1940. Every day now the Fiocca flat was cheerfully invaded by four or five English officers from Fort St Jean and every day they were well fed and provided with cigarettes and soap and other comforts to take back with them to their comrades.

One day a Captain Ian Garrow arrived. He was very tall, strongly built, clean-shaven and good-looking – a Scot of great charm and considerable cunning. When, a little later, contacts were made by escaping officers on the Spanish frontier and in Gibraltar, he created an embryo escape route. And having observed the generous and somewhat reckless way in which Nancy entertained the men from St Jean, he decided then to channel her hospitality and contempt for all Vichy authorities into his own escape-route business.

Nancy did not need much encouragement before she agreed, and so Henri's anguished fears for her, born on the first night when Englishmen had visited their flat, began to materialise. Yet when Nancy now began to ask him for considerable sums of money, to help finance Garrow and his contacts, he gave them – in spite of his own persistent need of liquid capital for business affairs – unfailingly. Thus the Fiocca flat rapidly became a planning centre for the escaping activities of British prisoners of war.

Steadily, after that, the Fioccas' life grew more unorthodox. Civilian contacts in the escape racket were brought along by the British officers and Nancy offered them all exactly the same open-armed welcome that she offered the officers, although she relied implicitly on her intuition and bluntly warned away any whom she did not like.

Christmas Day 1940 arrived. They invited fifteen officers, Antoine (the Corsican waiter) and a number of personal friends to dinner, and she and Henri gave scarves or ties to all the officers except Garrow. He had always been the perfect gentleman and he had constantly declared that he felt naked without a gentleman's hat. For him Nancy bought a brown homburg initialled I. G. G. She had looked forward mischievously to presenting Garrow with this last touch to his sartorial elegance, but to her dismay he was ill on the day and had to remain in the fort, so that Henri had to deliver the hat to him in hospital. Her disappointment at this detail was largely expunged, however, by the noisy success of the party as a whole and by Henri's present to her – another gold bracelet to replace the one she had lost after her birthday.

◆ ◆ ◆

Garrow, who had just escaped from the fort and was in hiding in Marseille, one day asked her if she would be prepared to take messages to other towns, most particularly Cannes and Toulon.

'Of course,' she said.

'It's a bit risky,' he warned.

'What isn't?' she retorted. 'Anyway, why shouldn't I travel to Toulon or Cannes, or anywhere else, if I want to? My papers say I'm a respectable married Frenchwoman. I've got every right to go anywhere I like. The police can look at my identity card till they're blue in the face. They still can't prove that I'm not Madame Fiocca of Marseille. I'll take any message you like.'

So began a regular routine of train journeys from Marseille to Cannes, and from Cannes back to Marseille.

One of their friends, whom Nancy and Henri particularly admired, was a Commander Busch. They had first met him in Marseille shortly after France fell and was divided into two zones. He was a refugee from the northern occupied zone.

Busch's father and grandfather had both been ruined by German wars. He had quickly shown which way his sympathies lay in 1940 by helping the men of Fort St Jean as much as possible.

Early in 1941 he met Nancy casually one day and she told him that she was going to Cannes.

'Will you deliver a package for me at Toulon, on the way, to a man who will be waiting?' Busch asked. Nancy said at once that she would. Later she delivered a second package. Then the Toulon contact asked her to take a package for *him* to Lyon. She agreed and also told him that she had a chalet in Névache that he could use for his men whenever he wished. She told him where the keys were always hidden so that if she was not there the chalet could nevertheless be entered.

When she delivered his package – a suitcase containing a radio transmitter – to the contact at Lyon, she also gave this man her Névache address.

Thus she became a member of a French Resistance organisation as well as of Garrow's group, and to her list of towns to be visited, Toulouse and Nice were now added. Her life was getting strenuous. To make it a little more secure she obtained, from a friendly police officer, new papers which, though they still identified her as Mme Fiocca of Marseille, tactfully omitted to mention the fact that she was also a British subject. Armed with these she went on more and more train trips, always with the greatest confidence. Each trip meant another group of men on its way from one place to another (eventually from France into Spain, then from Spain into Gibraltar, finally from Gibraltar back to England). Each trip meant more evaders on the move, often under Nancy's guidance, but it also meant more people who knew Nancy and so more chance of arrest or betrayal. Right throughout both circuits Nancy was now known as '*L'Australienne de Marseille*', the woman who always laughed. And though this was flattering, and the companionship of her fellow adventurers was agreeable, it was also dangerous.

To combat growing gossip about her activities, Nancy also lived an ostentatiously normal life in Marseille. She continued to meet all her friends, to entertain, to be seen in restaurants and hotels. Very few of even her most intimate friends knew that she led a dual life. Daily the strain of it grew worse – the sheer exhaustion of being two complete people every day when there were only twenty-four hours in a day – and yet still she accepted more and more responsibility on the circuits. Fortunately, she had a volatile temperament and the excitement of the life she led lent her extra energy.

So month succeeded month and the two organisations, which had started life as uncertain, stumbling infants, grew steadily to confident maturity. Meantime, in April 1941, Yugoslavia and Greece were both attacked by Germany and quickly occupied. Two months later Russia was also reeling under the first Nazi blows. Then came the next step in the path that led Nancy Fiocca so spectacularly through the War. She heard the odd story of a man called O'Leary who had just been sent by the Vichy authorities to the prisoner-of-war camp at St Hippolyte-du-Fort.

O'Leary, it seemed, had been arrested by a Vichy patrol on the coast and had told the patrol that he was a French naval officer attempting to escape to England. Promptly, therefore, the Vichy authorities charged him with desertion and sent him to Toulon for a court martial.

Thereupon O'Leary changed his tune. Halfway through the court martial, which was going very badly for him, he declared, 'I am sorry, but I have lied. In actual fact I am a British naval officer.' This plea was accepted and he was interned. The story reached

Marseille and there Garrow at once suspected that a stool pigeon was being planted upon them by the Nazis. From his secret hideout he went to St Hippolyte to inquire. Advice from O'Leary himself convinced him that O'Leary was concerned with espionage and that this fact would, on inquiry, be confirmed by London.

On his return to Marseille, at large but in danger, Garrow cabled London through his usual sources and then, impatiently and suspiciously, awaited London's reply. When it came it surprised everyone. It instructed him not to attempt to send O'Leary back to England via the escape route but, instead, to keep him in France and to accept him as his main assistant in the circuit.

O'Leary's escape from St Hippolyte-du-Fort was then contrived. But no sooner had he broken out of the camp than the alarm sounded. He was passing a convent and already he could hear cars and trucks pursuing him. He entered the convent, told the Mother Superior that he was an escaper and asked for sanctuary.

The Mother Superior said nothing – just opened a door and pushed him in behind it. Then came a pounding on the front door. The Mother Superior walked to it calmly and opened it.

'Have you a strange man in here?' she was asked.

'Gentlemen,' she replied, 'this is a convent!' The searchers departed and O'Leary was safe.

When Nancy heard this story she said at once to Garrow, 'Bring him here. I'd like to meet him.'

4 DISASTER

O'Leary's history – like that of everyone connected with Nancy Fiocca – was a fantastic one. On being captured by the Vichy shore patrol he had claimed first French then British nationality, and it was as a Briton that he had finally been interned. Actually he was Belgian.

He had crossed to Britain after King Leopold's surrender and had there been assigned to HMS *Fidelity*, to assist in clandestine operations along the coast of Occupied Europe.

Fidelity had originally been a French vessel which her commandant had taken to Britain upon the fall of France. There he had offered his own and his ship's services to the Allied cause – his name was Pérès and he spoke perfect English. He declared it also to be the desire of himself and his crew that half of any prize money they might receive should be devoted to a fund for purchasing Spitfires.

Pérès was a little surprised, therefore, when enrolled in the Royal Navy, to find that the rings of rank on his sleeve were different from those of other captains. Suspiciously, he inquired about this discrepancy and was informed that *his* braid rings indicated that he was a reserve officer, not a regular. They were, in fact, wavy rings rather than straight rings and he was Wavy Navy not regular Navy.

'If I am only Wavy Navy, then I and my ship do not fight,' he declared stoutly. 'I must be straight Navy.'

Unavailingly did numerous high officials explain to him that all ships which served as his was serving became Wavy Navy.

'If I am not straight Navy I do not fight,' Pérès repeated stubbornly, and he refused to sail his ship.

The matter was taken to the Admiralty and the Admiralty debated it at length. Eventually, anxious to get the ship into operations, it was agreed that Pérès should be allowed to become straight Navy.

Time, however, had flowed swiftly under the Admiralty's Arch. By then Pérès had found himself a most congenial companion ashore. He greeted the news of his success in this dispute over his naval status with the demand that now he must also be allowed to sail with the lady of his heart on board.

Again it was frantically explained to him that on none of His Majesty's ships were women allowed to sail.

'All right,' answered Pérès logically, 'then I do not go to sea.' After that he made discussion doubly difficult by suddenly forgetting all his English and talking only French.

In the end, complete with straight rings on his cuffs and his mistress on board – herself carrying the rank of an officer – Pérès sailed into the Bay of Biscay. The Belgian who masqueraded under the name of Patrick O'Leary sailed with him.

On a subsequent special landing operation, which it was his task to supervise, O'Leary was cut off from the *Fidelity* which, complete with her captain and her captain's mistress, then had to abandon him in the fading darkness. This was the man Nancy demanded of Garrow that she should meet, the man who was to assist in their circuit. He was brought by Garrow to her flat. She liked him at once and he liked her. Instinctively she realised, however, that he did not like Henri, which upset her. She decided, however, that that was a matter between the two men themselves and so determined, loyally, to continue her endless travels to Cannes, Nîmes, Nice and even Perpignan. She also continued her normal social life in Marseille and her charitable works for people like the Ficetoles.

Calling on Mme Ficetole one day she learnt that Monsieur Ficetole was anxious to start a business of his own as a carrier. He wanted to buy a horse and cart.

'Well, why doesn't he?' demanded Nancy.

'It is the money,' Mme Ficetole explained.

'Then I shall see Henri,' Nancy announced. 'Don't worry about it any more.' Tactfully changing the subject, she asked, 'How are the children?'

Mme Ficetole explained that they were not very well. The food available to a poor family in wartime Marseille was not good for growing children. Nancy made a note to do something about this too and then took her leave.

She went direct to Henri. The result was an interview between Henri and Ficetole. Several days later Ficetole was in the carrying business with a horse and cart. The horse he immediately christened Picon II!

At this time the mother of one of Nancy's closest friends died. As a compliment, she was invited to the lying-in-state of the dead woman.

'Must I go?' she asked Henri.

'Afraid so, my dear,' he told her. 'It would be considered very rude if you didn't.'

'But, Henri, I hate dead things. I'm terrified of them.'

'I know, Nanny, I know,' he reassured her, 'but just walk past the coffin and don't look.'

'Yes,' she agreed doubtfully. 'I suppose I could do that.'

Clad sombrely in black, she and Henri attended their friend's home. There the men lined up in one file, the women in a second, and then each file slowly moved past either side of the body of the old lady who lay pallid in her coffin. With her head turned desperately away from the casket, Nancy shuffled forward.

And then, at the very last second, the bereaved daughter, as a special sign of Nancy's esteemed position in the family, grasped her hand and placed it caressingly on the cheek of the old dead lady.

Nancy trembled, felt her knees melt, heard the pound of blood in her ears and waves of alternate clamminess and chill sweeping over her forehead and was horrified to find herself thinking – almost aloud – 'My God, I'm going to faint.'

Swaying, she forced herself to remain in the file of mourning women. The second she was out of the room she signalled Henri in the file of mourning men and, as he walked swiftly to her, almost sobbed at him, 'Quick, get me outside.' Gently but firmly her husband led her away.

Later, when Henri's own mother died and Nancy had to attend her lying-in-state – not to have done so would have been regarded as insulting in the extreme – Henri carefully kept his wife out of the room until all the rest of the family had paid their last respects. Then he shut the coffin lid firmly and led Nancy quickly past it.

'I feel such an idiot, Henri,' she apologised. 'I don't know, though, I just can't stand any sort of violence. Death always seems violent to me.'

'I know, Nanny,' he murmured. 'Don't worry about it any more.'

Another Christmas passed. It had seen the Japanese, encouraged by Germany's resounding victories over the Soviets, bomb Pearl Harbor, and the United States come into the War in Europe. This meant that, as well as the Fort St Jean internees and (more recently) RAF aircrew, there were now American aviators to be shuttled along the escape circuit. The Milice and the German and Italian commissions consequently redoubled their efforts to check all unauthorised movements and black marketeering. But the circuit carried on undeterred and evaders in increasing numbers continued to cross the Pyrenees and eventually to return to England.

Garrow's career (in jeopardy ever since he had escaped from Fort St Jean and gone into hiding) now came to an abrupt conclusion. He was arrested by the police and tried and sentenced to ten years' imprisonment in Meauzac concentration camp. First, though, he was to serve three months' solitary confinement in Fort St Nicolas in Marseille. It thus became O'Leary's task to take over command of the circuit from Garrow.

For the first two months O'Leary had to go north to organise contacts, and during that time Nancy still worked in Marseille. Then O'Leary returned and arrived suddenly at Henri's flat. It was about ten minutes before noon when he appeared at the door. Nancy let him in, offered him a drink, told him Henri would be home any minute for lunch and then asked him why he had come.

'I'm afraid I need money again,' he said.

'Will you ask him for it yourself, please, Pat?' Nancy asked him. 'I've collected more from him already than I should have done. He seems to have so many people to look after. But if you ask him, he'll give it to you. He likes you.'

'All right,' O'Leary replied. 'I'll ask him. I'm sorry we all call on him so often.' He and Nancy stared at one another as he spoke. She noticed the penetrating quality of his eyes and the curious flecks in their dark blueness; but she continued to stare so that he became disconcerted by the dispassionate candour of her gaze, and was glad when her eyes, still staring at him, suddenly lost their thoughtfulness and went blank. O'Leary then knew that in future, if he wanted financial support from the Fioccas, he would have to respect Henri more. He had understood from Nancy's stare that at last she was telling him that he must no longer take her husband's generosity for granted. A few minutes later Henri arrived home and he and O'Leary started talking earnestly together.

Watching them, Nancy felt a twinge of foreboding. O'Leary was a young man of about thirty, with sparse blond hair; tallish and authoritative. Henri was tall, strongly built, heavy, elegant, humorous and suave. They made an oddly contrasting pair. Finally, Henri took out his wallet and passed the other man a wad of notes. O'Leary, whom he had always liked, had now also won his confidence. His wife sighed heavily then as she realised that, though O'Leary accepted the money, neither the confidence nor the liking were returned by the Belgian.

In the midst of all her other activities Nancy, having just received a letter from Garrow in Fort St Nicolas, decided to add another and much more dangerous project to her list.

Garrow had written that after three months' solitary confinement he was very emaciated and consequently anxious about the outcome of his ten years' sentence. Nancy determined to visit him in the fort, to find out how he was, to feed him and eventually – if possible – to organise his escape.

Before lunch she had dispatched the letter which was to be the basis of all her future actions in this affair. *Mon cher cousin,* she addressed Garrow, *as the daughter of your mother's sister, I am most sorry to hear of your condition and will try to obtain permission to visit you.*

Knowing that all letters to Garrow would be censored before he received them, she felt confident that the authorities would draw the conclusion she desired from this odd and mendacious epistle. They would decide that Mme Fiocca's mother had had a sister who married a Briton and produced a son. Thus, Ian Garrow, the Scot, and Mme Fiocca, the Frenchwoman, would be first cousins!

When Henri arrived home for lunch he took Nancy to task. 'You've heard from Garrow, haven't you?'

'Yes, how did you know?'

'I saw his letter in the box this morning as I left for work. Recognised his writing on the envelope.'

'He's ill in Fort St Nicolas.'

'Nanny, I forbid you to try to see him.'

For some minutes Nancy did not reply. She knew exactly why Henri forbade her to see Garrow and she knew also that, in many ways, he was perfectly correct to do so. Her position grew daily more vulnerable. As an Australian working under the noses of the Milice and the Gestapo, to contact Garrow now, even as his ficti- tious first cousin, would hardly improve matters. Also, Henri and his own family were being irrevocably compromised by her activi- ties if ever they should be uncovered.

Nevertheless, there was the matter of her own conscience to be considered. France may have been defeated but Britain had not – and Nancy now felt very British. France may have been occupied but her soul had not – and, in this respect, Nancy also felt fanati- cally French. It was a matter upon which everyone had to take his own decision and there could be no other loyalties once the deci- sion was made.

'Henri,' she murmured, 'Garrow is ill. If anyone, even a dog, were in his position, I'd feel I had to do something about it. You might as well know that I've already sent him a letter making out that we're first cousins. He is my oldest aunt's son! If that works with the fort authorities, I intend on seeing him and doing everything I can to help.'

'Is that your final answer?' Henri asked quietly.

'Yes.'

'Then we shan't discuss it any more,' he concluded. 'I disapprove completely but you may count on me for anything you need. Now – where shall we go for dinner?'

It was not only Henri who was alarmed by Nancy's determination to help Garrow. To O'Leary her blatant pose as the cousin of a jailed Englishman seemed most dangerous. Furthermore, he disapproved strongly of the work she was doing with the Toulon group of French Resistance workers. And so, for some time after this the British organisation – convinced that she was leading too dangerous a life – kept clear of her.

She visited the fort three times a week as soon as permission had been granted for her to do so. She actually saw Garrow on her first visit and on two other occasions. To see him, however, was not her purpose: the main object of her visits was to take him food and to cheer him up by making him realise that he was not forgotten. Every day, when she did not actually visit the fort, she wrote to him – a thing that Henri found difficult to understand.

'You don't love him, Nancy,' he protested. 'How can you write to him so often?'

'Because I know how much letters, no matter who they were from, would mean to me if I were in his position,' she retorted.

He put his arm round her shoulder affectionately. 'You're a very kind creature,' he told her. 'Sometimes I think I'm not good enough for you. You go on writing your letters.'

The man in the next cell to Garrow, a Frenchman called Frank Arnal, was that week acquitted on his appeal against a similar sentence to Garrow's. He was released and came to see Nancy and promptly resumed his Resistance work.

Arnal encouraged Nancy from two points of view. First of all because he had appealed against his sentence and been released – if he had succeeded, why shouldn't Garrow? Secondly, because he had told Nancy that there was a guard at the Meauzac concentration camp (where Garrow would be sent if his appeal failed) who could be bribed so that eventually an escape should be possible. It had already been contrived once, Arnal told her, so there was no reason why it should not be contrived again.

O'Leary thereupon undertook to find a good counsel for Garrow's defence in his coming appeal. At the same time Nancy decided, as a special bolster to Garrow's morale, to send to him regular consignments of Scotch whisky.

She cultivated a hotelier known to have a stock of Scotch and she visited him every day. On each of her subsequent visits to the fort she would deliver, in her food parcel, a bottle of hair tonic or cough mixture or patent medicine. Every single bottle arrived intact and it was never suspected that none of these bottles was what it purported to be.

But then, to Nancy's great disappointment, Garrow lost his appeal. She made inquiries and found that the counsel whom O'Leary had hired for Garrow had not even troubled to appear on behalf of his client. Very angrily she went to see O'Leary and told him exactly what she thought of his lawyer. Having put him at a marked moral disadvantage by this furious and justifiable outburst she then made her offer.

'If I do all the preliminary work,' she demanded, 'will you get him away later on?'

O'Leary nodded.

'Out of France?' she persisted.

'Out of France,' he promised. So the breach with O'Leary's group was healed.

◆ ◆ ◆

At this time Nancy at last decided that it was no longer fair to Henri, with his business and family responsibilities, to have so many visitors, many of them now active enemies of Germany, coming into his home. For one thing, the flat opposite was owned by a Vichy commissaire and the commissaire was watching them much too closely. Accordingly, she asked Henri for the money to lease another flat well away from their home – a flat which O'Leary and the organisation could then use as their sole rendezvous.

Blissfully married, she had to pretend to the estate agent, who knew her well, that she now had a lover which made a second apartment necessary. Full of Gallic understanding, he made one available to her. Henri was highly amused at the deception.

Every day after that she ordered two gallons of milk (and meat and vegetables and bread in similar quantities) for this flat alone. She hired a maid to clean it and to deliver the food. She herself went to the flat only twice after she leased it. As Garrow's 'cousin' she was too conspicuous; and as a member of the Toulon group she was sometimes not even welcome. Henceforth all the planning for O'Leary's group was done at this apartment.

Nancy naturally took extraordinary care that as few other people as possible should know for what purpose the flat was used – the woman who had the apartment beneath it, for one. On the stairs one day, on Nancy's second and final visit to the place, this woman stopped her.

'Madame Fiocca, I have been worried about you,' she said. 'You have bad colic, yes?' Nancy was about to deny the colic strenuously when the extraordinary nature of the question suddenly made her cautious.

'How very kind of you to concern yourself,' she replied. 'How did you know?'

'Because your cistern goes twenty times a night,' the good woman told her. 'Every night, when I hear your cistern, I think to myself, that poor girl . . .'

Nancy suppressed the temptation to laugh. 'Don't worry any more, my dear,' she reassured the other woman, 'today I have been much better!'

Then she rushed upstairs and burst into the flat.

Half humorously, half angrily she rebuked the men inside. 'How often have I told you lot *not* to pull the chain unless it's absolutely necessary?' she demanded. 'Thanks to all of you, and your exaggerated sense of hygiene, *I* have been saddled with a terrible bout of colic.' The men looked puzzled and crestfallen. Very clearly she explained to them what she meant, and with considerable authority she concluded, '*You* should know as well as I do that we're all in too deep to draw attention to ourselves. In future, more security and less lavatory flushing.'

◆ ◆ ◆

When they had married, Henri had given Nancy a chalet near Névache. She and a friend, Mme Marques, chose this moment in the fine summer of 1942 to visit the chalet to buy a black-market piglet and to give the two Ficetole children a holiday in the country.

The piglet, Nancy arranged, would be fed by a neighbouring farmer and when it had reached full growth would be shared equally between them. A small piglet could easily become a 300-pound pig. That would mean 150 pounds of pork, bacon and ham each. And in hungry France it was well worth the money spent on the piglet and the train and bus fares all the way to Névache to get 150 pounds of pork.

The day the two women and the fattened Ficetole children were preparing to return to Marseille, three Frenchmen arrived, all of them in trouble with the Vichy police. They had been sent to the chalet by Nancy's contact in Toulon. Until arrangements were made to get them away again, Nancy would have to stay on at the chalet to look after them. She did so cheerfully, confining her three hunted guests to the upstairs rooms.

The next morning, she went down to the village to gossip and so find out casually about Milice checking points and other matters of esoteric interest to people such as herself. In the course of this gossiping the village teenagers complained to her that nowadays they could never dance because the authorities – acting on German orders – forbade all public assemblies. And a public assembly was any group of more than three people.

'You can't dance with only three people,' they grumbled, 'and the police won't let us use any hall around here.'

'I'll tell you what,' suggested Nancy, always anxious to undermine authority. 'Why don't all of you come each night to my chalet? There are no police for miles around up there and I've got a gramophone with lots of dance records.'

Thereafter there were illegal *refracteurs* upstairs and illegal dancers downstairs for night after night at Nancy's chalet. The Ficetole children loved it. And each morning Nancy and Mme Marques would go down on their knees and scrub all the dancers' heel marks off the white wooden floor – using much elbow grease and steel wool – so that no trace of these activities should ever remain to be seen by the suspicious eyes of either Milice or Gestapo.

Then the messages came that dispatched Nancy's three 'guests' on the next step of their journey, so she cancelled that evening's dance and she and her young friends and Mme Marques – with the fair promise of a pig fully grown by Christmas – returned innocently to Marseille.

◆ ◆ ◆

Receiving the news that Garrow was to be taken by train that afternoon from the fort to the prison camp at Meauzac, Nancy and Henri decided to cheer him up by seeing him off at the station.

They had been waiting only a few minutes when Garrow – looking ill but cheerful, and still wearing his smart felt hat – appeared. Nancy and her husband at once displayed the most extravagant affection for him. Chattering gaily to him as he was hustled into the train, making themselves as difficult as possible to the guards, they watched him take his seat and, as the train drew out of the station, they waved with outrageous ostentation. Eventually the carriage vanished from sight.

'That was good,' declared Henri in great satisfaction. 'Now he knows that he still has friends.'

'And when he gets out of Meauzac,' Nancy thought rebelliously to herself, 'he'll know it even better.' Feeling very confident of this, she armed herself that night with a false identity card, stating that she was Mlle Lucienne Carrier, and took the train to Nice.

There she took delivery of three American aviators whom she escorted across France to Perpignan. She left them knowing that within seventy-two hours they would be free in Spain. She herself returned to Marseille and became Mme Fiocca again. Though she was to revert to being Mlle Carrier on many subsequent occasions, she was for the moment concerned most with her status as Nancy Fiocca, first cousin to Captain Ian Garrow.

5 THE RESCUE

In early November 1942 the worst fate that the southern zone of France could imagine befell her. Savage and frightened by unprecedented Allied successes in North Africa and Egypt, and urged to do so by the traitor, Laval, the Nazis marched into Unoccupied France.

Their aim was to seize the French fleet that lay in Toulon, to fortify the Mediterranean coast against any further attempts at Allied landings, like the August one at Dieppe, and to operate from its ports with their own supply craft and U-boats. Last but not least, they wanted to wipe out the various subversive organisations that flourished in the South.

This was the time when Nancy chose to travel every weekend between Marseille and Meauzac – a phoney Frenchwoman blatantly sympathising with her phoney Scottish cousin, who was himself serving a ten-year sentence for illicit operations – and this was also the time that the Gestapo first began to talk among themselves of 'The White Mouse'. The White Mouse was Mme Fiocca!

Fortunately, Mme Fiocca was quite as unaware of these discussions as were the Gestapo of her real identity. She did know, however, that train checks and controls must soon grow tighter and the risks she ran larger. Nevertheless, she continued to visit Meauzac regularly.

Nor were train checks and controls the only danger confronting a Resistance worker at that time. More and more people were coming to need the help of patriots like Nancy: people of three types.

There were first of all *evaders*. They were Allied personnel, mainly airmen, who, having been shot down, had so far escaped capture and were trying to get out of France and back to Britain.

Next there were *escapers*. These were men who, having already been imprisoned or interned, had escaped from their confinement and were now trying to reach Spain and safety.

Finally, there were *refracteurs*. They were simply people who were in trouble with Vichy or German authority because they had broken an Occupation rule. They might merely be women who had been prosecuted for buying black-market food for their hungry families; or they might be Jews who (frantically avoiding the Nazis' net that would scoop them into the ovens of Buchenwald) had illegally obtained for themselves a Christian identity card rather than that marked fatally 'Jew'; or they might be any one of a dozen categories in between these two.

These were the people for whom escape organisations worked. But the work could not be done without money. In fact, the amount of money required to run the organisation was now becoming enormous. And because these were the days before such activities were financed from London, it became necessary to raise contributions from sympathisers in France itself.

Accordingly, members of the organisation would call on selected Frenchmen and ask them for donations.

'Look,' they would say, 'I know you can't just accept my word for it that this money will be spent the way I've told you, so you listen in to the BBC each night when the personal messages come over. One night you'll hear "*Message for Eileen . . . The cow jumped over the moon*", or any other message you choose. That will prove my bona fides and it will mean that the British government will guarantee your loan to us and pay it back at the end of the War.'

If these terms were accepted, the circuit member would then take the message agreed upon by the potential donor to a courier, who delivered it to a wireless operator, who sent it to London. From there the BBC would transmit that agreed personal message; and the Frenchman would then – perhaps – make his contribution. Or perhaps, if the organisation had not chosen him well, he would talk about the unusual suggestion that had been made to him and how he had refused it. More than anything else, this need to raise their own money (conversely, London's inability to provide it) was the cause of the mass arrests by the Gestapo that were to come later. Raising money bred risks. And O'Leary needed lots of money.

Henri Fiocca himself, for example, gave more than £6,000 to the movement, as well as a personal allowance to Nancy of £25 a day, £20 at least of which was spent on subversive work and only £5 on household requirements. Garrow's rescue was a typical case of the expenses incurred. The key move in Garrow's rescue was to be the payment of a bribe of 500,000 francs to one of the camp guardians.

How to contact this guardian was the difficulty. That was why Nancy, taking the bull by the horns, had decided to visit Meauzac every weekend armed with food parcels, arriving on Saturday afternoon and leaving on Sunday afternoon. Having made herself thoroughly conspicuous by taking parcels to Garrow so often, she felt sure that the corrupt guardian would eventually make an opportunity to contact her.

For weeks nothing happened. Then, one Saturday afternoon a uniformed man flashed past her on a bicycle and a note, wrapped round a stone, thudded to the ground near her feet. At last her plan had worked. Looking quickly in all directions to see that no one was watching, she stooped down, picked up the message, unfolded and read it.

'Oh no,' she muttered to herself. 'This gets more like E. Phillips Oppenheim every day.'

The note read melodramatically: *Meet me at midnight on the bridge at La Linde.* And the more she thought about this cryptic little billet-doux, the angrier Nancy grew.

'How the hell will I know who he is? All I've seen is his back,' she snarled to herself. '"Meet me on the bridge," he says. Of course curfew doesn't matter! "Meet me at midnight," he says, when curfew's at ten thirty.' So she grumbled her way back to her room.

But by midnight, slipping through the shadows, evading gendarmes and all other passers-by who might arrest her or report her for breaking curfew, she was on the bridge at La Linde. And she waited there until 2.30 in the morning without the guardian ever turning up. Furiously she slunk her way back to bed and the next day took a train to Toulon.

Travelling home from there that afternoon she found herself in a first-class compartment with two companions. One was a little French soldier, still in uniform, and the second was a German officer. Nancy, who had spent the morning in Toulon arranging all sorts of plans of which the Gestapo would certainly have disapproved, now felt full of righteous indignation at the German's presence.

On the lapel of her costume she wore an insignia given to her by the touring Australian Rugby team of 1938 – a kangaroo. She removed her overcoat and thrust her bosom aggressively at the German officer, flaunting the unmistakably British insignia. He took no notice. The better to make her point, she dragged a Penguin book, printed in English, out of her large handbag, and ostentatiously read it. Still he took no notice. Nancy, conscious of the complete 'authenticity' of her forged French identity papers, felt gloriously secure, but disappointed that her studied rudeness had made no obvious impact on the Nazi officer.

Then the ticket collector came to their compartment. Stolidly he examined the German's ticket and Nancy's ticket and passed them back. But he declared that the little French soldier must leave.

'This is a first-class compartment. You have only a third-class ticket.'

'But all the third-class carriages are full,' the soldier protested. 'Here there are plenty of seats.'

'That doesn't matter,' the collector told him. 'You cannot travel in this compartment with a third-class ticket.' Thereupon Madame Fiocca, full of outraged fury, fell upon him.

'How dare you,' she demanded, 'as a Frenchman, tell one of your own countrymen to go when you leave this German gentleman sitting here in peace?' Confident that the German would understand every word she said, but equally confident that her behaviour was no more than that of a normally high-spirited and patriotic Frenchwoman, she elaborated considerably about the outrageous hardships endured by decent French soldiers since France had fallen. Finally, she finished her speech. 'And if you won't let this man stay in here on his ticket, when there are no seats in the third class, then I personally shall pay the difference in the fares so that you cannot throw him out.'

With the inspector dumbly shaking his head, she then passed over a handful of franc notes and the little soldier stayed where he was. They smiled at one another and then both scowled at the German. Ten minutes later he got up and moved to another compartment. In high satisfaction Nancy finished the journey to Marseille – until she remembered her long and fruitless wait for the guardian the night before. Then she grew angry again.

Arnal called on her at her flat immediately after she got home. 'He gave me a rendezvous,' Nancy stormed without any explanation, 'and then he didn't turn up.'

'The guardian?' Arnal guessed tentatively.

'The guardian,' she snapped. 'From midnight till two-thirty I wait on his accursed bridge. I break curfew. I walk miles. I freeze to death. And then he doesn't even turn up.'

With difficulty Arnal soothed her. 'And what now?' he asked finally.

'I'll go back next weekend, of course.'

So the following Saturday saw Mme Fiocca sitting stolidly in the train to Meauzac, beautifully dressed as always and hatless as Frenchwomen usually were in those days. As soon as she reached Meauzac she walked to her favourite bistro and ordered a drink.

A guardian sauntered over to her.

'Haven't I seen you here before?' he asked.

'Probably.'

'Haven't I seen you at the camp too?'

'You could have. I've been there, often.'

'You visit the English captain, Garrow, don't you?'

'Yes. He is my cousin. My mother's sister's son, you understand? I take him food parcels.'

'That is what I had heard, Madame.' He grinned. Cautiously he peered round the bistro and then whispered to her, 'Five hundred thousand francs and a policeman's uniform.'

Five hundred thousand francs, at the rate of exchange in those days, was more than £2,500.[1] Nancy had known that this would be the figure, though, and she now showed no dismay.

'How much deposit?' she demanded.

'A hundred thousand.'

---

1   Approximately £80,000 in 2020.

'Give you fifty.'

'Now?'

'I can't now. I've only got ten thousand on me.'

'I must have the fifty thousand now,' he insisted.

'This evening,' Nancy stalled him calmly.

'All right,' he said. 'This evening. Here.'

Nancy then rang Henri long distance to their home and said enigmatically, 'Henri, I've come to Meauzac without any money. Could you telegraph me forty thousand francs this afternoon?' That was £200.[2] As tonelessly as she had asked for the money, Henri replied, 'At once.'

The postal service of France was one organisation in the country that had always functioned perfectly. Wars and occupations never made any difference to its efficiency. By late afternoon Nancy had cashed Henri's telegraphed order for 40,000 francs. In the evening she gave the guardian his full 50,000 deposit.

'You'll get the rest, plus the gendarme's uniform, next weekend,' she promised.

The next day, when she visited the camp, she was led not to Garrow's cell but to the office of the commandant.

'Madame,' he announced brusquely. 'I am informed that you have just received a large amount of money from Marseille. Why?'

'Me?' she exclaimed. 'A *large* amount of money? I have received no large amounts of money, I assure you.' She registered polite but bewildered astonishment at the very suggestion.

'The Post Office have told me, Mme Fiocca,' he shouted, 'that yesterday afternoon you received forty thousand francs by telegram. That is a very large sum. Why was it sent to you? Why?'

Giving him the benefit of her longest and coldest stare, Nancy then registered disdain.

---

2   Approximately £6,500 in 2020.

'Monsieur le Commandant,' she explained, 'perhaps to you forty thousand francs is a lot of money! I don't know. But to me, I assure you, it is nothing . . . pin money in fact.'

'Pin money? Nothing?' he gulped.

'Nothing at all,' she declared. 'I needed it for drinks at the bistro!'

Utterly overwhelmed, as much by his own sense of snobbishness as by Nancy's arrogance, the commandant capitulated. Quickly she pressed home her advantage. 'Now, mon Commandant, if you have nothing further to say, I should like to see my cousin.'

'Of course, Madame,' he agreed. He called a guard. 'Take this visitor to Garrow,' he ordered. Looking him straight in the eye, she corrected him.

'To my cousin, the *Captain* Garrow,' she insisted quietly.

No sooner was she alone with Garrow than she hissed, 'Next weekend. The money and the uniform. It's all settled.'

When she left the camp that afternoon she went straight to the Post Office and then complained to its staff, with the greatest possible indignation, about the shameful breach of confidence of which they had been guilty when they had informed the commandant of her telegraphed money order. Before she had finished everyone in Meauzac knew the story and Nancy herself was almost convinced that she was telling the truth.

On the way back from Meauzac to Marseille she stopped at Toulouse and met O'Leary. She told him about the uniform. He replied that he would get one made, but said that first he wished to discuss the details of the escape plan with the guardian. He therefore agreed to travel to Meauzac with Nancy the following weekend and arranged to meet her in Marseille mid-week.

The following week was a busy one. First of all, the Vichy authorities organised a well-attended anti-British demonstration at which some arrived to participate, others, like Nancy and Henri, to jeer. Very quickly Henri was locked in sarcastic argument with one of the Vichyites.

'*Eh bien*,' the Vichy man concluded his diatribe, 'look what these accursed English did to our Joan of Arc – burnt her! Always they are the same.'

'True, true,' Henri agreed placidly. 'It's a great pity. If they hadn't burnt her, doubtless she would be able to save France today!' The Vichy protagonist gave him a furious glance and then abruptly moved elsewhere to continue his demonstration.

Then, on 27 November, during the same week, the Germans attempted to seize the French fleet in Toulon. In spite of Laval, and Laval sympathisers among the commanders of the fleet, patriotic French sailors suddenly rallied against the proposed coup and successfully scuttled one battleship, two battle-cruisers, seven cruisers, twenty-nine destroyers and torpedo boats and sixteen submarines. The reaction of the Germans to this act of superb defiance was naturally a bitter one. Angrily they began to scour the countryside and towns for saboteurs and Resistance workers and this meant that Garrow's rescue, planned for Saturday week, was going to be a tricky business.

When O'Leary met Nancy in Marseille, they agreed that, since no one at Meauzac knew Henri, O'Leary should travel to Meauzac as Nancy's husband. O'Leary provided himself with false papers to this effect and so, whilst Nancy later talked with Garrow inside the camp, O'Leary talked with the guardian at the bistro.

The guardian told him that unfortunately all the uniforms of the camp police had been changed because of an escape recently executed by the same method. O'Leary took details of the new uniform and promised that it would be delivered the following Saturday. Then he and Nancy left.

Next weekend Nancy did *not* visit Garrow – but the uniform was delivered to the guardian in the village as agreed and then he smuggled it into the camp and hid it in a lavatory. He also gratefully accepted the balance of his bribe from O'Leary's organisation.

Thus, whilst Nancy was deliberately conspicuous in Marseille, Garrow, many miles away at Meauzac, slipped into a lavatory, changed into a beautifully fitting gendarme's uniform and attached himself boldly to the old guard as it was relieved by the new, and was marched out of the camp.

The only danger point was the main gate. There he had to pass a sentry who should know both the faces and the correct number of the old guard quite well. Garrow covered his face with his handkerchief and compelled himself to saunter out of the gate. There was no challenge.

With his nerves screaming at him to run, he had to continue walking slowly down the road away from the camp. He turned a bend in the road and there saw the car that O'Leary, through Nancy, had promised would be waiting for him. He was driven to Toulouse, given a few weeks to fatten up and strengthen his legs for the long walk that lay ahead and then he was passed from hand to hand into Spain along the escape route he had once himself largely controlled. In quite a short time he was back in England. Thus Nancy's bargain with O'Leary had been honoured, on both sides, to the full. She celebrated this successful outcome of her plans by making five more trips in two weeks as Lucienne Cartier and so adding twenty more triumphant escapes to her already impressive total.

6 THE WHITE MOUSE

Garrow escaped from Meauzac on 8 December 1942, and for a few days after that Nancy, since Marseille was littered with Gestapo agents, made frequent appearances as the harmless socialite wife of Henri Fiocca.

She was cleaning up in her flat when a gendarme knocked on the door. He told her that Captain Garrow had escaped from his concentration camp and he watched Nancy's reaction to this news very closely.

'Has he?' she demanded, half amazed, half enthusiastic, which was not at all what the gendarme had expected.

'You look very pleased, Mme Fiocca,' he accused.

'Pleased!' she exclaimed. 'I'm delighted! Wouldn't you be if *your* cousin had just escaped?'

This entirely disconcerted the gendarme. 'I suppose I would,' he had to agree.

'Good,' she announced. 'Let me give you a drink.'

After the gendarme, suitably refreshed and considerably puzzled, had left, Nancy rang Henri at his office.

'Do you know what?' she shouted excitedly at him. 'A very charming gendarme has just called in to tell me that my cousin Garrow has escaped from Meauzac.'

'No!' exploded Henri, registering supreme astonishment.

'Yes,' his wife assured him. 'Au revoir for now, dearest.'

'Au revoir.' Whereupon they hung up.

'So if any of you Gestapo apes are tapping my wires,' Nancy muttered to herself, 'just put that conversation in your pipes and smoke it!' The instinct to cover every dangerous track with innocent and obvious footprints had long since become second nature to her. The moment she had seen the gendarme at her door she had known why he was there. Instantly she had realised that the only *innocent* thing to do was to look delighted and then to ring up her husband to tell him the wonderful news. This was the kind of subtle mental reflex – an unfailing ability to convince herself of her own innocence in any situation – that was to save her life many times in the next two years.

Perhaps it was the Garrow affair that developed this talent of hers to perfection. Certainly she was to use it again very shortly.

Christmas was approaching and Nancy decided that pork would be an excellent idea for a Christmas dinner with all their friends. She accordingly bought herself a new ski suit and headed off boldly by train and bus to Névache – to her chalet and, she hoped, a fully grown piglet.

The 'piglet' exceeded all her finest expectations. It had become a huge porker, weighing more than 300 pounds. Ruthlessly Nancy ordered its immediate execution and division into two. Before this task could be carried out, however, four Resistance men crept into the chalet with her, having been sent on to her by the French organisation at Toulon.

She was about to take the bus from Névache to Briançon, complete with a huge suitcase full of pig weighing well over 100 pounds, with her four 'friends' as company, when news arrived in the village that the Germans were planning to block all the roads to Briançon that day and to check all traffic.

The villagers, who knew all about Mme Fiocca's pig, assumed that the Germans were hunting her only on charges of black marketeering. Since they approved whole-heartedly of black marketeering, they helped her to persuade the bus driver to depart from Briançon hours before the scheduled time, so that he would pass the crossroads at which the Germans planned to check all traffic before the Germans even got there.

Nancy herself had had word, though, that the Germans were setting a trap not for black marketeers, nor even for the four men in her care, but for herself alone. They were looking for a woman, a strange woman, whom they styled 'The White Mouse'.

She therefore made a quick decision. The half pig and her four charges would go by bus to Briançon. Even if the Germans arrived at the crossroads in time to check the bus – which was very improbable since it was leaving early – they would be looking only for a woman. Men and pigs would be all right. She herself would ski from Névache to the Briançon side of the crossroads and would pick up the bus there, beyond the checkpoint.

She set off herself at once by ski and, on a long cross-country run, managed safely to bypass the crossroads. Soon the bus came lumbering along and she climbed inside. The Germans arrived at the crossroads a mile behind them some time later. They caught no one. The mystery of The White Mouse remained unsolved.

Just before they arrived at the terminus, Nancy, with her four evaders and the pig, got off the bus and caught a taxi to the station at Veynes, rather than go to the obvious one at Briançon. Briançon station was being heavily controlled at the time and, had they gone there, they would all certainly have been trapped.

At Veynes, the four evaders being now well on their way, they split up, agreeing to rendezvous outside the station at Marseille, where Henri would have sent a truck. Nancy, still in her ski suit, boarded the Grenoble-Marseille express, and the taxi driver lifted her enormously heavy suitcase up on to the luggage rack for her.

For some time she travelled alone and without too much anxiety. Then the train stopped at Aix-en-Provence and she was no longer alone: she was, in fact, sharing her compartment with a very obvious German in plain clothes. As there was a German headquarters at Aix-en-Provence, she had very few doubts that he belonged to one of the Nazi services. And at Marseille she heard there was a curfew.

Overhead was almost 200 pounds of illegal pork; behind her, in the train somewhere, were four men she had helped escape; in the valley near Briançon a special raiding party were looking for her. This, she decided, was as pretty a kettle of fish as ever she'd been in. But what would an innocent woman do? First, look completely disinterested in the young gentleman opposite; second, never even think of whether he might be Gestapo or not since, to a legitimate traveller, it could not matter one way or the other; third, forget the danger of Marseille's curfew.

Convinced now that she was just an ordinary traveller, she gazed placidly out of the carriage window. The German found her calm good looks soothing and attractive. Like most of his compatriots in France, he was lonely for decent company.

'It's very cold, isn't it?' he commented. His French was perfect. Perhaps he was not a German, she thought. She decided to test him by her answer.

'Well, we French people don't have the fuel any longer to heat our trains like you do yours in Germany,' she stated mildly. 'That's why,' she lied, 'I always travel in these skiing clothes.' He did not deny her observation about German trains. So he *was* a German. Instead he chose to talk about her skiing clothes.

'They suit you.' He smiled. She smiled back. She decided then that he would help her with her bag at Marseille. The young

German flirted and Nancy did not discourage him. He asked if he could see her again in Marseille and she said 'of course' and made a date.

They rattled into Marseille station. Nancy looked out along the platform and, as the train clanked to a halt, saw that it was stiff with German police, French police, black-market police and customs officials. She began to pull at the handle of her huge suitcase.

'Allow me,' the German said, as she had intended he should.

'Thank you,' she agreed. He reached up, tugged at the case and looked faintly astonished at the way it moved only a few inches forward on the luggage rack.

'If it's too heavy for you,' Nancy told him, 'leave it for me!' After that, of course, nothing would stop the young German from carrying her suitcase. Lurching heavily, he followed her on to and along the platform. He listed noticeably to starboard.

'The way you are carrying my bag the police will think it's full of black-market stuff,' Nancy complained. 'You'll get me into trouble. *Faites comme ça.* Swing it like this,' she ordered . . . and mimed someone carrying the lightest of handbags.

With a heroic effort he straightened his back and shoulders and walked erect.

'*Bon, bon,*' Nancy commended. '*C'est bien comme ça.*'

At the barrier only the customs stopped them. They wanted to look inside the suitcase. Nancy knew, though, that no German officer could possibly allow himself to be caught carrying contraband – or even risk being caught. And she was certain that the German officer now knew as well as she did that contraband was exactly what he was carrying. Arrogantly he produced a Gestapo card for the customs officer and walked through the barrier, the bag unopened.

When she had promised him faithfully that she would meet him later that week, he eventually agreed to leave her.

'Thank you for carrying my bag,' she said.

'Delighted,' he told her and smiled broadly. Then he walked away and Nancy sighed at the thought of his disappointment when she would fail to turn up at her date with him in three days' time.

Her four evaders joined her the moment he had gone.

'Who was that?'

'Gestapo,' she answered curtly.

'But he carried your bag.'

'Well, you didn't think *I* was going to, when there was a willing man around, did you?' she retorted. 'The cursed thing weighs a ton! And this curfew has stopped Henri coming along to help me. Now you lot hang around.'

Soon she learnt why the station was so cluttered with police and soldiers. Someone had blown up something and the Germans were after blood. They had imposed an early curfew and were 'controlling' everything. So it was no use expecting Henri or anyone else to meet her and help with the pig, or with the four men. What to do?

After much brain-racking she remembered Carlin at the nearby Hotel Terminus. Carlin was Ficetole's brother-in-law. Carlin was contacted and came to the station. He helped carry the suitcase and he led all five of them by dark back streets to the rear entrance of a hotel requisitioned entirely for German officers. These officers would arrive on the 6 a.m. express next morning. He guided them through the basement kitchens and up the servants' staircases. He showed them into an empty room and invited them, all five of them, to lie crossways under, not on, the bed.

At 5.30 a.m. – half an hour before the Germans were due to arrive – a friend of Carlin's collected them and led them out through the same staircases and kitchens and into the back streets again. The four escapers thanked Nancy and left her to travel on to Toulon, where she had given them another contact. Then Henri's truck arrived and drove her home with the pig.

Nancy, a Cordon Bleu cook, now made piles of pork savouries and pâté. She prepared all the pork and threw a series of parties, which were invariably given on a Friday.

The bath was the reason for this. The ham and the gammon portion of the pig's carcass was in the bath being cured. This process took forty days of constant turning in strong brine. After forty days it had to be hung in cheesecloth until it was dry. So, for forty days, the bath was almost always full of brine and pig.

But this was not the hardship it might seem. Because of German restrictions there was no central heating in the flat and the hot-water system worked only once a week, on Fridays. So, on Fridays, the salted carcass would be taken out of the bath and laid tenderly on newspapers in the hall. Then as many of the Fiocca circle as possible would be invited to the flat. They would each have a glorious hot bath and, after that, a delicious meal of the pâté and savouries that Nancy had baked. As the meal began, Henri would carry the pig back into the bathroom and again lay it gently in its cradle of brine.

Other friends, who had also acquired illegal foodstuffs, reciprocated; and so began what Nancy always regarded as the warmest, friendliest time of her life in Marseille. Black-market restaurants, haunted by the Gestapo, had become too dangerous to patronise so, instead, people shared their hoards of food in the comparative safety of their own homes. Parcels of cured ham were dispatched all over Marseille when Nancy's pig had eventually spent its full term in her bath and dried out in cheesecloth. She particularly looked after the Ficetole family.

Walking home with Henri and two of her friends one night, after just such a meal with another friend, all four of them were depressed by the fact that they had to make their way by foot. Petrol rationing had immobilised their cars and taxis were the province mainly of the Germans. They came to the long, steep hill that led up to their home.

'This is almost enough to take the edge off all that lovely food I've had,' Nancy complained.

'This is the worst atrocity the Germans ever committed,' confirmed her husband, who hated walking as much as ever.

Every step of the way they complained. Then, not quite halfway up the hill, about fifty yards ahead of them, they noticed a black Mercedes Benz and, standing round it, a group of officers in Gestapo uniform. Nancy was ahead of the other two, who were lagging lazily. Panting, she reached the Mercedes just as the last officer was climbing inside.

'No, this is too much,' she said facetiously as he looked round at her.

'What is?' the German demanded.

'All you lucky men in that lovely car, and I'm walking.'

The German looked at her in amusement and then suggested gallantly, 'Perhaps Mademoiselle would like us to drive her home?'

'Of course,' she accepted promptly. And so, to their horror, Henri and his two friends saw Mme Fiocca roar off in the dreaded black limousine of the Gestapo. Frantically they ran all the way back to Henri's apartment block and ascended to the flat. Henri fumbled with the key as he tried to open his front door, his hands trembling with nervousness. But eventually the door yielded and they burst inside. There, placidly helping herself to a drink, they saw Nancy.

She turned round and grinned mischievously. 'Much quicker than walking,' she told them. 'Easier too!' Then she began to laugh helplessly.

'Oh dear,' she choked, 'if only you could have seen your faces when I drove off in that car.'

This escapade with the German officers and the Mercedes Benz was not just a gallant piece of bravado peculiar to Nancy. It was characteristic of the majority of loyal Frenchwomen at that time. They were at once objects of envy and despair to the Germans.

The conquerors poured into garrison towns all over Southern France from November 1942 until January 1943. By that time they had occupied the entire zone very securely. Then the officers brought down their wives or acquired low-class mistresses; and for these women the German officers had only one ambition – that they should attain French chic.

So, noticing that all the Frenchwomen went hatless, the officers' women also stopped wearing hats. Immediately the Frenchwomen started wearing hats again. But they made it impossible for the officers' women to copy their example because the hats they wore all sported a green feather. The green feather symbolised a green bean and 'the green beans' – *les haricots verts* – were what the French had nicknamed the Germans! For any woman in Marseille to wear any hat at all after that was to fling subtle insult at the Reich. The officers' women had to remain hatless.

But the Frenchwomen did not stop there. When the officers' women obtained the best French stockings, the local women went stockingless. When their rivals also went stockingless, the Frenchwomen took to wearing revolting knitted stockings in which they still contrived to look chic. At this the opposition gave up the unequal struggle and victory went to the conquered.

It was a woman's war they started fighting now, these daughters of France. They were quick to sense that peculiar quality of loneliness which afflicts all soldiers away from home. They managed to make the Germans feel lonelier than any other army has ever felt before. Also they had the capacity to taunt like navvies, to be even more arrogant than the Nazis themselves and – if the need arose – to kill quite ruthlessly.

Theirs was an attitude of magnificent defiance and convinced superiority. They were frivolous, cunning, hostile, courageous and utterly lacking in any discretion. They were acutely conscious of recent German defeats in Africa and at Stalingrad and took no pains at all to disguise their pleasure in those defeats, and, in four years of living with them, many of their characteristics seemed to have rubbed off on to Nancy Fiocca.

Hitherto all the Gestapo attempts to capture The White Mouse had been directed from Paris alone. Now both the Paris Gestapo and the Marseille Gestapo were operating in Marseille and looking for her. Fortunately, however, as so often happened in Nazi organisations, there was inter-departmental jealousy. The Paris and Marseille Gestapos did not cooperate. Each wished to bring off her capture alone. So far, then, neither had succeeded, but recently, sensing that all was not entirely well, Nancy had been lying low.

For three days, for example, she had heard strange clickings whenever she spoke on her telephone and often the phone had rung, only to go dead when she answered it.

It was all very mysterious – and ominous. So finally she forced herself to sit down and take stock of her position. The Vichy commissaire who lived opposite her flat; the camp commander she had crossed at the time of the bribing of Garrow's guard; the authorities at Fort St Nicolas who had read her letters to Garrow and checked all her visits; the Gestapo roadblock planned to catch 'a woman' outside Briançon; the Gestapo officer with whom she had travelled by train – who had carried her suitcase full of pig, and whom she had failed to meet as she had promised.

Yes, it all added up. Particularly now, with this business of the telephone. She was under suspicion. Briskly she stood up. She'd call

Henri. But no, she couldn't call Henri; the phone was tapped. Visit him at his office, then? No, it would be better if she did nothing unusual, just kept to her normal daily routine. That being the case, it was time for her to call in at the bistro opposite her flat.

She and the proprietor (who was one of her best contacts) talked cheerfully for a few moments until there was no one else around them. The proprietor then lowered his voice and murmured, 'Some odd-looking people have been asking questions about you.'

'What about?' Nancy asked softly.

'The gendarme who saw you at your flat after Captain Garrow escaped is the trouble. And I think you're being followed.'

'Thanks for the warning,' she said quietly. Someone else came into the bar and stood close by. 'Some cigarettes,' she asked loudly.

'Sorry, Madame, we have no cigarettes.'

'No one nowadays has any cigarettes,' she complained. 'Ah, well. Goodbye,' and so she walked home.

As soon as Henri returned she made him sit down and then sat close to him.

'Henri,' she said, 'I think someone is watching me.'

He looked at her carefully before he answered. Then he said quietly, 'Then we must get you out of Marseille, Nanny.'

This was a solution that had not occurred to her.

'Do you think so?' she asked. 'I don't know what to do. Don't you think perhaps I could just lie low for a while?'

Henri was now emphatic. 'No. No, I do not think so. It's not safe. You must leave. I tell you what. I'll get in touch with O'Leary. Somehow we must get you out of France. You've done too much. More than your share.'

'Don't be silly, Henri,' she retorted. 'You know I won't leave you.'

'It would be better,' he said reasonably. 'And later, perhaps, I could join you.'

'In England?'

'In England,' he promised.

'Now that,' she murmured, 'would be just marvellous.'

'Good, then, it's agreed. So now I'll get in touch with O'Leary. Before you know where you are, you'll be over in London.'

PART TWO: INTERLUDE

7 ARRESTED

The decision having been taken, everyone now worked swiftly to put it into effect, but dangerous though her situation was, Nancy was still in the mood to take risks.

'I'm going to send on all my clothes,' she announced to her startled husband.

'Send them on?' he repeated in astonishment. 'Where?'

'Spain,' she answered. 'Via Cook's! I'll send them addressed to "Nancy Wake, c/o Cook's, Madrid". No one here knows that I'm Nancy Wake. As far as the Germans are concerned, I'm Nancy Fiocca, and I am French.'

'But, Nanny, it's such a risk. Someone at Cook's is bound to know who you were before we married. Someone will inform on you.'

'No, they won't, Henri. Anyway, they're such beautiful clothes. All bought for me by you. And if they stay here either the Boche will get them or the moths will eat them. And you can hardly bring them out with you when you come!'

Finally, far from convinced, he agreed. The clothes were packed into large trunks and labelled as planned. Ficetole was to call with his cart (drawn by the horse, Picon II) and take the trunk to Cook's Travel Agency in Marseille after Nancy had left the town.

'Nanny,' Henri said, 'you know that if anything happens to me there's plenty for you in your safety deposit box here in Marseille, don't you?'

'I'm not in the least concerned about money,' said Nancy. 'Just you follow me to England as soon as possible.'

'I will,' he lied cheerfully, 'but just you remember the money.' Indeed, she was well provided for. In the deposit box, in gold, notes, securities and shares, there was a fortune worth about £60,000[3] and Henri's box contained an equal amount which would also be hers if he died.

Picon was Nancy's next problem. He always hated her to go away and he always fretted whenever he saw her packing. Consequently, Claire was sent out on long walks with the little terrier whenever such packing had to be done. And when, eventually, Henri would follow her out of France, Nancy had arranged that the dog would be looked after by friends.

In spite of all her cunning, though, when the last moment came Picon knew. He looked at her miserably with brown swimming eyes and he followed her frantically from room to room, never allowing her out of his sight. Unable to bear the deceit any longer, and terrified anyhow that she would break down when she had to say goodbye to him, Nancy dispatched him on yet another walk with Claire.

Then she took a hurried farewell of Henri. 'See you in England,' she said. He stroked her black hair, kissed her damp eyes and repeated his lie. 'In England, Nanny. It won't be long. Here's some money and take care.' She stuffed the wad of notes inside her bra, smiled wanly, kissed him again and so left for Toulouse – there to lie up until the circuit was ready to receive her and put her on her way to the Spanish frontier, Gibraltar and finally London.

---

3   Approximately £2 million in 2020.

In Toulouse she stayed, as ordered, at the Hôtel de Paris, which was run by a Mme Montgelard who not only worked with the organisation but was also the least security-minded woman in the whole of France. Mme Montgelard revelled in sheltering both German soldiery and Allied evaders simultaneously under her roof. Although this terrified her friends, it apparently added piquancy to her own life.

Whilst she waited at Toulouse, Nancy also worked. She did several trips as a courier for O'Leary, carrying money and bread tickets to Perpignan near the Spanish frontier. Everything nowadays had to be delivered by hand and Nancy saw nothing wrong in acting as a postman herself at this crucial time in her career. Until her third trip.

On that trip, as she was returning to Toulouse, the train was suddenly stopped and everyone in it was arrested and bundled into trucks. Nancy's truck was halted by traffic in one of the squares in Toulouse so she promptly leapt out with several others and ran. Blindly she bolted down the first street that offered escape, but fate was against her. A mob of students had been demonstrating in another part of the town and their demonstration had been broken up. They too had bolted. Fleeing students came one way, fleeing train passengers another. They collided, could not move or pass one another and were almost all recaptured by the two pursuing forces. Nancy herself was knocked heavily to the ground and when she stood up found herself facing a rifle. Meekly she went to jail.

Soon she was being interrogated by the Vichy police, an ordeal she had anticipated with no pleasure at all since she had no valid reason for being on any train between Perpignan and Toulouse. However, since they had discovered her identity card and found out that she was Mme Fiocca of Marseille, she decided that that should be the crux – and almost the entirety – of her story.

'I've been on a business trip with my husband,' she declared. 'No, I haven't the faintest idea where we were going to stay in Toulouse. I leave all those arrangements to him.'

'Where is your husband now, Mme Fiocca?'

'I haven't the faintest idea. We had a terrible argument in the train and he left the compartment. Then the train was halted and I haven't seen him since.'

'Do you really expect us to believe that?'

'I don't care whether you believe it or not. It's the truth and I have nothing more to say.'

'But how do you explain the fact that your husband is not here? After all, everyone who was on the train has been brought here.'

'Not everyone,' Nancy answered with some relish. 'Quite a few got away in the square . . . My husband must have been among them.'

She was put in a cell on her own and there, in privacy at last, she admitted to herself that things looked black. She was called out for another interrogation.

'Mme Fiocca,' the commandant said, 'we do not believe your story. In fact, we know that you do not come from Marseille at all, but from Lourdes, and that actually you are a prostitute.'

'If you check in Marseille you will find that I am well known there,' Nancy retorted aggressively, 'and not as a prostitute.'

'We have checked Marseille,' the interrogator replied, 'and they know of no Mme Fiocca.' Nancy knew then that she did not have a chance. If they were prepared to lie about Marseille, then obviously they intended to frame her; and if they intended framing her then they must already have a charge in mind. The whole thing was hopeless – which being the case she determined that henceforth she would say nothing.

A so-called chief of the Lourdes prostitute police appeared and calmly identified her as one of the street girls of that city. Nancy snorted with rage but refused to speak. What was the point? She had never been to Lourdes in her life.

Soon the nature of the offence they wished to pin on her was made apparent. A film featuring the tenor, Tino Rossi, had been showing in Toulouse. Someone had blown up the cinema (obviously not approving of the alleged pro-Fascist sympathies of Tino Rossi). The Vichy police wished to convict Nancy as the person responsible.

For four days they alternately beat her up and questioned her, trying to make her confess to this crime or to admit where she had planned to stay in Toulouse. Knowing exactly what would happen to Mme Montgelard if she mentioned the Hôtel de Paris, Nancy said nothing.

'Obviously you are a saboteur because your papers are false,' the interrogator snarled. Nancy, knowing her identity as Mme Fiocca to be completely genuine, ignored him and was struck across the face for her insolence.

'You must be guilty or you would talk,' he shouted. Still she remained silent, so he hit her again.

Then she did speak. 'Look,' she said, 'if you want to frame me, frame me. Send me to your labour camp. But stop asking silly questions and knocking me about. You call yourself a Frenchman – you're worse than the Boche.'

Somewhat subdued, the man now took a different line. 'Whom did you see on the train?' he asked. Nancy invented the most nondescript travellers possible and then described them with loving detail. France must have held at least ten million people who looked exactly like those she mentioned now.

'What class did you travel?'

'First, of course. What other would I travel?'

'Ladies don't travel first class without a hat. You wear no hat and you are a prostitute.'

'My friend,' she snapped briskly. 'How much do you earn a month? Almost nothing. You wouldn't know how a lady dresses or what she does. I shall say no more.'

Although they again beat her up, she did not say any more. She became sullen and they eventually realised that they were wasting their time questioning her further. They put her in a cell with a woman who *was* a prostitute and left her there till morning. She had no bed and nothing to eat or drink.

In the morning she was dragged into the corridor and told to sit on the floor until the interrogator was again ready for her. Completely resigned to her fate now, numb and indifferent, she leant against the wall. And then, suddenly, standing between two policemen, she was electrified to see O'Leary. Electrified and appalled. 'So,' she thought, 'someone's talked and they've got the lot.'

O'Leary, to her complete astonishment, smiled at her brightly. She ignored him. 'The idiot,' she fumed to herself. 'I get myself bashed up for days on end because I won't admit knowing anyone round here and *he* comes in and gives me away smartly by grinning at me.'

O'Leary went into the office and stayed there some time. Wearily Nancy wondered how badly he would be tortured. Later, however, he emerged quite unscathed and had the gall to smile directly at her again. Furiously she cut him dead.

A moment or two later he disengaged himself from the two policemen who accompanied him and walked down the corridor to where she sat. Grinning at her cheerfully, he hissed out of the corner of his mouth, 'Smile at me, you fool. You're supposed to be my mistress!'

Completely bewildered, Nancy gave him a brilliantly false white-toothed smile which looked almost as sick as she felt.

He left her and returned some time later with a covered dish on which there was a steaming hot meal.

'Don't worry,' he whispered. 'Françoise sends her love.'

Unable to understand anything any longer, Nancy contented herself with eating an excellent meal.

When she had finished, she was called into the office of the Commissaire of Police. He ticked her off soundly for having lied to him and then, to her utter astonishment, said, 'Now go', whereupon she was handed into O'Leary's charge and he led her calmly out of the jail and into the street.

◆ ◆ ◆

Standing in the road, not fifty yards from the jail, she then dragged the truth out of the fair-haired Belgian. This is what happened.

Word reached the circuit three days after Nancy was caught that she had admitted nothing, betrayed no one and told a story which was meaningless. Nevertheless, some of the circuit had still wanted to break up and go under cover.

'Nancy won't talk,' O'Leary had said from the beginning. 'We'll wait.' And when the news had reached them of her stubborn silence he had declared, 'That settles it. We stay here. And what's more, if it's possible, we'll get Nancy out.'

Quickly O'Leary worked out the details. Then, masquerading as a Frenchman, and a member of the Milice, he sallied boldly into the jail and demanded to be taken into the commissaire's office. There he told the commissaire that Nancy was Mme Fiocca and that he was her lover. The reason why she had refused to talk, he explained, was to protect him, O'Leary, from the rage of her husband. They had had an assignation, he and Mme Fiocca, in Toulouse.

Knowing that portion of O'Leary's story which stated that Nancy was Mme Fiocca of Marseille to be true (even though he had himself earlier denied it), the commissaire at once accepted as authentic the whole of this beautifully Gallic situation. O'Leary was not going to leave it at that though.

'Monsieur,' he said, producing the false papers which declared him to be a member of the Milice, 'I am a personal friend of Monsieur Laval's and I know that he would appreciate it very much if you did not inconvenience Madame Fiocca any further.' The mention of the name of the arch-tyrant of Vichy convinced the commissaire still further, but he was officially minded enough to seize on this very feature of O'Leary's story as one upon which he could safely check and so cover himself against the responsibility of releasing Nancy.

'If you will just wait whilst I ring Monsieur Laval's office and confirm what you say, I shall be happy to release Madame,' he offered at once. O'Leary's answer was furious.

'You cannot ring Monsieur Laval,' he stormed, 'because Monsieur Laval has gone to Paris and will not be back for weeks.' He had ascertained this invaluable fact before he invented his story. 'And I hope you do not doubt the word of a friend of Monsieur Laval, because, if you do, you will find that things will go very badly with you indeed.'

There was a lot more that he was prepared to say but it was unnecessary. Convinced of the truth of O'Leary's outrageous story, and terrified by the mention of Laval's non-existent friendship with this man, the commissaire had at once promised to release Nancy.

Nancy was momentarily stunned by the sheer audacity of the action. 'You shouldn't have done it, Pat,' she said. 'Thank you, my dear, but you should never have done it.'

'I decide that,' he replied seriously. 'And if you hadn't been worth it to us, I shouldn't have worried.'

'Well,' she declared simply, 'someday I might know how to thank you. Right now I can't think of a single thing.'

Silently they walked along the road together, then suddenly Nancy halted.

'Pat,' she exploded, 'they've still got my papers.'

'Doesn't matter. We'll make you a better set.' He grinned.

'I don't care about that,' she shouted. 'But they now say I'm innocent so they should have given me back my papers. Let's go back and get them – it's the principle of the thing!'

With the utmost difficulty O'Leary managed to persuade her to forget her principles and not to go storming back into the jail from which she had so recently escaped, but instead to return with him to the hiding place he had prepared for her.

Nancy was taken to the flat of the Françoise who had cooked the hot meal she had just eaten in jail and whose love O'Leary had sent her.

Françoise Dissard was about sixty years old, wonderfully ugly, wore her grey hair in two uncompromising plaits over her head, sported old-fashioned clothes and spent all her time raging at the Boche.

She was the spinster aunt of a young man who languished in a POW camp in Germany; this nephew and her cat were her two chief passions in life. She spent hours each week preserving food and then actually canning it for her nephew. Amazed at her skill, Nancy would watch the old lady (round-shouldered, a cigarette in a bamboo holder always clenched between her broken teeth) as she plodded round her shambles of a flat with a soldering iron in her hand and tin after tin of food to be sealed.

As far as Nancy could see, Françoise never slept. When she was not cooking she was soldering, or drinking the blackest of black coffee, or slanging the Germans – her eyes glinting with hatred through her glasses – or stroking her cat and lighting another cigarette. A very indomitable old lady was Françoise.

In the next few weeks Nancy made five unsuccessful attempts to cross into Spain but a series of inexplicable arrests foiled her on each occasion by breaking up the circuit and sending both contacts and guides to ground. After each attempt Nancy would return to Françoise's flat and sleep on the floor whilst fresh plans were laid.

The sixth attempt was delayed for three days whilst Françoise engineered the escape of ten men – American and Canadian servicemen, a big man from Nîmes called Gaston and one of the guards himself – from a nearby jail.

The guard, who was to join the escape, was provided with a bottle of doped wine. This was administered to the jail commissaire, who soon passed out. The cells were unlocked by the guard, who had all the required keys. He then handed the keys to Gaston whilst he himself coolly and confidently took command of the actual break-out from the jail.

All went well with the escape and the ten men duly arrived at Françoise's flat. For three days, whilst Toulouse seethed with search parties, the men lay low in the flat. Nancy spent the time washing their clothes, which were prison soiled and had been badly muddied in the break-out as well, so that their next move could at least be attempted in respectable dress. Also she had to persuade Gaston to surrender the huge jail key which he insisted on keeping as a souvenir.

Reluctantly he handed it over and Nancy then flung it into the river. Gaston, wanted for the fact that he had been caught assisting at an Allied dropping of parachutes, was too 'hot' to be allowed to wander around their flat with a jail key on his person.

Thus, washing clothes all day, playing cards all night, Nancy, Françoise and the ten escapers passed their time.

The guard slipped away first, then Gaston departed and hid up locally. The remainder accepted orders to split into two parties and head for Spain independently. The second group left with Nancy and O'Leary as their leaders.

Apart from O'Leary, Nancy's party consisted of a French Resistance radio operator called Phillip, a New Zealand airman and an ex-policeman known as Guy. A little anxiously they took the train to Perpignan on the frontier.

Nancy was dressed as smartly as ever, determined to attract no unwelcome attention by looking hunted. She wore silk stockings, Cuban-heeled shoes, a smart navy-blue dress, a camel-hair coat and no hat. Her nails were well-tended and polished. Over her shoulder she carried her large handbag: in it some walking shoes and also a small leather purse containing all her jewellery.

These jewels were themselves worth a small fortune. Her engagement ring boasted a large diamond, pure and almost blue. There were brooches, Henri's Christmas gift gold bracelet, a platinum watch, eternity rings, a wedding ring and four other rings. These and the money in her bra were all she had with her of her once opulent life in Marseille.

The train sped along smoothly. All seemed to be going well and gradually they relaxed. Perhaps the recent plague of arrests had now ended and there was no need to worry. Nancy slipped her bag off her shoulder and took out a cigarette. O'Leary lit it for her. At that moment the door of their compartment slid open and a railway official rushed inside.

'The Germans are going to check the train,' he warned urgently and then slipped out again. Throughout the War the employees of the French railways were constantly helpful with warnings such as this and Nancy and O'Leary knew better than to disregard one now.

Already the train had begun to slow down. And yet it was not scheduled to stop anywhere at all near here.

'Quick,' said O'Leary, 'jump for it.'

Nancy did not hesitate for a second. She crawled through the window, flung herself away from the carriage and crashed on to the metalled track. Picking herself up, she rushed stumbling towards the vineyard that flanked the railway track. Machine-gun fire slashed through the vines around and above her. Nevertheless, she straightened up and ran faster, all the time collecting her wits and working out just where she should head to reach the mountain that had been fixed as their emergency rendezvous in the event of just such a disaster as this.

Although the German fire continued to be heavy, Nancy never faltered. She had her directions now and she ran on steadily, panting but determined, through a mile of vineyard until she began the muscle-tearing ascent of the mountain itself. It did not cause her the least surprise to find that she had reached the emergency rendezvous first. Collapsing on to the ground she recovered her breath and waited for her companions.

Guy was the first to arrive.

'Where are the others?' he asked.

'Don't know.'

'How did you get here so quickly?'

'I ran,' she told him, 'like a deer!'

'I'll go and look for the others,' he said. He left and never returned. He was captured, sent to a concentration camp and died of typhus. Shortly after he had left her, the others arrived. It was only then that Nancy realised that as she had jumped out of the train she had somehow lost her handbag and her jewels.

O'Leary then shepherded his small party into a deserted barn, where a sentry was posted, whilst the others, on a freezing February night, with only their coats to cover them, endeavoured to sleep. They huddled close together for warmth and when one turned over the whole lot turned. They stayed there for two days, very uncomfortably, until the neighbouring countryside quietened down; and then they set off to walk to Canet-Plage.

Nancy had no walking shoes and no papers – both had been in her large handbag – and they spent five days, travelling only at night, getting to Canet-Plage. During that time they slipped past numerous control posts and slept the day in sheep pens. They all developed scabies. When they reached Canet-Plage they were filthy and consequently felt horribly conspicuous, so they cleaned up in a known safe hotel before they boarded the train for Toulouse. Thus they reached Françoise Dissard's flat once more and there held a conference.

'There have been too many arrests,' Nancy declared. 'The Germans know too much. You know what I think? I think we've got a German counter-agent working in our circuit.'

This was the most dreaded of situations for any Resistance organisation, and yet it seemed the only possible explanation of all their recent disasters – of Nancy's six thwarted attempts to reach the frontier, for instance.

O'Leary nodded in agreement. 'We'll have to lie low and get you out as quickly as possible,' he ordered.

'Then I'd better get my clothes clean again straight away,' she remarked practically.

So Françoise took Nancy's clothes to an express dry cleaner and her shoes to a cobbler. Until they came back she would have to wander round the flat clad only in her underclothes and her camel-hair coat.

On 2 March O'Leary went down to the café he used as a meeting place for his contacts. There he was to meet one of his most recently acquired agents, a man known as Roger. Roger had repeatedly asked the privilege of meeting the 'Boss' and at last his request was to be granted.

O'Leary had not been in the café thirty seconds before the Gestapo arrived and arrested him. His trusted agent Roger was, in fact, Gestapo agent Number 47 and had worked with the organisation as a spy. At last the secret of their constant betrayals was out.

When word reached them that O'Leary had been arrested and that Roger had vanished, Nancy and Françoise were quick to realise who had been responsible for the disaster. They thanked God that Roger had never met them or come to know their identity. But they must move quickly. They decided that the only course of action open to them was to disperse, to break up the organisation and take cover.

Since Nancy still had no clothes, she took refuge in the nearby house of a man who, before the War, had been a pilot with Air France. When she had been taken to the house she had felt apprehensive. After all, she didn't know the ex-pilot or his mother and they had never heard of her.

But when it was explained to them that Nancy was both British and in trouble with the Germans, the mother had at once said, 'Come in,' and offered shelter for the night. Françoise and the rest of the organisation then set off by train from Toulouse. Half an hour later one of Françoise's men, Bernard, remembered that the Gestapo, through O'Leary's arrest, might search his own home and find a diary list of his old Air Force comrades. Nancy's temporary refuge was on that list. Bernard immediately turned back and made his way to the endangered house.

Nancy borrowed a dress and left at once, and she and Bernard boldly boarded a train heading towards Marseille where Nancy proposed to warn the other members of the O'Leary organisation about the defection of Roger.

In Marseille she found that all her contacts and agents had already got wind of the disaster and were reported to be at her second flat. Quickly, head thrust forward, she walked towards it, passing her own home on the way.

With her heart in her mouth and tears in her eyes, she compelled herself to continue straight past the block where she knew Henri would be at that moment. She longed to go inside and see him but she could not be sure that the block was not under observation or that she herself was not being skilfully trailed. To visit him would only endanger his life unjustifiably.

Feeling very depressed she carried on to the headquarters flat. She found it full of escaping airmen, warned them of the break-up of the circuit and then – still without papers – took another train to Nice. She took two of the airmen with her.

As the train drew out of Marseille she thanked God for Henri's wad of notes that she had stuffed inside her bra weeks ago when she had first left Marseille. Without her papers this money was now doubly valuable. The train gathered speed. She became suddenly and deeply convinced that this time she really was saying goodbye to the city that had been her life and her love for almost five years and, smitten with unaccustomed loneliness, she began to weep.

Remembering Bernard, and the other two escapers who were also on the train with her, and now largely dependent on her leadership, she finally pulled herself together. Life and the War might have grown sad, but she and her men were heading for Nice, and, if they arrived, there they would carry on living and continue waging war. In future, though, for her it would always be the habit of war that would be dominant because, having fled from her husband and her home, she no longer had a real life of her own.

8 ESCAPE TO SPAIN

It was to the home of Mme Sainson that Nancy and her friends, once they had reached Nice, now walked. 'Sainson' being French for 'Samson', Madame's Resistance *nom-de-guerre* was inevitably 'Delilah'.

There can have been no more reckless enemy of Hitler's Reich in the whole of France than Mme Sainson. Both she and her husband were active members of the Resistance, her flat was always full of escaping airmen and the whole population of Nice knew that if ever they saw anyone who looked foreign or lost, the place to send them was to her apartment in Rue Baralis.

She had a daughter aged twelve and a son aged fourteen, both of whom had frequently carried messages and helped her outwit the Germans. Once, when the flat was surrounded and being searched, and in it was a radio transmitter that would have meant death to them all had it been discovered, it was her young daughter who carried it out of the house. Deceptively childlike and innocent, she walked straight past the sentries at the front door with the transmitter concealed in a pail of rubbish.

On another occasion Mme Sainson had sheltered thirty evaders at once in her flat. It was an uncomfortable and dangerous time; but all thirty were eventually sent safely on their way towards freedom.

In 1942 alone, sixty-three men passed through her hands. From the end of 1942 onwards it was Nancy who always took delivery of her 'guests' and each woman had conceived an undying admiration for the other.

Mme Sainson's brother, Raoul, had escaped to London in 1942 and her husband was to be arrested in 1943 and later executed. Yet right through until the end of the War she carried on – with a maximum of gossip and ostentation – her escape-route work.

She was a humorous, volatile woman with heavy black eyebrows, calculating brown eyes and strong white teeth. Running her husband's garage in her spare time, her greatest pleasure in life was to give the fuel the Germans left with her (for the exclusive use of their own vehicles parked there) to the fishermen of Nice. She would replace the missing quantity with water! She worked in close association with the district priest and her lack of any sense of security was the despair of her chief, Arnoul.

Her worst weakness was a passion for being photographed with groups of Allied escapers. She would take them down to the beach for a breath of fresh air and then she would ask the nearest Italian soldier to photograph them. Once she even suggested that three of the enemy soldiers should join her group. The result is a handsome portrait of a mischievously smiling Mme Sainson with three slightly disconcerted-looking Americans, who spoke neither French nor Italian, for whom three flattered Axis soldiers are making a willing background.

When Arnoul heard of this episode he was extremely displeased, but the expression of his displeasure made no impression at all on his exuberant subordinate. Unrepentantly she showed him the photograph and remarked that she thought it a very good likeness, except for the Italians, who were imbeciles and of no importance.

This, then, was the atmosphere towards which Nancy and her four friends walked from the station at Nice. They entered the apartment doorway, climbed up the stairs and Nancy looked at the doormat. It lay squarely against the door. This was one of Mme Sainson's only three gestures towards security. If there was any danger, she kicked the mat crooked, then she chained the door firmly (which was her second precaution) and laid a hand grenade ready inside the door (which was the third). Anyone mad enough to knock when the mat was crooked merely invited Mme Sainson to open her door the few inches allowed by the chain and to deposit an exploding bomb at their feet.

'We're safe.' Nancy sighed with relief and knocked. Mme Sainson opened her front door and peered out suspiciously. 'Nancy!' she exclaimed with delight. 'How are you? Come in.' Without asking for any explanations she ushered in the troupe of strangers behind her friend as well.

'A brandy?' she offered. They all accepted. 'I'm sorry, Nancy, that we have no pastis!' The two women laughed uproariously at this and the men looked puzzled. Mme Sainson hastened to explain.

'Nancy is very fond of pastis,' she said, 'but of course it is forbidden. Once she had a small flask of it and the police caught her with it. They ask her, this is pastis, no? And Nancy says, "Certainly not, it is only perfume and anyway I never drink," and puts it in her handbag and they believe her and let her go! Ah,' she concluded, '*elle est formidable, cette Australienne! La plus formidable de la Résistance!*'

Between the two women there was a strong bond of affection and confidence. This was not surprising. They were very alike. Arnoul regarded them as his two best agents and respected their talent for imagination and initiative in the work they did.

Fortunately for him his respect was amply returned – although that was not surprising either. At the age of sixteen Arnoul had won a British Military Medal in the last year of the First World War. In

1940, to quote him, he 'had been obliged to go very quickly from Paris where the Germans did not like him'. Friends in Nice gave him a job running a macaroni factory and, under cover of that, he continued his Resistance work.

In 1941 Claud Bourdet, then leader of the Resistance in that area, became a national Resistance officer and appointed Arnoul (whose real name was Major Comboult) as his successor.

Thereafter this slim man, who looked ten years younger than his real age, ran the organisation in Nice. Occasionally Mme Sainson would have him wringing his hands in despair at her recklessness but more often he blessed the fates that had given him so courageous a lieutenant. Whenever, in her profligate fashion, she took in excessive numbers of 'boarders', so that she was unable to buy sufficient food for them all on the black market, he himself would make up the deficiency with huge donations of macaroni. To over a hundred evaders, as a result, he was to become known disrespectfully as 'The Macaroni Man' or Monsieur Macaroni. Americans and Britons particularly found the diet he provided hideously monotonous. But they were grateful to him that they ate at all – and to Mme Sainson that they had a roof over their heads and a hostess who apparently loved entertaining them.

Let it not be thought, with all this gossip and lack of security, that the Gestapo never heard mention of Mme Sainson. They did, frequently. In fact all the time. And quite often they took her away for questioning. But Mme Sainson had a great facility for tears, and as soon as they picked her up, and right throughout her interrogation, she would sob moistly and noisily. Invariably they decided that she was a cowardly blabbermouth, worthy only of contempt, who boasted of non-existent Resistance work to boost her own prestige – and so they would release her. Immediately she would stop her weeping and return grimly to work.

Nancy stayed with Mme Sainson for three weeks. During that time she bought new clothes, acquired a set of false identification papers and endeavoured to find out exactly what the position was about the circuit.

Soon she discovered that guides were again escorting escapers across the Pyrenees. Bernard, therefore, made some exploratory trips and eventually declared that the time was ripe for Nancy's seventh attempt at getting out of France.

He declared that he wanted to go to England with her and she suggested that the New Zealander and two American airmen should accompany them. She herself escorted the non-French-speaking Allied airmen to a big store to be photographed so that false papers could be made for the three of them.

In her spare time she cooked or gossiped with Mme Sainson, or went to the cinema with the Sainson children, whom she adored, so the days passed quickly and happily and eventually she was almost sad to have to leave. She and her party took the train from Nice to Perpignan.

At Perpignan they picked up two French girls who also had a pressing need to leave the country. The next difficulty that confronted them was to locate guides. Because of the breakdown of the circuit, they had no passwords and no contacts. Nancy, however, knew the address of one of the guides so she volunteered to try to persuade him to take her party into Spain – a dangerous business because, without a password, it was quite possible that the gentleman concerned would regard her as a spy for the Gestapo and shoot her out of hand.

Eventually she contacted the guide and, without any preamble, said, 'Look – I haven't got a password. You don't know me, but I know you. You've worked for O'Leary and I've worked for O'Leary too. Now don't give me any nonsense – I want to go to Spain.'

Such blunt candour was too much for the guide. He asked a few cautious questions. Nancy gave the correct answer to each. He went with her to collect the rest of the party and then they began the trek into Spain.

◆ ◆ ◆

They walked in the darkness for about three hours, then they met the main group of guides. These were all men who, before the War, had made their living entirely by smuggling across the frontier. Then it had been contraband; now it was bodies. Some of them were a cut-throat-looking crew but they knew their job – and their mountains – perfectly.

Nancy and her party were hidden for the rest of the night in a hollow on the hilltop and at dawn were pushed into the back of a coal lorry. Coal, loose and in bags, was then packed all around and over them. The lorry drove off. Soon they entered the twenty-kilometre strip of French territory which the Germans had made a forbidden zone to anyone who did not actually live in it. At the end of this zone lay the frontier. On the other side of the frontier was another forbidden zone to a depth of fifty kilometres. These seventy kilometres in all, and the Pyrenees (which were heavily patrolled with sentries and dogs), were the danger areas.

The coal truck was frequently checked on its run through the French zone but no attempt was ever made to search the coal in the back. At last the truck halted and they were told to get out and take cover in the bush. Wearily they flopped to the ground and allowed a sickly sun to warm their grimy bodies.

At sunset two guides and a dog called for them. The senior guide was a Spaniard whose Resistance name was Jean. He was wanted in France by the Gestapo for espionage and in Spain by the police for murder. He was tall, thin and dark, about thirty years old, and seemed unperturbed by the price that lay on his head on both sides of the frontier.

The second guide was a young woman, Pilar. She was a good-looking peasant, as strong as an ox and just as taciturn as Jean. The dog belonged to her and it knew its way backwards and forwards across the mountains even better than the Spaniards did. Somehow Nancy felt that the presence of this dog, a mongrel fox terrier, was a good omen. Sadly, though, she wondered how things were going with Picon . . . and Henri . . . and her friends.

All of them were instructed to remove their shoes and put on rope espadrilles instead. These were better for rock climbing and quieter. They had to go by the rockiest paths because these alone could foil the soft-padded police dogs of the Gestapo. They had to march silently because sentries on the dark mountainsides relied even more on hearing movement than they did on seeing it.

They set off. For forty-seven hours on end they marched and climbed with only ten minutes' rest every two hours. Jean and Pilar were implacable about this – and the little terrier pranced with impatience at every stop.

Each time they rested they had to take off their wet socks and put on dry ones – otherwise the wet socks would have iced up and frostbitten their feet. They would keep the wet socks in their pockets and then put them on again, after removing the dry ones, just before the march resumed.

Jean allowed no talking or coughing or smoking. If anyone wanted to cough he had to smother it completely under his coat or with his fist, anything, so long as there was no noise.

All of them began to be afflicted by colic. They had eaten some black-market lamb and it had apparently been tainted. The trip became hellish. One guide always went ahead, preceded by a silent,

95

prancing mongrel dog, and the other always flogged them on from the rear.

They clawed their way up into the highest, craggiest reaches of the Pyrenees, using their hands and their feet equally, panting and despairing. They were hungry, which was bad, but they were also thirsty, which Nancy considered worse. She ate handful after handful of snow. The others argued with her about it but she ignored them. Nothing would stop her walking but she must have something to drink. It was a bitter, alpine climb.

Time after time they would ask Jean or Pilar how much further.

'One more mountain,' they were invariably told. But each time they crossed a mountain, a valley and another mountain lay ahead. Ruthlessly they were driven on.

On the second part of their forty-seven-hour trek they were lashed with a biting snowstorm. A blizzard raged and the ice and snow cut into them like needles. But they pressed on through it. One of the Americans cried out that they must halt, he couldn't go on. Nancy slapped him savagely and he went on. One of the women said she could go no further. Nancy whispered to Jean, and Jean calmly tripped her into an icy stream. Then she had to go on or freeze to death.

But finally it ended. They reached a hut, lit a fire, dried their clothes and waited until nightfall. Ahead lay a river. When they crossed that river they were out of German-controlled Europe and into Spain. Nancy slept badly as she waited on this last leg of her dash for freedom. There were several alarms, but nothing came of them.

Then, under cover of darkness, they eluded the sentries, crossed the river and left the sentries behind them.

'Henri, my dear,' Nancy muttered as she reached the other side, 'I hope you'll be as lucky in your journey as I've been.'

9 WELCOME HOME

While Jean went ahead into Barcelona to warn the consul that British and American subjects had arrived somewhat unexpectedly in neutral Spain, Pilar took the party to a farm.

There they were given their first meal in thirty-six hours – baby rabbits and chicken, with a batter of egg, flour and breadcrumbs, deep fried in boiling oil and then garnished with mayonnaise and garlic. They ate their fill, dried their clothes and then slept till dawn.

As the sun rose they were all told to go and hide in the fields. They were well fed during the day and returned to the house at nightfall. Jean reappeared and announced that the consul had promised to send a car to a place near the farm the following morning. This car would collect all the escapees – and their worries would then be over. In the meantime, afraid of police in the area, he had suggested that they should spend the night in the barn, rather than in the house. Happily, they all climbed into a haystack.

A few minutes later Bernard whispered urgently to Nancy, 'This accursed colic; lend me some of your toilet paper.' Nancy reached into her bra and produced two sheets. 'The last,' she told him gravely. Hurriedly he left – followed by one of the women who was having the same trouble.

The haystack now held Nancy, Jean, Pilar and her dog, two Americans, a Frenchwoman and the New Zealander; and that was the moment the Spanish police – suspecting the farmer of hoarding produce – chose to swoop on the farm. Stamping round in their heavy boots, looking fearsome in their medieval three-cornered black hats, they found nothing in the house or under the farm machinery that lay scattered round the bam. They were about to leave when one of them casually prodded the haystack with a pitch-fork. In the process he prodded Pilar.

With a shriek of rage and pain Pilar bounded out of the stack, hotly pursued by her mongrel dog. Sure-footed she leapt from one piece of farm machinery to another and then out of a window. The *guardias civiles* all started firing at her like madmen – but they all missed. The last sight Nancy had of her was of a lithe figure vanish-ing into the dark field. Streaking ahead of her, dashing non-stop on the route to France he knew so well, was Pilar's mongrel dog!

Deciding not to wait until she too was stabbed with a pitch-fork, Nancy calmly climbed out of the haystack and sat down on a plough. She was not going to worry. She spoke no Spanish and she had no idea what would happen, but she was not going to worry. Quickly the rest of the party were winkled out and a policeman came and examined Nancy suspiciously.

'Americano,' she assured him blandly. At that the Spaniard burst into a blood-curdling diatribe of which she understood not a syllable, except that she gathered he did not approve of her story.

With difficulty the Spaniards persuaded their undisciplined prisoners to fall in and start walking. They marched about three miles to a town called Besalu. They were thoroughly happy and sang rude songs in French and English all the way because they were confident that at any moment the consul would intervene and then all would be well.

A little to their surprise, however, the consul did not materialise and instead they found themselves bundled unceremoniously into a top floor cell in Besalu's jail. The cell was about six feet wide by ten feet long; there was straw on the floor and a can in the middle; it had obviously been constructed in the days of the Inquisition; it was freezing cold and there were eleven inhabitants in it already – so that now the cell held seventeen. They were not comfortable that night and they slept badly.

When morning came there was still no consular intervention. Jean explained this unfortunate diplomatic lapse by pointing out that there was a festival on (and, of course, no one in Spain ever transacted any official business whatsoever during festivals) so there would be no one available with whom the consul could negotiate the prisoners' release.

'How long does this festival last?' Nancy demanded.

'Three days,' Jean answered lugubriously.

For that time not only the government officials but also the jail officials took a holiday. No one thought of bringing the seventeen prisoners in the upstairs cell any food at all. On the third night, however, Nancy was taken rudely out of the cell and led downstairs.

'Why me?' she wondered as she followed the sentry. She was not at all pleased with this sign of special notice. And when, downstairs, they chained her ankles and wrists and then questioned her at great speed for several hours, she was even less pleased. She made no attempt to understand a word they said and only occasionally said anything herself. When she did speak it was always to announce that her name was Nancy Farmer and that she was an Americano. She relied on the British Consulate to hear about her interrogation, and to realise that the name Nancy Farmer indicated the initials NF and that NF meant, in reality, Nancy Fiocca.

Exhausted by their attempts to question her and make her talk, the Spaniards suddenly offered her a drink.

'Whisky,' one urged enticingly in curious English. 'Scotch!' Nancy looked at the bottle. It was pure Scotch whisky, made in Spain.

'No, thank you,' she said. 'I'm hungry.' She made unmistakable gestures to indicate that she wanted food, not drink. So they offered her food – which only convinced her that they were going to take her outside after a last meal and shoot her. She knew that Spain was full of Nazi agents and that the government and police were often bullied or bribed by the Germans into doing what suited the Reich. Now she was certain that the Gestapo, realising that she had escaped them in France, had arranged that the police should execute her in Spain. Accordingly, on the principle that if she put off the last meal she would also postpone the execution, she refused to eat.

For a while they left her alone and then they returned to the fray – this time with a little tailor who spoke bad but comprehensible English. He informed her that he was to act as interpreter.

'Well, now, you don't need an interpreter to be shot,' Nancy told herself, immediately sensing that somehow or other she had gained an advantage over the Spaniards. Again she was offered food. This time she chose to be aggressive. Filled with that sense of superiority towards the natives that afflicts some Britons overseas, she announced arrogantly, 'I'll have nothing to eat or drink, thank you, unless all my friends in the cell get some too.' This the tailor volubly translated.

All her friends were at once dragged downstairs, chained up and fed. Again Nancy complained through the interpreter. 'How dare you expect us to eat with chains on our wrists?' The chains were removed. After which they ate a huge and cheerful meal and topped it all off with two of the bottles of pure Spanish Scotch whisky. Then they returned to their cell, Nancy included, and there they were each of them very sick indeed into the can, because pure Spanish Scotch is not good for the stomach.

In the middle of the night Nancy was again led out of the cell and the tailor-interpreter told her she was to be taken to sleep in a hotel in the village. Assuming that this move must have been prompted by consular intervention in Barcelona, she made no attempt to escape during the night but satisfied herself with being as rude as possible to everyone through the medium of the tailor. The Spaniards accepted her rudeness meekly, thereby confirming her suspicions that all was now well.

In the morning she was joined by the rest of the party. They were herded into a bus and sat in pairs, each pair chained together. Prisoners sat on the left-hand side of the bus, ordinary passengers on the right – an arrangement to which the ordinary passengers seemed quite accustomed.

Jean, knowing that he was wanted in Barcelona for a murder he had allegedly committed during the Spanish Civil War, was now getting anxious. He was chained to a Belgian priest and he sat by the bus window. He passed the word along that he would attempt to escape somewhere en route to Gerona, which was the bus's destination. Guards sat by the front exit and on the full-length back seats as the bus rattled on its way.

Nancy, sitting immediately in front of Jean, heard him desperately fiddling with the chains on his wrists. Then, after a while, she heard the quiet clicking cease and had to fight with herself so that she would not turn round to see how he was faring.

Some minutes later, the guard by the front exit looked casually back along his half bus of prisoners – and suddenly his face registered first dismay and then utter horror. Jean's seat was empty, his window wide open. The guards on the rear seat were talking animatedly amongst themselves. They had been too engrossed in their own discussions to observe Jean's disappearance through the window.

The bus jerked to a halt. All the *guardias* piled out on to the road, and away in the fields to the left Jean was to be seen, leaping and bounding like a deer, bolting to safety. Amid a fusillade of rifle shots from the guards and roars of encouragement from Nancy and her friends, the Spanish guide vanished out of sight. The police blundered into the field after him, slow and cumbersome in their boots. Rifle shots rang out intermittently. Finally, the guards returned, looking self-conscious and ridiculous, and Nancy knew that Jean was safe.

At Gerona they were told that they were to appear before the governor, charged with illegal entry. On this score the British Vice-Consul, a man called Rapley, advised them to be tactful but not to worry – the Germans having just been routed in Tripoli, the Spaniards were in no mood to be anti-British!

The case was, in fact, heard that afternoon when a large fat man who sat behind a large fat desk made the motions of going through a formal trial. A present in the right direction having already ensured that he would return a favourable verdict, it was difficult for Nancy to take the fat man as seriously as he took himself.

'You were well-treated in prison?' he suggested.

'I was not!' she assured him stoutly. 'There were seventeen of us in one cell and the lavatory was filthy!' Rapley flashed a look of reproach at her and she remembered his instructions about being tactful.

'Sorry,' she announced cheerfully. 'We were very well-treated, and the lavatory was lovely!' Apparently, the governor did not consider this tact. He looked furious and dismissed them peremptorily into Rapley's hands. After a gift of £1,000 there was, of course, little else that he could do, but at least he did it with the worst possible grace. So Nancy took the train to Barcelona and for the first time since 1940 knew that she was really free.

◆ ◆ ◆

The British Consul at Barcelona provided Nancy with plenty of money so that, having no financial worries, she stayed for a while in Barcelona and then travelled down to Madrid. The first thing she did when she arrived there was to call at Cook's and ask whether perhaps they had a trunk for her, addressed to 'Miss Nancy Wake' and dispatched by Cook's at Marseille. The trunk was there and triumphantly she ordered it to be sent to her hotel.

The loyal Ficetole had done well when, with his cart and Picon II, he had collected the trunk from her flat. He had first taken it to his own home and there, searching out suitable words from advertisements in the paper, had found three large words which he had then cut out and laid on top of the clothes inside the trunk. When Nancy, in her bedroom in Madrid, opened the trunk, the first thing she saw was Ficetole's message. Very simply, very touchingly, it read: *Love from Henri.*

Complete with her trunk Nancy proceeded on to Gibraltar and there, ten days later, was put aboard one of the ships in a large convoy heading for Britain. Standing by the ship rail, near the gangway, she was soon engaged in conversation by a young man, who obviously approved of her dark good looks, when suddenly she noticed a familiar figure coming up the gangway towards her. It was Micheline, the girl whom, three years earlier, she had escorted home to France from the convent at Weybridge. Micheline was no longer a girl but now a married woman with a baby in her arms. Excitedly Nancy called her name and the young mother rushed forward and embraced her.

As Nancy took the child out of Micheline's arms to give her a rest, they chattered together about how they had contrived their respective escapes and why. Finally, Nancy turned round to introduce Micheline to the young man with whom she had been talking. But, depressed by all the symptoms of motherhood he had observed, and mistaking Micheline for Nancy's hired nurse, the young man had fled.

'I think you've disillusioned him,' Nancy laughed.

'Too bad,' Micheline replied. 'By the way, where's Henri?'

'He'll be following soon – I hope! How is Mme Digard?' Whilst the two young women continued discussing their families,

Gibraltar began slowly to fall behind them. By sheer chance Nancy was returning to England in June of 1943 with the same girl who had been her companion when, in 1939, she had left it.

Theirs was a large convoy of seventy vessels in a month when the Bay of Biscay was to be the main target area for U-Boat packs that had just been forced to withdraw from the North Atlantic. The ten-day voyage was depressing and interrupted by constant alarms and attacks from the air. But Nancy felt too exhausted to be frightened and was indifferent to all the hazards of sea warfare. She simply could not believe that anything would happen to her now that she had come so far.

She was perfectly correct. The ship docked safely at Greenock on 17 June 1943, and the passengers slowly filed along. Soon Nancy reached the immigration official's desk.

'Name?' he demanded.

She told him.

'Passport.'

'I have no passport.'

'You what?'

'I have no passport. It hasn't been terribly fashionable to carry British passports in France since 1940.' The official glared at her suspiciously.

'What documents of identification *have* you got then?' he inquired curtly.

'None. The War Office put me on board this ship. You people should have been notified of my arrival by them.'

'Well, we haven't,' he snapped. 'You'd better get back on the end of the queue.'

Nancy had no intention of returning to the end of any queue. Instead she found an officer who was being repatriated and who had by then become a friend.

'Do me a favour,' she said. 'Send this telegram for me when you get ashore.' She handed him the message she had written out. 'And for God's sake don't let the immigration people know I've been talking to you. They're convinced I'm a spy.'

Her friend got safely ashore and duly sent off the telegram, which was addressed to Captain Ian Garrow at the War Office. It told him in no uncertain terms exactly what Nancy's trouble was.

Whilst she waited for the message to have its effect, Nancy also made herself quite odious to all the officials who kept her in custody and by the time the War Office had sent someone along to collect her, she was no longer talking to any of them. She was placed in a special carriage, all alone, on a train to London. On the outskirts of the city she was taken off the train and driven in a War Office car into the West End. A room had been reserved for her at the St James Hotel. Later she was entertained with a large dinner party at Quaglino's. Very late that night she went to bed.

'*You'll never get back,*' the customs man had threatened her, when she had insisted on sailing to Boulogne with Micheline years earlier. '*If you go now you'll never get back!*'

Luxuriously she pulled the sheets up round her ears and relaxed in the bed. Well, she'd done it. She'd worked on an escape circuit for two and a half years (1,037 men altogether were to escape from France along the route she helped create). She had engineered Garrow's escape from imprisonment and she had herself been rescued from jail. She had survived a hundred roadblocks, train checks, control points and dangerous journeys. She had escaped traps, ambushes, the Milice, the Spaniards and the Gestapo. She had fought for her husband's France and now, at last, she was home. But the War had not ended yet. Nor, though she was blissfully unaware of the fact, had her part in it.

10 THE MAD HOUSE

In safety at last, the reaction to endless months of danger, and to the past few weeks of lack of sleep, set in swiftly. For days on end Nancy wanted only to lie in bed or to be alone. Each evening she slipped out on her own into London's crowds and hid from the people who wanted to entertain and fete her. After a few drinks she would return to the flat she had rented and go miserably to bed.

It was not until the middle of July that she began to feel her normal cheerful self again. By then, however, she had become convinced that Henri would not be able to follow her out of France, so she called on Free French Headquarters in London and suggested to them that they might care to send her back there as a saboteur.

Unfortunately, at this time there was considerable antipathy between General de Gaulle and Churchill, and this antipathy was mirrored in Free French Headquarters by the violent suspicions they entertained there against the British War Office.

The French were slow to accept Nancy's offer – not because they doubted her value but, frankly, because they suspected that she had been sent to them by the War Office only to spy on their activities and then report back to the British.

That such spies had been planted in the French headquarters was quickly proved. A War Office representative called on Nancy and asked her why she had offered herself to the French rather than to themselves – a matter that should have been as unknown to them as it was confidential to the de Gaullists.

Nancy was not lost for a good reason as to why she had not volunteered for MI9. She strongly disliked one of its chief executive officers and she said so. 'I'd never consider working for him,' she declared bluntly. 'Hate the sight of him.'

'Why not join Buckmaster's group, then?' they suggested.

'Never heard of it, that's why. What's Buckmaster's group?'

'SOE,' they told her. 'Special Operations Executive.'

Straight away an appointment was made for her to be interviewed by a Major Morell on behalf of SOE. He infuriated Nancy, who had seen more Resistance work than most, by asking a lot of questions which she described to herself as 'bloody silly' and which were best summed up in his final query.

'Why do you want to go over to France?' he asked. 'Is it because you think the job's glamorous?'

'For God's sake,' Nancy exploded, 'if I want glamour I can get much more of it here in London than over in Occupied France.' So saying, she stalked out of the office and went to lunch with Ian Garrow.

'How'd it go?' he asked curiously. With great venom she told him. Garrow laughed and they then talked about other things. After lunch Garrow telephoned Major Morell and told him about Nancy's indignation. Morell was undisturbed.

'Just wanted to see her reaction,' he said.

Soon after that Colonel Buckmaster (who had known of her work for some time) himself asked that Nancy should be enlisted in his group. Another appointment was then made and, unhesitatingly, she accepted the invitation. Enlisting under her maiden name of Wake, she signed up for service at the headquarters of a group known most misleadingly as the FANYs.

The initials FANY stand for First Aid Nursing Yeomanry. The unit had been created in 1907 to enable wealthy women to serve their country in a state of congenial company, mild discipline and attractive uniform. All FANYs were of the same class; rank was quite unimportant and the uniform was flattering. Thus, when Nancy joined the unit, there was a general's wife who held the rank of private, all ranks wore silk stockings (elsewhere forbidden) and a large proportion of their numbers were in no way connected either with first aid or with nursing – they were, in fact, young women training to be dropped as saboteurs into Nazi-dominated Europe. It was a unit ideally suited to a woman with the temperament of a Nancy Wake.

◆　◆　◆

That weekend Micheline and a friend called Alfred came to stay with her so Nancy shared her room with Micheline whilst Alfred slept in the front room. She went to bed early and slept soundly, and as she slept she had a most curious dream.

She saw one of her best friends in Marseille – called Dédée – standing at the door of her flat, saying, 'Come in.' Nancy went inside the flat and looked around. 'Where's Paul?' she asked.

'In there on the bed,' Dédée announced flatly. 'Go in and see him.'

Nancy walked through into the bedroom. Lying stretched out on the bed, quite dead, was Dédée's husband.

'But, Dédée,' Nancy whispered, 'he's dead.'

'I know,' she replied indifferently. And yet Dédée and her husband had been gloriously in love for fifteen years.

Then, shrieking, Nancy woke up. She rushed out of her bedroom into the sitting room. Alfred seized her and asked what was wrong. Micheline followed her anxiously.

'It's Henri,' she sobbed. 'I've just had a dream. He's dead. I know it, and I wasn't there.'

Desperately the other two tried to quieten her but, inconsolable, she wept on. It was 16 October 1943, and Nancy was illogically certain that her husband was dead.

For several days Nancy was haunted by the certainty of her dream. Then common sense and the arguments of her friends began to make her see how unreasonable her fears had been.

'Why,' her friends asked, 'decide that Henri is dead when the dream you had was about Dédée's husband, Paul?'

'Because Dédée and Paul were so much in love. She could never have looked at him like that.'

Could she have looked at Henri like that?

No.

'Then what are you worrying about? You ate too much for dinner, that's all that was wrong. Forget it, Nancy.' And so the conversation switched from Nancy's dreams to Italy's declaration of war against her one-time ally, Germany.

Slowly, then, she forgot it, but always after that she found herself hollowly incapable ever again of feeling close to her husband. Instinctively she took refuge in the thought of getting back to France and resuming her war against the Germans.

Her training course started. They began in an establishment known respectfully to its inhabitants as 'The Mad House'. First came the obstacle course.

'These are your instructions,' the conducting officer told her. His name was Denis Rake and he had once been an actor and his father had been executed with Edith Cavell in the First World War for espionage against the Germans. 'This is an obstacle course. Each obstacle has a sign showing its point value. The total number of points possible for the course is eighty-five, but you pass if you score fifty. Decide for yourself where you want to start and which obstacles you want to attempt.' Then she was shown the course.

There were trees to be climbed, gaps to be jumped, high slack ropes to be crossed with only another slack rope above to be used as a handhold, difficult walls to be scaled, a seventy-foot rope to be slid down, a dizzy platform off which one must jump to catch a rope six feet away and so slither down to safety. Nancy looked at all these obstacles with marked distaste.

'Which would you like to attempt?' she was asked. The answer that came quickest to her mind was 'None of them'; obviously, however, that was not what the officer hoped to hear. Cautiously she made her choice. She passed the test, but with no distinction and even less enthusiasm. It occurred to her that in all her two and a half years of Resistance work so far she had never been required to scale a fifty-foot fireman's ladder and that she would make quite certain that such a frightful contingency should never arise in the future.

Having thus tested her nerve and her strength, Nancy now found that the organisation wished to test her for imagination and resourcefulness.

'This plot of land is a minefield,' Rake told her. 'It is extremely dangerous but you must cross it somehow.'

Overhead was a horizontal wooden bar about fifteen feet above the ground. Nancy looked at it curiously and decided that it must be there for a purpose. Suddenly it occurred to her that it could be used for swinging – and swinging meant a rope. She searched round the 'minefield' and eventually, hidden in a pile of rubbish, found the rope. She tossed one end of it over the bar, caught it as it swung back, tied the two ends of the rope together, grasped the rope high and then flung herself – her knees drawn up – into space across the 'minefield'. At the furthest point of the rope's arc, she let go and thudded to the ground safely beyond the danger zone.

Next she was taken to a rectangular pool of water. The water was only about six inches deep and the pool was twenty feet long by ten feet wide.

'This pool is sulphuric acid,' she was told. 'If the acid touches any part of you, you will be badly burnt. You must cross it.'

Nancy had overheard some gossip among earlier contestants concerning this obstacle and she knew in advance what to look for. It never occurred to her that this was cheating. She wanted desperately to get back to France and she would use any methods now, just as she would then. She made a pretence of fumbling round to find stepping stones and finally, in good time, unearthed three blocks of wood, each about a foot high and eight inches wide. Planting them carefully in the 'acid', leap-frogging her way, she walked the length of the pool on top of them. Rake, the conducting officer, duly pronounced her to possess individual imagination and resourcefulness.

But she was also, it seemed, required to possess a *group* sense of imagination and resourcefulness. For this purpose she and five men formed a group and they were then asked to manoeuvre heavy weights over high obstacles, to cross ponds that were apparently uncrossable and to project themselves somehow over a barbed-wire barrier six feet thick, six feet high and 'electrified' . . . all within a specified time. Each test required *all* of the group to achieve the crossing (none could be used as a human springboard and then left behind) and the tests certainly demanded the highest degree of cooperation and enterprise among the six team members.

Nancy, to her delight, found herself with a mad collection of irrepressible team mates and had no trouble at all with the course. They passed their tests with flying colours.

The next test was to be the one Nancy hated most. It was the room-searching test. Here the 'room' was marked out by a series of imaginary lines and, occasionally, by ropes. The candidate was supposed to search, in this non-existent room, for a non-existent paper that was somewhere concealed in the non-existent furniture.

'Ducks,' Rake reproved gently, 'you've just walked straight through a wall!'

'Hell,' his candidate exploded, 'where *is* the wall?'

'Runs right down there, old thing. Oops – now you're standing on the sofa.'

'Bloody nonsense,' she muttered to herself. 'If they want me to search a room, why don't they give me a room? It's no good, Denis. I never could play at make-believe.'

'Sometime you might have to,' he threatened.

'I doubt the Germans will ever hide imaginary papers in an imaginary room,' she observed moodily. 'And if they do, I can't see London asking me to go and find them. Give me a real room and real papers and I'll find 'em for you in no time.'

Rake grinned and understood her point. He had every reason to. He too had already worked in France. He had landed on the Cote d'Azur and had quite often, when in Cannes, taken cover in the hospitable home of none other than Monsieur Miracca, manager of the Palm Beach Casino. Miracca had asked no questions, provided Rake with a bed and a room (from which he could tap out his messages to London) and never mentioned these extraordinary visitations to anyone. After a long tour of very successful operations, Rake – described by his chief, the dissimulating Colonel Buckmaster, as the 'incomparable Denis' – had returned to Britain and now helped to instruct new recruits to the cause, like Nancy.

Next there was an obstacle race. Denis Rake stood at the beginning of a maze of impediments, all marked clearly *A* or *B*.

'You will cover the course as quickly as you can,' he instructed in a whisper, 'and you will go *over* everything marked *A*, *under* everything marked *B*. Do you understand?'

Others preceded her along the course and she was a little perplexed to observe some of them going under and not over A's, some going round and not under B's. Well, she had been told over A's and under B's – that was how she would do it.

All went well till she came to a car tyre that was not marked at all. 'Over or under?' she pondered. 'Through,' she decided boldly. Halfway through she felt her trousers start to drag off. Almost undressed she fell out the far side, but she continued the course. Under, over, under, over. Colonel Buckmaster and a psychiatrist watched carefully from the sidelines.

She came to another tyre and looked in amusement across to Buckmaster. 'Not again,' she shouted. 'This time I'd probably lose them entirely.' Howls of laughter accompanied her as she crawled under the tyre and completed the course.

'Good girl,' Denis congratulated her.

The final ordeal at the 'Mad House' was an interview with the psychiatrist. Understanding nothing of psychiatry Nancy decided in advance that she would not enjoy this interview. Impatiently she sat in his waiting room until the candidate ahead should be finished. The door opened and she came out. As the door closed behind her she ran quickly across to Nancy and whispered, 'Blots. They show you hundreds of blots and ask you what they look like.'

'Well, what do they look like?' Nancy whispered back.

'Blots! But you don't say that. You say corsets and butterflies and head waiters and things like that.'

'Why?'

'I don't know, but you do.'

The doorknob rattled and the woman fled. A little puzzled, Nancy entered the psychiatrist's office.

He asked her a long series of questions, none of which she considered had anything to do with subversive work in France as she understood it. She therefore amused herself by lying.

'Are your mother and father happy together?'

Nancy, recollecting how her mother had been alone in life for twenty years, replied, 'Very.'

'Was *your* home life a happy one?'

Nancy, remembering her two attempts at running away, replied, 'Perfectly.'

'Have you ever indulged in fantasies – you know . . . wished your mother was dead or tried to draw attention to yourself by lying, or anything like that?'

Nancy, who had, at the age of five, stuffed a small cushion down her front and announced that she was going to have a baby (because the pregnant lady next door received so much kind attention) responded gravely, 'Never.'

The questions continued and the colourful answers came back readily. Then she was shown the series of pictures made by blots of ink being folded in a sheet of paper so that they squelched symmetrically out on either side of the fold and produced curiously insect-like results. There were about a hundred of them, nightmarish, spidery, of various colours.

As each one was shown to her the psychiatrist asked her to name the immediate object with which her mind associated it.

'Blot,' said Nancy. 'Blot . . . blot . . . blot . . . blot . . . blot . . . blot.' Every single picture to her looked, she claimed, only like a blot. Expressionlessly the psychiatrist put the papers away. 'Surely you can see something?' he suggested.

'Certainly,' she agreed. 'Someone's thrown a bottle of ink or something.'

He told her that he would speak a word and she must respond with another word which her mind associated with the one he uttered. The duel was short.

'Roses' . . . 'Red.'

'Sugar' . . . 'Sweet.'

'Soda' . . . 'Whisky.'

Quietly he put away his list of words, wrote in his dossier and then suggested that Nancy might play with some blocks. He was a large young man and now Nancy looked at him curiously.

'You're not English, are you?' she asked.

'No – New Zealander.'

'Don't you think you'd be more use fighting the Japanese in the Pacific than mucking about with all these ridiculous blots and blocks over here?' she demanded severely. 'Because if you don't, I do.'

Knowing the value of the job he did, he just smiled amiably and replied, 'Perhaps! Well, that'll be all for now, thank you,' and so dismissed her. Cussed interviewees told him just as much, by the quality of their cussedness, as did the compliant or over-anxious by their desire to please. He was perfectly satisfied that Ensign Nancy Wake would make good training material – and he said so in his report.

From the 'Mad House' Nancy and three other young women were to proceed to a second training centre in Scotland. They waited in Welbeck House to be taken to the station by their conducting officers – a man for the male candidates, a woman for the females. Nancy entered the lounge just as Denis and one of the women were in the midst of a violent personal argument. She sat down and pretended not to hear. Almost immediately Rake stormed out of the room, slamming the door behind him.

His antagonist then began a tirade of abuse about Denis. She didn't like him; she didn't think he knew his job; she didn't think he would be any good in France and anyway he was impossible.

Nancy, who knew that Rake had already done a wonderful job in France, and who had the highest regard for him both as a person and for the work he had done, said quietly, 'You're talking nonsense; anyway, leave me out of it, he's a friend of mine.'

'He was insufferable to me. You heard him. I've never been so insulted. I'm going to report him and you'll be a witness to what he said. I'll fix him, you see.'

'For God's sake, woman,' Nancy hissed, her eyes blazing unpleasantly, 'shut up! What *you* need, you know, is a couple of good stiff drinks and to forget the whole thing.'

'You've had a few yourself, haven't you?' she suggested disagreeably. Nancy, who had had one double whisky an hour before at lunch, decided to be contrary.

'A few,' she replied.

The woman promptly reported the affair to an officer in the organisation who was a friend of hers. She claimed that Rake had been rude to her and that Nancy had witnessed the incident but was drunk and would not admit having heard the disputed words. A message was sent to Nancy asking her to wait in another room. Unsuspectingly she did so. Then she was called into the officer's room.

He looked at her sharply and began to question her with considerable hostility about the Rake affair. Nancy returned the hostility with interest.

'You been drinking?' he demanded.

'I have.'

'Well, we don't like our girls to drink,' he said. Nancy looked at him very coolly and then used an army word which seemed the only suitable means of expressing her feelings at that moment.

'Ensign Wake,' he stormed, white-faced with anger, 'I am not accustomed to that kind of rudeness.'

'Neither am I accustomed to your kind,' she retorted. She was ordered to leave the building at once and to return to her flat. Very soon a telegram arrived from SOE saying: *Send back your FANY uniform to HQ at once.* She rang up SOE, told them that the uniform was in a box, neatly packed, and that she would gladly surrender it if it were called for. But to one person only: to the officer who had been rude to her! Her career as a saboteur, it seemed, was finished.

She waited in her flat all of the next day for the pleasure of handing the uniform over to the man she now disliked more than anyone else in England. To her disappointment, he never arrived. She had dinner that night with a colonel who had once sheltered in her Marseille home before escaping from France and who now got her side of the story. Inquiries started. Garrow was questioned about her character and explained her extraordinary volatility, her passionate loyalty to anyone who had actually served in the field and her fierce courage when people questioned her convictions. She was asked to attend SOE's office for an interview with Major Philipstone-Stowe the next day.

The interview went smoothly, and Philipstone-Stowe concluded it by saying, 'Are you still prepared to go to France?'

'Provided I never see *him* again, yes,' she replied. It was then agreed that she should go to another course in Scotland.

SOE sent Nancy to Scotland unaccompanied by other trainees. Moreover, she was afforded a male conducting officer on the journey rather than the usual woman. There were to be no other women on the course. At the end of her journey she was consequently awaited by her instructors-to-be with the deepest distrust. Any woman whom SOE would send escorted by a man to a unit in which there were only men, her receiving officers decided, must be a veritable old dragon. They felt confident that she would be about sixty years old and certainly toothless. They were pleasantly surprised when she arrived.

There followed a wonderful six weeks in Inverie Bay. PT at dawn was the only snag and Nancy soon found a way out of that. On the third morning, when she was called, she surveyed the chilly darkness and shouted through the door, 'Not this morning. I don't feel well.'

The men were understanding. They knew that such indispositions were inevitable with women! Whilst they leapt and pranced and grunted and froze, Nancy lay snugly in bed, nothing at all the matter with her.

When her indisposition had continued for many days beyond the expected time, a young doctor was sent to see her. He was very shy and very tactful. 'Is anything wrong?' he asked. 'Anything you'd like to ask me about?'

'Nothing,' she assured him truthfully.

'Would you . . . Would you, er, like me to examine you at all?'

'I wouldn't,' she vowed. He left her and she continued not to do PT until eventually the hour was changed to 9 a.m. when it was light and reasonably warm. Then she miraculously recovered and joined her comrades in their violent exercising.

She learnt about explosions and detonators and about dismantling and reassembling Bren guns and their three main causes of stoppages. She practised firing with a Sten gun and achieved the reputation of being a crack shot because her bullets never went high. She omitted to explain that she had weak wrists which meant that her barrel always tended to drop so that she couldn't fire high, anyway.

She trained in silent killing, raids on other students, night exercises, radio transmission by Morse and how to move across country.

She was wonderfully happy throughout because the companionship was completely loyal and undemanding.

She regarded silent killing and unarmed combat with some horror as dirty and violent. But when the thought occurred to her that it could easily be a choice between the silent killing of a Nazi or herself in a concentration camp, she studied hard at the dirt.

There was an obstacle course. The best man in the school took only two minutes; Nancy took four and missed out three obstacles in the process.

There was a cross-country race. Nancy completed only three legs of it and then found herself far behind the rest of the field. She remembered that in the mess there were to be crumpets for afternoon tea and she was very partial to crumpets. By the time she completed the course all the crumpets would have been devoured by her greedy colleagues – she knew it!

Abandoning the cross-country course, she took a shortcut back home and entered the mess by the front door. By great good fortune this turned out to be the finishing post and the officers in charge thought she had finished first. She accepted their compliments gracefully, went into the empty lounge and ate all the crumpets!

In the grenade classes she did not shine. She loathed the rigid overarm throw and did everything she could to avoid practising. The drill was simple. The class sat in a trench and took it in turns to climb out, remove the pin from a grenade, hurl it forward and then leap quickly back into the trench whilst it exploded. Nancy's turn eventually arrived.

'What do I do?' she stalled. The sergeant instructor glared at her and then answered with terrible sarcasm.

'Pull the pin, throw the grenade into the trench and run,' he advised. With a dead-pan face Nancy pretended to believe him. The class in the trench – including the sergeant instructor – were last seen fleeing for cover whilst Nancy laughed helplessly above them.

A fisherman, who had spent forty years as a trawlerman in the worst northern seas, taught them how to handle a rowing boat and, from it, to pick up parachutes and containers that might have landed in lakes and reservoirs rather than on the ground. In his forty years of stormy trawling, the old fisherman had never had an accident. On his first trip with Nancy she capsized him and the boat and they had to swim to shore.

Nancy regarded herself as most inefficient in matters of this kind but endured her failures cheerfully. When her colleagues roared with laughter at the mishaps that befell her she was undeterred.

'Maybe I can't do it,' she would laugh herself, 'but at least I'm good for morale. You people have never been so amused in all your lives.'

'But, Führer,' one asked, for that was what they had christened her, 'what will you do in France? You can't climb this wall. What will you do if you have to climb a wall like this in France?'

'I have never seen a wall like this in France,' she told them easily. 'And if ever I do – even if the whole German army's after me – I shan't even try to climb it. I'll let the Germans climb it if they want to. But I'll just stay on my side of it and talk myself out of trouble. Come on – time to change for dinner.'

They dined in full uniform. Nancy always arrived at the table first because experience had taught her that being just a fraction of a minute late allowed her companions to prepare practical jokes on her. In rapid succession her colleagues followed her to the table.

'*Sieg heil!*' they declaimed, saluting her with Hitler's outstretched arm. Gravely she saluted them back. It was their ritual. Then they sat down to eat. The world, she felt, was a nice place. She had got used to the idea of Henri staying in France whilst she trained in England. She was accustomed now to the lack of news from him. Soon she would be near him, back in France. All in all, she had never been happier in her life.

After a grand finale of a thirty-six-hour trek – in the course of which one Pole broke his leg – they all moved down to Manchester to learn how to jump in parachutes. They arrived on a Sunday just in time to watch a Frenchwoman from another school doing her preliminary jumps from a tower.

'Führer,' the men said, 'don't let us down. You must jump better than her or we'll beat you!'

Nancy jumped from the tower very reluctantly. As far as she could see it was just a splendidly alarming way of breaking her ankles, which would stop her jumping from a plane later in the week, which would stop her jumping into France eventually. But she jumped as she was told and her friends didn't beat her.

On the Tuesday they did their first jumps from a plane. They were very subdued as they flew high above the ground, sitting in two rows, facing inwards towards that ominous hatch. 'Remember,' the instructor said, 'elbows close to your sides; legs together.'

Wafting down through space, Nancy decided that parachute drops were not so bad after all. Then she heard shrieks from the ground below.

'Remember what your mother told you,' an officer roared, his head bent back, his hands cupped round his mouth. She leant downwards. 'Bah,' she bellowed in reply. '*Merde!*' But she snapped her legs together as instructed and landed perfectly. So did everyone else. They were all very excited and laughed when Nancy begged that they be allowed to go up again at once and do another jump.

On Wednesday morning they did do another jump, but from a balloon instead of a plane.

Up in the balloon all was silent and insecure and Nancy grew steadily more unnerved. The instructor noticed her *malaise* and decided to take her mind off what had to be done.

'Do all Australian girls have such lovely pearly teeth?' he asked pleasantly.

'Shut up,' Nancy snapped back ungraciously. 'Oh, this is awful. I'll be killed, you know. I'll never do it again.' But she did. The weather continued to be too bad for flying and, if the boys on her course were to finish their jumps in time for weekend leave, the balance of descents would have to be made from the balloon. They implored her to jump from the balloon.

'Think of it, Nancy,' they begged. 'Weekend leave in London.'

'What's it worth?' she demanded. They consulted together and agreed that it would be worth a double whisky from each of them if she jumped.

'All right,' she agreed. 'But I wouldn't do it for any other men in the world.'

She jumped for the last time at night in the worst of a long day's bad weather. She caught no sight of the earth until suddenly it smacked her in the face and promptly she was knocked unconscious.

As she came to she saw anxious eyes peering down at her and felt affectionate arms supporting her. She swore violently. 'Ah,' the men sighed in relief, 'she's all right.' In great good spirits they all set off together for London.

There they ate at the Celeste Restaurant, which was out of bounds to them because it was a leave rendezvous for the Free French, whose security was known to be terrible. They had a huge meal and then celebrated all over London. They ended up at the Astor doing parachute rolls across the dance floor and singing, '*Gory, Gory, Alleluyah – What a helluva way to die*', much to the astonishment of the nightclub's other clients and with a lack of security that would have done credit to the Free French themselves.

Down Park Lane they whooped, up Piccadilly and at last to Nancy's flat. Micheline was there with her child, so she and Nancy cooked a meal for the men and then shared the bedroom again whilst the others slept all over the sitting-room floor.

Much of the group's behaviour in London had been childish, much perhaps not very funny. But they had led a hard life, they took risks – they were going to take even greater risks – and their *esprit de corps* was as high as their *joie de vivre*. Their antics were a childish relaxation against the days when they must be purely adult. Their frivolity was a safety valve against the knowledge they all shared that Ravensbrück and Belsen could lie ahead of them just as surely as did France.

Certainly Nancy saw nothing foolish or excessive in the behaviour of those with whom she had spent the past two months. On the contrary, she was touched by their unfailing gallantry and chivalry and she loved them for their magnificent gusto and vitality. Enthusiastically she played her part in their nonsense.

◆ ◆ ◆

Their next school was in the New Forest and dealt with security. Nancy hated it. She learnt to identify all types of German planes, German regiments and German badges of rank – and she found all of it boring in the extreme.

She cheered up a little, however, at the exercise designed to simulate a Gestapo interrogation. She and her group were told to prepare a story and then all would be questioned on it, in Gestapo fashion, to try and bring out inconsistencies in their various versions.

The group agreed that they had all gone to the local doctor's home to play tennis. They had all gone there in uniform. They had had afternoon tea in the drawing room. And since they had done all this, they could *not possibly* also have blown up a bridge at 3 p.m.

At the last minute they decided that they were not wearing uniform, they had gone in civilian clothes. Then, individually and quite harshly, they were questioned.

Nancy's turn came. She answered a series of questions with the confidence born of experience. And then, disaster.

'What were you wearing?'

'Uniform,' she replied promptly – and, too late, remembered that the group had changed their minds and finally agreed on civilian clothing. Ferociously her blunder was noted down and then, even more aggressively, the questioning continued.

'What did you do after the tennis?'

'Had tea.'

'Where?'

'In the drawing room.'

'On what sort of table?'

'What do you mean?'

'Was it a round table?' Nancy cursed herself that she hadn't thought to bring this point to the notice of her group.

'No,' she said.

'Square then?'

'No.'

'Well if it wasn't square and it wasn't round, what shape was this table?'

'Between the two,' she averred – and refused thereafter to be shaken from her story. She regarded her performance on this occasion as a shameful fiasco but she had learnt her lesson and was never to be tripped up again. Rather contritely she went on weekend leave.

11 WITCH ON A PARACHUTE

Her next course was the manufacture of explosives from the sort of ingredients that could be purchased quite innocently anywhere in France at either hardware shops or chemists.

'The secret of these explosives,' the instructor told them, 'lies in being absolutely accurate with your weighing-out. The slightest fraction too much or too little of any one ingredient and there'll be no bang!' In a savage kind of way it was amusing to see the entire group sitting round on the floor, pudding bowls between their knees, weighing scales at their sides, carefully mixing their mortal brew.

When they had finished their scrupulous preparations they would go out and test the result. It was a tedious business but the lessons were obviously valuable. Should supplies fail to arrive by parachute from London, these saboteurs would never be compelled to abandon altogether their attacks on railways, rolling stock, machinery or communications. A little 'home cooking' would keep them operational.

There was another woman on the course and her name was Violette Szabo. She and Nancy became firm friends and shared a room. Being more accustomed to cooking than the men, a strong spirit of rivalry developed in the old manor house between the males and females of the bomb-making species. Practical jokes grew daily more numerous – and Nancy and Violette, more often than not, were the target of these pranks.

Finally they retaliated. Employing all their knowledge of hand-to-hand combat and surprise attack, they fell on their instructor. Whilst he fought back bitterly, all the men on the course watched the battle with professional interest. But he could not match the trained skill of the two women. Triumphantly Nancy waved aloft his trousers. The instructor had been de-bagged, the women had won their battle and blue-striped underpants were his crestfallen acknowledgement of defeat. Honour, for the women, had been restored.

A little time later the instructors and staff at the manor house held a party – for instructors and staff only. The 'course' were a little incensed, not because they felt that they had any right to be invited but simply because they hated missing a party. Nancy and Violette, being particularly incensed, decided to take action.

They stripped their conducting officer's bedroom of every piece of furniture and clothing except his tin hat. After an excellent evening the officer padded unsteadily up the hall and flung open his door. Bewilderment spread over his face. He was sure he had followed his normal route home, but this was not, he knew, his home. He bellowed for his batman, who came running.

'Where's my room?' he demanded drunkenly. 'Take me to my room.' The batman gave him an odd glance, retreated to a safe distance and explained that this *was* his room.

'Don't be bloody silly,' the officer roared. 'How *can* this be my room? Nothing in it but a tin hat.' Irritably he scooped up the hat and examined it. It was, he saw, his own tin hat. His forehead rutted as he compelled his beer-drenched brain to think. Then his face cleared. 'Aah,' he pronounced ominously. 'Those ruddy girls!'

He led a counter-attack on their room, but they had prepared for it skilfully. A barricade of chairs, beds, tables and wardrobes made the door impenetrable, and Nancy and Violette, looking dangerously confident, made entry via the windows unthinkable. The onslaught was repelled and finally the old house subsided into quiet sleep.

At last the course came to an end. The group were fully trained. Any day now the office in Wimpole Street might tell them: 'Tonight you leave for France', and every day, regularly, they must call in to the office to collect their orders . . . to inquire had they yet been 'posted'?

Whilst Nancy and two young French colleagues 'did the town' with Violette, Buckmaster discussed with his assistant Vera the potentialities of Ensign Wake after she had been parachuted back into France. Vera expressed frank doubts that Nancy would be successful.

She admitted that Nancy had done a wonderful job in Marseille between 1940 and 1943. But, she pointed out with considerable logic, in Marseille Nancy had always possessed a ready-made background in the home and life of Mme Fiocca; she had always been able to get strength and means from her husband. How would she fare now, Vera wondered, when she would be compelled to live against a background that was false – a mere cover story – and when she would be compelled to seek her finances and weapons only where the RAF might care to drop them? Frankly, Vera was not confident that Nancy would survive long.

On the other hand, no one could doubt Nancy's ability to fight nor, if she were captured, to keep her mouth shut – her behaviour when arrested by the Vichy people in Toulouse had proved that. So Buckmaster, relying on Nancy's progress reports and his own intuition, decided to send her to France at once. Nancy was the first of her group to be posted.

Clothes were made for her by a French tailor in London. Elizabeth Arden face cream, her favourite, was packed for her in French cosmetic jars. She was given her cover story and interrogated fiercely in an attempt to shake her on it. She was given her code name and required to write it down fifty times, *Hélène, Hélène, Hélène*, she wrote, over and over again. Then came the matter of her own personal code. It was to be based on any quotation or verse she cared to choose as one she couldn't forget.

'Bible, Shakespeare, anything you like,' it was suggested to her. Nancy grinned evilly. 'I know a verse the Germans will never suspect,' she announced.

'Tell me,' the coding officer suggested. Nancy told him.

> *'She stood right there,*
> *In the moonlight fair*
> *And the moon shone through her nightie.*
> *It lit right on . . .'*

'All right, all right,' the officer laughed. 'I know the rest.' He quoted the last two lines. 'Correct?'

'Correct.' Nancy nodded. 'Let the Boche try and crack that!' Soberly the vulgar limerick was entered in SOE's official list of code keys.

'I'm sure you'll do well, Nancy,' Buckmaster told her. 'You've got excellent reports.' He scuffled through a pile of papers and then glanced up at her. '*Her morale and sense of humour,*' he read, '*encouraged everyone.*' He paused again and then said quietly, 'You'll leave, we hope, on Friday.'

A tremendous party was thrown on Thursday night. After it, Violette returned home with Nancy. They parted on Friday morning.

'Au revoir, Violette.'

'Au revoir, Nancy. *Merde!*' They kissed and Nancy watched her walk lightly along Baker Street. She was never to see her friend again. Beautiful and fragile, Violette was ambushed in a field in France; her ankle was too badly injured to move. Carefully she shot it out with the searching German troops, wasting not a single bullet. When she fainted they captured her. She was executed at Ravensbrück, still calm, having betrayed no one.

At Buckmaster's office that Friday there were last-minute and frantic changes in the plans. An entire new series of orders, 'safe houses' and lies had to be committed to memory. Nancy retired to the flat bathroom and studied desperately. But it was no good. After the party of the night before she could learn nothing, so it was decided that she, and her colleague Hubert, should leave instead on Saturday.

The following evening she reported back again, her story and orders at last safely committed to memory. She knew her targets, her contacts, her dropping point, her safe houses, her codes and her cover story – knew them all perfectly. Her cover story, back to the time of fictitious grandmothers and great uncles, was a masterful fabrication of the probable and the uncheckable. It contained deliberate but convincing inconsistencies, because life itself is inconsistent. It was supported fully by all the documents required of a Frenchwoman in Occupied France.

Buckmaster handed her a silver powder compact. 'A going-away present,' he said gently.

'Thank you.'

Kissing her, he wished her '*Merde!*' in the French fashion.

The other men in the flat kissed her warmly as she left. They looked very glum. They hated seeing women go to what they knew lay ahead. One especially, an American trainee called René Dusacq (once a Hollywood stuntman), was almost in tears.

'You're just jealous,' Nancy laughed at him, piling into a car with Hubert and Vera. Quickly they drove to the airport. There a security officer wanted to search them both. Hubert agreed, was searched and pronounced free of such incriminating possessions as London theatre tickets or English labels. He nevertheless parachuted into France with a British regimental badge in his overcoat pocket which he discovered, to his horror, days later.

Nancy refused to be searched. She wore a smart civilian outfit, silk stockings and three-quarter-heeled shoes. On top of them, for warmth and pocket room, were a pair of overalls. Next came a large camel-hair overcoat, very full in the back for concealing anything she might need to conceal. Over that was her parachute harness. To check all of this would have taken hours.

'Look,' she raged. 'I've got nothing on me except what you people have made me and the money and papers you've given me.' They compromised by binding her ankles to provide some support against the shock of a fast parachute landing in high-heeled shoes.

All sorts of inconsequential thoughts now filled her head. The London flat was one of them. She had forgotten to make arrangements about the rent while she would be away.

She sat down and dashed off a note to her bank manager, asking him to settle monthly but giving him no explanation.

'What on earth are you doing?' the security officer demanded.

'Writing to the Germans to tell 'em I'm coming,' she replied. 'Here – post this when you get back to London.' Then she was ready to go.

At ten o'clock they were out on the strip. Nancy looked bulky with her huge handbag (which contained their plans and about a million francs in cash) against her seat, revolvers in each of her trouser pockets, a parachute on her back and a tin hat over her shoulder-length black hair.

Clumsily she was handed up into the belly of the Liberator that was to fly them to France and Hubert was hauled up after her. Her code name for the trip was to be *Witch*.

'Thank heavens these things are warmed,' she muttered to Hubert as the American bomber rumbled across the aerodrome. The dispatcher, a lean good-natured Texan, sidled up to her.

'Say,' he asked, 'are you really "Witch"?'

'I am. And don't get your letters mixed.'

'Gee,' he muttered, 'a woman! We ain't never dropped a woman before.'

As a tribute to her femininity, he brought her a Spam sandwich and a cup of coffee. Their Liberator droned on through the night. After she had finished her meal she lay on her side and tried to sleep. Hubert did the same and they both failed miserably. Then they hit bad weather and were flung about by the explosions of ack-ack. Nancy abruptly got rid of the Spam sandwich and the coffee. For the next three quarters of an hour she continued being extravagantly airsick. The dispatcher gazed at her compassionately.

'Look, Witch,' he urged, 'if you don't wanna leave we can easily take you back.'

'And do this lot again,' Nancy moaned. 'Brother, you just get me to our dropping point and let me get out of this thing.' It was, she felt, a very unheroic beginning to her life as a saboteur.

At five past one in the morning of 29 February 1944 they arrived over their dropping point. Hubert and Nancy peered through the hatch as they whirled 400 feet above it. Bonfires blazed, torches winked, faces were clearly visible.

'My God,' Nancy murmured. 'It looks like the Blackpool Illuminations! Every German between here and Russia will know we're coming.' Hubert did not reply.

'I wonder if Maurice Southgate is there?' she asked. Southgate was an agent in Montluçon who was to introduce them to the leaders of the Maquis in this area. London had said that he would contact them. Hubert said he didn't think so.

'Sure you don't wanna come back?' the dispatcher offered anxiously.

'Sure!' she snapped. The plane lurched wickedly, a light flickered on and the dispatcher, thumping Hubert on the back, shouted, 'OK – JUMP.'

Hubert vanished. Nancy felt a slap. 'JUMP.'

'Elbows in,' she thought – and vanished through the trap. There was a jerk as the chute opened off the static line and then, fast and smoothly, she was sailing down.

'Legs together,' she muttered as the ground rushed up towards her. And then, 'Blast. I'm going too far over.'

She whistled down beyond the remotest fire and landed comfortably in a hedge. With some difficulty she extricated herself from her parachute, which had been caught in a tree, and bolted into the neighbouring field. She could see no lights, no reception committee, only black, silent night.

Then shouts and screams rent the air. 'An ambush,' she decided, frantically shedding her overalls and ankle bandages. But even as she started to slink away into the bush she heard Hubert's voice.

'Here's her parachute.'

She broke through the hedge and observed a short, good-looking Frenchman who examined her disembodied parachute curiously. The Frenchman saw her coming and greeted her formally, not quite disguising his disappointment that she was a woman when he had expected a man.

'Madame Andrée?'

'Yes.'

'Tardivat,' he introduced himself.

'Where's my friend?'

'Don't worry. He is safe.'

Nancy laughed in relief and he smiled back. He looked humorously up at the parachute.

'I hope all the trees in France bear such beautiful fruit this year,' he declared, bowing gallantly towards her. She began to drag her parachute down out of the tree.

'Careful,' he warned, 'you will tear it.'

'Going to destroy it anyway,' she grunted.

'No, Madame Andrée,' he protested, 'such beautiful nylon is not to be destroyed.' In spite of all her arguments he refused to allow her to carry out this fundamental step in parachutage security. Remembering the fires and noise and activity that had awaited her reception, Nancy decided that the stories she had heard about the Maquis lack of security were all lamentably true. To make things worse, there was no sign anywhere of their contact, Southgate.

'Be it on your own head,' she warned. 'Isn't it time we left this funfair?'

'Ah, yes, of course,' he agreed, folding her parachute carefully. 'Come, we have a car for you.'

'A car!' Cars, they had been taught, must never be used. They were the exclusive province of the Germans and for anyone else to be seen driving them was to invite disaster.

'Certainly. At least, a *gazogène*. Come. I will take you to your friends.' He guided her across the field to a waiting car and introduced her to the driver and his wife.

Bouncing off into the darkness in the charcoal-burning car, Nancy looked across at Hubert and smiled reassuringly. Alarmed though she was, she felt as if she were back home. But how must he be feeling, faced with all this fearful lack of security?

'Well,' she announced cheerfully, 'we're here.' For years in France she had been Mme Fiocca; for months in England she had been Nancy Wake; now, back in France again (for how long?) she had become Mme Andrée to the Maquis and Hélène to London

135

and she had at least three other pseudonyms as well for emergencies. To a normal person all of this could well have been confusing, but women like Mme Andrée had not been trained by SOE to become normal persons.

'I wish we had our wireless operator with us,' Hubert grumbled. 'What can we do without a wireless operator?'

'He'll be here soon, Hubert. With his feet you couldn't expect him to *jump* in; and you couldn't expect any plane to land in these awful mountains. Don't worry. He'll be here soon.'

'Why should he be? The Lysander was going to land him somewhere near Châteauroux. That's a hundred and twenty miles away. He'll probably be weeks.'

Hubert was very depressed by it all and Nancy had to admit that things were less encouraging than she had hoped. No Southgate to introduce them to the Maquis and no wireless operator to keep them in contact with London. But she *did* have her bagful of money and their D-Day plans and she was full of confidence. The car lurched darkly on.

PART THREE: WITH THE MAQUIS D'AUVERGNE

12 A MURDER IS PLANNED

Nancy and Hubert had dropped near Montluçon, between Hérisson and Cérilly, and were now being driven by their hosts to their home in Cosne-d'Allier. They travelled about ten miles, during which time their hosts told them their life stories, including the fact that they had been refugees from the north in the earlier days of semi-occupation and that now it was safe enough for them to drive because they could always see the headlights of a German car approaching them. Since they themselves drove without headlights of any kind, the road ahead of them just inky darkness, the two British were prepared to believe that any approaching German vehicle would easily be identified. Nevertheless, they felt happier when they reached their destination.

Their hosts' home was over a radio shop. 'Hope our operator isn't too long catching up with us,' Nancy remarked, reminded of him by the radio sets she saw as they went upstairs.

'Nothing we can do till he gets here, anyway,' Hubert repeated. They went into the kitchen and were given a large meal.

'I've never been so empty,' Nancy vowed.

'After your behaviour on the flight across, I'm not surprised,' Hubert laughed.

They rounded off the meal with coffee and brandy – a *pousse-café*. Then, since it was about four in the morning, Nancy suggested that they might all get some sleep.

She and Hubert were led proudly to the main bedroom and there shown a large double bed.

'Do they think we're going to sleep together?' she demanded in English.

'Looks like it,' Hubert declared.

'Well,' said Nancy, 'we're not! You'd better find a sofa or something.'

But their hosts had no sofa and they could not understand this British reluctance to share a bed. Every time Hubert dossed down on the floor, the French couple would burst into the room again and chide him for his shyness in avoiding the attractive English girl. Finally, too tired to argue any more, Nancy slept under the bedclothes and Hubert, covered with everyone's overcoats, slept on top of them. Discovering them like this in the morning, their hosts showed the most obvious symptoms of surprise but made no comment.

For several days they hung round Cosne-d'Allier waiting for the arrival of either Southgate or their radio operator. On the first day, distrustful of everything, they did not even leave the upstairs rooms. On the second morning, however, Nancy peered through the shutters at the clear sunlight outside.

'Better get out and get used to it,' she announced finally, and so, feeling decidedly strange, she went downstairs and walked through the small village where everyone greeted her and everyone knew who she was and where she had come from and why. This in no way added to her self-confidence.

'The first thing we do, when we get in touch with these Maquis leaders, is tighten up their security,' she told Hubert. 'This is awful. The way everyone knows us just drives me straight up the wall.'

Hubert nodded. 'Wonder where the hell Southgate is?' he muttered distractedly. Maurice Southgate, who was in charge at Montluçon and who, according to London's plans, was to have met them as soon as they landed and introduced them to Laurent, one of the leaders of the Maquis d'Auvergne. It would be Laurent's role then to take them to Gaspard, chief of the whole area.

Gaspard was in command of four groups, numbering about four thousand men, in the departments of Allier, Puy-de-Dome, Haute Loire and Cantal. After Nancy and Hubert had met all these groups, and sized them up and inspected their forces, they were to cable London and advise whether the whole Maquis was worth financing, arming and training in preparation for D-Day.

But four days had passed and still there was no Maurice Southgate to introduce them to Laurent, and no wireless operator to send any messages to London. They seemed doomed to remain inactive in Cosne-d'Allier forever.

However, their inactivity was not allowed to persist. News reached them that day that Southgate's group in Montluçon had been the victims of mass arrests, which explained his delay. A special messenger then arrived to confirm the news. Not only that, but he told them that their wireless operator had regrettably landed on the other side of all this Gestapo turmoil and that he would have the greatest possible difficulty getting through to them – if, in fact, he had not, as seemed probable, already been captured. Then he left them. Southgate himself never did get to Nancy and Hubert to introduce them, as planned, to Laurent. First he had grievous troubles of his own on his circuit, and later he was himself captured by the Germans. After that there was only one thing for Nancy and Hubert to do – they must arrange their own introductions to the leader of the Maquis d'Auvergne.

Nancy went to her host, the radio mechanic.

'Jean,' she said, 'take us to Gaspard.'

'I can't,' Jean told her, 'but I will take you to see Laurent. He will know how to find Gaspard.'

'Always Laurent,' she thought. Well, it was a start at least. 'Thank you very much,' she said.

They drove that day to Laurent's hideout. When Nancy questioned the advisability of driving by day, Jean told her that it was safe enough. He knew all the secondary roads and the Germans, he claimed, preferred to stick to the Routes Nationales. Secondary roads were too dangerous for them. Nancy, taught by London to travel only by bicycle or train, or on foot, was at first not entirely convinced. The nature of the country through which she now drove, however, soon changed her mind.

The ancient province of Auvergne is a highland district. There are mountains as high as 6,000 feet, there are plateaux, gorges, heavily wooded slopes, jagged volcanic rock formations. Most of the year it is cold and wet; all the year round it is inaccessible and ideally suited to guerrilla warfare. Not for nothing is it known traditionally as the Fortress of France. In this sort of terrain, she felt, the Maquis were at a decided advantage over the Germans and cars were emphatically more sensible than walking, which would be exhausting in the extreme, or bicycles, which would be pointless.

They found their first contact and he, recognising Jean, led them to a second; the second led them to a third. So it went on. It was the sixth or seventh contact who eventually guided them to a house in a tiny village. Laurent, wanted for the shooting of several Germans in Clermont-Ferrand, was taking no risks. Their guide told them that the Maquis leader had been in this house for four nights.

He was a tall, darkly handsome man of about thirty. His speech was uneducated but his mind was obviously acute. He greeted the two Britons with reserve and looked secretly amused as he noticed that one of them was a woman.

Since it was already early evening he suggested that his visitors should sleep the night in his room and then go with him to find Gaspard in the morning. Nancy, determined to be quite independent, said that she herself would prefer to sleep in the car.

Also, knowing that Laurent had already spent four nights in this same house, she pointed out that if she could find him so could the Gestapo. Accepting the validity of this argument, Hubert and Jean decided to join her in the car. They spent an uncomfortably sleepless night and were, in consequence, more than a little irritated when a very fresh-looking Laurent called for them in the morning.

In their *gazogène* they then followed Laurent, who drove a petrol-powered car. He drove fast and extremely well and they had difficulty keeping up with him. Eventually he left them behind, to wash themselves and breakfast in a mountain village, saying that he would go ahead and contact Gaspard.

Gaspard made a rendezvous with them for several days later in a château at Mont Mouchet near St Flour, a considerable distance away. Having delivered this message Laurent then presented Nancy and Hubert with a petrol-powered car he had 'obtained' for them, so that Jean could drive back in his *gazogène* to Cosne-d'Allier to look after his radio shop.

Following a guide in another car, they arrived at the château at Mont Mouchet at about midnight. They discovered that all the Maquis in that area drove petrol-powered cars and, in fact, scorned anything else as slow and unreliable. They stole all their cars, the guide told them. 'That's just what *this* mob looks like,' Nancy muttered to Hubert, as she studied the crew who now received them. 'Professional car thieves.'

Gaspard was not there and they were shown into a room of their own to wait for him. Swiftly, when they had been left alone, Nancy looked round.

'Well, at least we've got a bed each,' she grunted. Hubert, who was ill, did not reply. 'Rough-looking lot, aren't they? Hardly welcomed us with open arms, did they?' Still Hubert didn't answer and Nancy looked at him anxiously. She was not to realise until later that Hubert, just out of a Regular Army Unit and talking only the purest academic French, felt not just physically ill but also mentally lost in the highly irregular and colloquial presence of the Maquis. Just as she had decided to ask him what was the matter, the door burst unceremoniously open and a voice informed them that food was ready and that Gaspard was 'expected'.

In the company of fifty surly and suspicious-looking Maquis, whose personal dirtiness was only exceeded by that of their table manners, Nancy ate an uncomfortable meal. As soon as they had finished, she and Hubert retired to their room.

'Well, what a ruddy awful lot,' she exploded. 'They eat like pigs.'

Weakly Hubert agreed. 'They're the end,' he said. Rather discouraged they crawled into their respective beds, and went to sleep.

All the next day they hung around and still there was no sign of the 'expected' Gaspard. Frenchmen had a reputation for being unpunctual at the time, but in this respect Gaspard, apparently, was excessively French. Nancy filled in some of her time trying to persuade one of the Maquis guides to go out and look for her wireless operator and to send him on to her should he find him, but the guide gave no sign of being willing to cooperate and she did not feel confident that she had had any success.

'The hell of it is,' she moaned to Hubert, 'that without our wireless we can't do a thing to help Gaspard or ourselves or anyone. And if Gaspard's anything like his men he'll only be out for what he can get from us.'

'You've got a lot of money,' Hubert pointed out.

'Yes, and they're not getting a cent of it,' she retorted, her hand gripping the huge purse clasp firmly. 'Not until we're in touch with London. Otherwise they'll spend the lot for us, we won't have organised anything and then they'll dump us.'

'Well, you're in charge of the money, you decide,' Hubert remarked listlessly.

Late that night, as they lay on their beds, a wild hullabaloo shook the château.

'Gaspard, I should say, has arrived,' Nancy diagnosed. 'Well, he's held us up for two days. Now he can wait till the morning to see us.' She turned over and went to sleep again.

In the morning they met him. He exuded arrogance, self-satisfaction and energy. He was surly. He was a bully and, Nancy decided, he was a bluffer. Glancing across at Hubert, she knew that his reaction to Gaspard had been the same as her own.

Gaspard was evasive in his answers to all their questions about his troop dispositions, arms needs, future plans and the methods he would employ to carry out the instructions she brought him from London. Intuitively she decided that he had no intention of cooperating with London at all. She believed him to be an ambitious man who would try to trick her into giving him huge sums of money, into obtaining for him powerful supplies of arms, and who would then use all of them for his own private war.

Her suspicions were confirmed that afternoon. She and Hubert sat outside a window of the château and eavesdropped shamelessly on Gaspard's round-table conference with his lieutenants. Money and arms were what this conference wanted; but nothing could have been further from their minds than cooperation with London – all this Nancy heard.

As soon as the conference broke up, Gaspard came to see them. 'Now,' he said with a great show of candour, 'I shall put all my cards on the table.' He then suggested to them, for their consideration, the decisions just taken at the conference, but not the motives behind those decisions.

'I am sorry,' Nancy lied, 'but we have no money so we cannot finance you.' She saw Gaspard did not believe her. 'And we have no wireless operator so we can't cable London to send you arms.'

Next morning Gaspard held another conference, and again Nancy and Hubert eavesdropped from outside.

'The woman is the trouble,' someone said. 'Of *course* she has the money. Let me seduce her and I'll kill her as she sleeps and take the money afterwards.' This was agreed – whereupon a second Maquis offered to murder Hubert also. The two British agents grinned tranquilly at each other. This was the first amusing thing that had happened to them since they had left London.

'Don't know who my "admirer" is, but he flatters himself,' Nancy whispered. 'No one out of this scruffy lot could get within miles of me.'

Her would-be seducer approached her and, after flattering her with every compliment to which he could lay tongue, suggested an assignation that evening. Nancy stared at him appraisingly and indicated that she did not think much of what she saw.

'I presume you would like to sleep with me,' she stated bluntly. He answered that he would be enchanted.

'Now, that's very gallant of you,' she thanked him, 'but you see I have no desire at all to be murdered in my sleep and then to have all my money stolen.'

'Madame Andrée! How could you think such a thing?'

'I heard it.'

'Impossible.'

'Then I dreamed it! Now isn't that an extraordinary thing to dream?' Again she stared at him – this time coldly – until his eyes dropped. When he looked up at her again he was smiling. Holding out his hand he said, 'You win, Madame!' After that there were no further attempts at their assassination by Gaspard's group.

That evening one of Gaspard's lieutenants, Judex by name, had planned a raid on a sports store in St Flour, and having gained the respect of Gaspard's men by her victory over her proposed seducer, Nancy now forced home her advantage.

'Judex, let me come with you,' she begged. Judex stared in momentary surprise and then agreed.

The raid was well planned and, although St Flour was garrisoned with German troops, their timing was so skilful that they met no obstacles on their way into the town. Blatantly they broke into the store, drove up their trucks and removed most of the stock of tents, blankets and boots. The proprietor was a collaborationist and they had no compunction in robbing him. Nancy herself worked with relish and excitement. She was, for the first time, impressed by Gaspard's men. Much more important – they were impressed by her! Triumphantly they all returned to the château.

Realising at last that he could neither bluff nor intimidate Nancy into giving him her money, nor into revealing to him the targets London had planned as his for D-Day, Gaspard now gave up arguing and thumping his fist at her. He had learnt to respect her, but she would not give him what she had, and she could not, without a wireless operator, provide him with what London would send, so, regarding her as utterly valueless, he bundled her off elsewhere.

He sent her and Hubert to another group under the control of a man named Fournier at a place called Chaudes-Aigues. He and Fournier disliked one another intensely and Gaspard was secretly pleased at the thought of unloading these stubborn and useless foreign agents on to him.

Fournier was as quick as Gaspard to realise that, for the moment, Nancy and Hubert were of no value to him. But he was a courteous man and an efficient one. In spite of the fact that he was chronically bad-tempered and endlessly arguing with his wife, he was always fair and he used his brains. Nancy respected him for this and also because she knew that he financed his group's activities almost entirely out of his own peacetime savings.

Politely Fournier suggested that, since they had no wireless operator, they might retire temporarily to a safer place until they could become operational. He then had them driven to a hotel in Lieutadès some distance away and there Nancy and Hubert spent several idle days wondering why on earth they had ever come to France.

'For all the good we're doing,' Nancy vowed, 'we might just as well have been parachuted into Brighton.'

On the third day she was sitting listlessly on the wall of the local cemetery when she heard a car approaching. She wondered if it was a German patrol car and, if so, just what she would say when they questioned her. But she was too miserable to be worried so she stayed where she was. A loud laugh shattered the stillness of the cemetery and then, astonishingly, a beautiful, clear voice shouted across to her in English, 'What you doing there, Duckie? Picking yourself a grave?'

With a shriek of joy, she flung herself off the wall and rushed to the car that had halted by the graveyard. 'Den-Den, you darling,' she greeted him. 'How lovely to see you. Where on *earth* have you been?'

The new arrival was Denis Rake, once her instructor at the Mad House, veteran already of long service in the South of France, now (after endless hazards) rejoining her as a wireless operator. Their war, at last, could begin.

13 OLD ENEMIES AND NEW FRIENDS

Denis had had terrible difficulty catching up with Nancy and Hubert. 'My dear, swarms of Germans chasing me everywhere,' he vowed. Now that he had arrived, all three of them felt elated, as if nothing were beyond them. Indeed, with the means of contacting London suddenly at hand, their status among the Maquis had been transformed. They had immediately become a source of power because they had Nancy's money and plans, and Denis's ability to summon arms, explosives and advice, and the specialised knowledge needed to instruct the Maquis in the use of every weapon that London could send them. Even Gaspard, they knew, would at last be glad to see them.

But Gaspard, playing his own game (even whilst he had endeavoured to relieve Nancy of her money) had already made contact with another agent, a Frenchman called Patrice. Patrice, however, knowing that Nancy was supposed to be Gaspard's official liaison with London, had refused to arm the ambitious Frenchman. Then Gaspard heard of a British team headed by an officer named Victor. Promptly he began to woo that group. But Victor also received instructions from London that Gaspard was to work only through Nancy and accordingly rejected his advances.

So eventually Gaspard found that he had lost the Frenchman, Patrice, lost the Englishman, Victor, and dismissed the Australian, Nancy, to Fournier! And Nancy, far from being deceived by his duplicity, had understood perfectly what he had been doing and had determined to bring him to heel.

'I'm a wake-up to him, Den,' she declared. 'He just wants everything we can give him, except orders. Well, we've got to show him that London is boss, not him. So we'll arm Fournier first and Gaspard can wait!'

They drove in Denis's car from the cemetery at Lieutadès to Chaudes-Aigues, where they found Fournier. Whilst Denis worked systematically to install his radio, rigging up an aerial, finding batteries and looking up codes, Nancy told the balding little Maquis leader that his group were to be the first to receive arms, at which Fournier was ecstatic with pride and pleasure – and with delight at having scored a point off Gaspard!

As Nancy and Denis coded their first message to London, he kept interrupting with new weapons he would like and more explosives that would be useful. At last, in spite of Fournier, the coding was completed. Surrounded by entranced Frenchmen, Denis began his accomplished transmission. Open-mouthed, utterly amazed, the forest-fighters listened to the magical tapping of the Morse key that could bring them Sten guns, grenades and bazookas from across the channel. They breathed heavily and stood rigidly beside the Englishman until their tension transmitted itself even to Denis.

'Tell them all to clear out,' he demanded. 'They're making me nervous.' All the spectators left – except Fournier. He refused to budge so Denis continued his tapping. But suddenly he stopped, checked his time schedule and then whispered hoarsely to Nancy, 'God Almighty. Don't tell anyone, but I'm sending now at the time scheduled for *tomorrow*, not for today. Got me dates mixed, Duckie. Afraid there'll be no one even listening to this lot at home.'

Howling with laughter they went through the pretence of asking for some further instructions from London and then disconnected the set.

'We must wait a little,' Nancy giggled to Fournier in French. 'London wants us to contact them again tomorrow.'

'But why do you laugh?' the perplexed Frenchman inquired.

'Oh,' Nancy answered truthfully enough, 'just something Denis said. He was on the stage once, you know. Denis is always making me laugh.'

Fortunately, Denis did not repeat the mistake of his first transmission. Every day of every month had a special time at which he would be expected to 'come through' in London. Two minutes to six one day, thirteen minutes past seven the next . . . and so on. But always different times so that the Germans with their detector vans could not easily pin down a transmitter. From now on Denis, a superbly trained agent, was scrupulously careful always to check his dates and the scheduled times for transmission on each date.

Soon supplies were pouring down upon Fournier's men. On six successive nights Nancy supervised parachutages which delivered everything the group required. Word of this military bounty spread throughout the district and hundreds of recruits flowed in to join them. Nancy's work was on its way.

Waiting for messages was one of her worst duties. Whenever a parachutage was due, the BBC would issue the special code phrase that she had previously sent to London as one suitable for the occasion. Without any preamble it would come over the air, after each of the news sessions. She would hear simply . . . 'The cow jumped over the moon.'

'The cow jumped over the moon' would be the phrase she had asked London to transmit when they planned to dispatch to her whatever she had asked them for in that particular message to them. Also in her message to them she would have given the name of the field (a fruit).

Perhaps she would transmit the message thus: 'Hélène to London. Want boots, Sten guns, money for 500 men at Strawberry. The cow jumped over the moon.'

When she heard the bare BBC message 'the cow jumped over the moon', she would know that that night, on Strawberry field, the RAF would drop boots, Sten guns and money for 500 men.

But there were five news sessions a day, and if on any one of the five the message suddenly stopped coming through, then the parachutage would be off, so all the news broadcasts had to be listened to. And if London wanted her urgently, then they simply broadcast: 'Personal to Hélène . . .' and then whatever it was they had to say.

It was a good system – but it chained Nancy and Denis to their receiving set for months on end – particularly at this moment when so many hundreds of recruits to the Resistance movement were flooding in to her at Chaudes-Aigues.

This influx of recruits was increased by two tragic incidents.

Nancy had set up her headquarters at Chaudes-Aigues and she was sitting in the sun one morning, close to the roadway, when a car drove quickly past. Indifferently she saw that there were two strange men sitting in the front seat. She would not have remained indifferent had she known that the man who sat in the seat nearest her was Gestapo agent Number 47, alias Roger, the spy who had brought about the arrest of O'Leary a year earlier in Toulouse.

Roger was being driven by another Gestapo agent and their mission was to locate and then either capture or assassinate Gaspard.

They drove twenty miles past Nancy to a point where they were halted by Patrice, the French agent, who was guarding the road with another Resistance worker. Roger gave Patrice the correct password and then asked to be taken to Gaspard.

Patrice and his colleague got into the back of the car and guided Roger along the road that led to Gaspard's headquarters. They had almost arrived when suddenly Patrice noticed the ring that hung from the ignition key. It was engraved with German lettering! This could mean only one of two things – either that the two men in the front seat were Resistance workers who had captured a German car, *or that they were, in fact, Germans.*

Patrice bent his head towards his companion and began to whisper. Roger, watching them intently in the rear-view mirror, observed their growing suspicion. Just as Patrice reached for his revolver, Roger turned round, shot the second Resistance man through the head and then fired at Patrice. At exactly the same moment Patrice shot first the driver and then, three times, Roger.

The car skidded to a crashing halt and was immediately surrounded by Gaspard's men who had heard the firing. Both Patrice and his friend were dead. The German driver was slightly hurt. Roger, in spite of a bulletproof vest, had three hideous wounds in his stomach.

The Germans were taken to Gaspard's headquarters and tortured by Judex for information. Word was sent to Nancy, telling her that two Gestapo agents were being interrogated at Mont Mouchet; perhaps she would care to come and ask some questions.

Nancy hastened to Mont Mouchet by car. As she walked into the château she smelt burning flesh and stopped dead.

'What are they doing to them?' she demanded.

'Getting information.'

'I don't want to see it,' she said. 'Why don't they just execute them?'

'We had to find out who they were. They had our password.'

'Do you mean you have *already* found out who they are?'

'Certainly. The leader is a man called Roger. His Gestapo number is 47.' The filthy smell of charred flesh filled the corridor again.

'For God's sake, shoot the poor devil,' Nancy urged. There was no answer. 'I'm going,' she said. 'Tell Gaspard I've no questions.'

Jerkily she walked away into the woods and was sick. The wheel had turned full cycle. Roger had trapped O'Leary, who by now had probably been tortured to death. Roger had been the link in the chain that had caused Nancy's flight to England. Now she was back in France and Roger was himself trapped and being tortured.

A shot rang out from the far side of the château. 'Thank God,' she whispered. Roger, a brave man on the wrong side, was dead. Telling no one that she knew who Roger was (in fact she never admitted to anyone that she had been in France previously) she slumped into her car and was driven back to Chaudes-Aigues.

When Roger failed either to return, or to send back a message to his own Gestapo headquarters, the Germans launched a massive attack against the whole of Gaspard's over-concentrated and under-armed three thousand men at Mont Mouchet. The attack was skilful and the defence, of necessity, was inadequate. Gaspard's men had not even been instructed as to an emergency escape route or reassembly point in the event of their being overwhelmingly assailed.

And the assault was overwhelming. At last Gaspard had to pay the price of the pride that had made him so ostentatiously mass all his men in the one place, for his arrogant treatment of the agents from London, which had left him unarmed, for his political ambitions which had unbalanced even *his* simple knowledge of military strategy. For all his faults, however, Gaspard was an exceptionally brave man. He led and fought in the battle that befell him like a tiger.

His group inflicted severe casualties on the attacking Germans and then – having lost about a hundred and fifty men – were given the order to scatter. That was when Gaspard's lack of attention to military details cost him so much.

With no definite route in mind, with no recognised point of reassembly, the three thousand Maquisards straggled aimlessly through the fields, losing most of their treasured equipment on the way and scattering over a huge area. The more intelligent and forceful of Gaspard's men decided on their own escape route and rendezvous. They simply chose the shortest way to Chaudes-Aigues, their rendezvous being Fournier's group which had been fully armed, as everyone knew, by Mme Andrée.

Every day more and more of these men filtered through. His overtures rejected by Victor, Gaspard eventually headed towards Nancy.

Finally they all arrived, those who had survived, and thus Nancy found herself the only source of communication between no less than seven thousand Resistance fighters (all congregated in the one area just north of Freydefont) and London. At her first conference with the leaders of these men she announced that the Maquis' security had been terrible, that the lack of emergency planning at Mont Mouchet had been unpardonable and that henceforth she would be, for all of them, *chef du parachutage* and that, as such, she would arm them only if they conformed to her concepts of military preparedness. Mutely her announcement was accepted.

This, plus Gaspard's humbling, plus the control she exercised over supplies of money and arms, plus the fact that she and the incapacitated Hubert alone knew all the plans for all the groups on D-Day, now established Nancy securely, if not legally, in the Maquis d'Auvergne as a leader. In little more than a month she had grown from a seemingly useless female agent, with a handbag full of coveted money, into probably the most powerful individual among seven thousand fighting men.

But she was not convinced that Gaspard would keep his word. Therefore, in despair at his stubbornness in flunking more politically than strategically, Nancy decided next to visit a certain Colonel Thomas in Clermont-Ferrand.

Thomas was a soldier of the French Colonial Army who had organised a group of regulars to be ready for combat when D-Day should arrive. He had refused to lead his men out into the fields until then – and, since his men were already trained and organised, there was indeed little point in his doing so. He was also a strong critic of Gaspard's policy of forming large groups in the one area simply for the effect they had on the morale of the civilians in that area, but regardless of the military risks involved. Nancy hoped that she would be able to persuade him to come to Chaudes-Aigues to argue with Gaspard.

The road to Clermont-Ferrand was too dangerous by car, so she had to go by train. Wearing her usual navy-blue outfit and camel-hair coat, she boarded a train at Montluçon.

She was expecting a BBC message at the time. She had her small receiving set in one coat pocket, her battery in the other. The various leads ran under her coat. The leads to the tiny earphones, which plugged right into the ear like a hearing aid, ran up her back and under her hair. Her hair covered the earphones.

So, sitting in a carriage full of German officers, she listened to the BBC.

Her expected message did not come through and, when she met him, Thomas would not agree to parley with Gaspard. Tired and a little bad-tempered she returned to Montluçon and was then driven home to Chaudes-Aigues. It was all in the day's work.

Fortunately, even if Thomas would not talk to Gaspard, she now had the power to control him a little by virtue of her contact with London. And, having acquired the power, she at once set about exercising it. Fournier, still delighted with the treatment she had afforded him, supported her completely.

Whilst her headquarters remained in the valley at Chaudes-Aigues, the mass of the Maquis were distributed nearby in groups, each under its own leader, on top of a large plateau which over-looked the valley and the one road that led into it. The plateau commanded all the other mountains and valleys that surrounded it and the Maquis controlled every path, track and road that led up to it. They were ensconced in the strongest position in the district and they knew it.

Nancy took possession of the best petrol-driven car she could find and had herself driven to every leader and sub-leader of each of the groups on the plateau. As soon as she arrived at each small head-quarters (usually in one of the tiny plateau villages) she got down to business. Her three years' previous experience of Resistance work gave her a secret and unconfessed knowledge of the difficulties encountered and the finances required by a Maquis group. When they tried to bluff her about their expenses, she simply blinded them with a science they had been sure she could not possess.

Accurately she assessed their qualities and then their needs. Mercilessly she budgeted for them. Here, twenty francs a man a day; there, forty; somewhere else, thirty-five. Shrewdly she judged their fighting calibre from the condition of their camp. Having judged, she would then say that she hoped to get them so many of this type of weapon and so much of that kind of explosive and francs to the sum of such and such.

When all her estimates were made, she would allow herself to be entertained. Successively in tents, kitchens, inns, the open air, she consumed huge meals and a stream of brandy – which was where the French had hoped finally to unseat her! But, unfortunately for them, Nancy had been born with a brain as susceptible to alcohol as a block of concrete. She was not a habitual drinker, she had not 'trained' to achieve her endurance and she didn't ever care whether she had a drink or not. But if she did, no amount of alcohol could knock her out. To the Maquis, drinking was what duelling used to be to German students – a point of honour! Outwitted on all other scores, in their conferences with her they relied on this last weapon to preserve their male superiority. Placidly she sat down with them to join battle and implacably she drank them all under the table. And it was as vital to her authority that she did this to the Maquis as it was that she improved their security.

As she drove off from each camp in the morning Nancy would smile freshly at her jaded group leaders and say, 'Well, we have agreed on what you need. Now I must see what my chief in London says.' This gave her time to reconsider her estimates, to change them if necessary and – if she did so – to blame her 'chief' across the Channel for the reduced assessment.

Another duty was to select suitable fields for parachutages and to completely reorganise the methods of reception. Vivid memories of her own comically publicised descent into France spurred her on. The comedy could too easily have been tragedy, and supplies from England were too precious to squander on the Germans through gossip about where and when they were due and fiery blazes of light while they fell.

Accordingly, she vetted every single field in the district and gave each field the name of a fruit. She then cabled to London the Michelin map reference and the fruit-title of each field. In France she kept the names secret to herself and Denis alone. The Frenchmen might then ask for a parachutage. She might agree and she would even accept from a message that the BBC could transmit to warn them that that night the planes would arrive. But, having accepted it, she invariably (without telling them) changed it to something else. The Maquis would never hear their message because it was never sent. But she would hear her substituted message – and then she would organise a reception party. Thus only Nancy and her wireless operator knew what night would be the night of the parachutage. Nancy herself always organised the reception committees and usually she attended them personally. With fifteen containers falling from each plane, and sometimes fifteen planes a visit, she was kept busy night after night, in one part of the country after another, but she thrived on it.

Money began to arrive from London. Whenever it did, she had to be there to receive it. She would take the entire sum with her in a car and pay it out each fortnight to individuals whom she had herself appointed as paymasters. She insisted on a receipt (which she usually destroyed) but the Frenchmen were impressed by the practice and were not to know that she only did it to make the ceremony seem more official. She paid out as much as 15,000,000 francs a month (the equivalent then of about £85,000[4]) and her group were always, to a man, certain of their ration allowances and even, where required, of family pensions which Nancy infallibly delivered in person to the households concerned.

When all the men were at last armed and on a subsistence allowance, she turned her attention to two other aspects of their life. The first, provisions; the second, emergency action. Food, clothing, cars and fuel had often, in the past, been stolen quite unscrupulously from anyone merely unfortunate enough to be at hand. In consequence, the Maquis were getting a bad name among decent French farmers. Emphatically Nancy laid down a new rule. A fair price was to be offered for everything they required. If that price was accepted, it must be paid. If it was not accepted, the object of the transaction could at once be taken for nothing! Collaborationists could be robbed whenever it seemed desirable; the Germans must be robbed whenever possible. The ruling about emergency actions was that every group whenever they took up any position, must, before they did anything else, plan an escape line

---

4   Approximately £2.5 million in 2020.

from that position and a fresh rendezvous for all those who should escape. Remembering Gaspard's sad fate, the Maquis accepted her ruling willingly and set about devising escape routes from the plateau where they were then encamped.

So much did Nancy teach the Maquis, but the Maquis also taught her.

She had been trained by SOE to travel everywhere in France either on foot or by bicycle or train. The Maquis, however, never considered using anything but cars and – in that district – they were right. For one thing, the work of organising the four groups could never have been completed in so huge a zone without a car; for another, London's orders usually arrived so late that only drastic measures and speed could put them into effect in the required time.

The Maquis also taught her that though German garrisons were scattered, Frenchmen were not; though Germans were hostile, Frenchmen were usually not; though the Germans were strangers to the countryside, Frenchmen were not.

These points were by no means as obvious as they seem. What they meant, in fact, was that, in this district at least, provided one kept off the main roads and out of big towns, the Maquis were in control. To have appreciated this point, as Nancy quickly did, was to gain a degree of confidence in her increasing travels that enormously enhanced the speed and efficiency of her work.

April 1944 was coming to a close when Nancy embarked on a second grand tour of her group leaders. She drove by secondary roads in a car that bristled with Sten and Bren guns but still, occasionally, she bumped into German opposition and had to shoot her way out of it. And this worried her – not because of the shooting but because such German activity was ominous.

'Gaspard's mob are still too much of a lump,' she explained to Denis. 'He's attracting too much attention. He'll have to disperse a bit.'

'If it's him that's causing this sort of thing,' Denis agreed, 'he certainly will. All those guns going off, Ducks, I was terrified.' Denis, of course, had blazed away as willingly and as effectively as anyone and what Nancy most loved about him was that, whilst being frankly alarmed by many situations, he invariably stood his ground and fought it out in all of them. She was very glad she had Denis with her.

'Well, we'll have a go at him when we get back,' she promised.

The tour was successful. She found all the groups well-armed, their arms well cared for, their feet well shod, their stomachs well filled. They were dying to fight.

She discussed with each leader the exact location of German underground telephone cables (all to be severed on D-Day) and possible small ambushes until then that would subject the groups to little risk but relieve them of boredom.

The seven thousand men were now assuming personal characteristics. Tardivat, away in the forests of the Allier, was the adventurous one – an experienced army officer who led his men dozens of times in forays against German convoys. They would allow the whole convoy to pass them and then shoot up the last truck.

Laurent, too, Nancy admired for his daring. She found him a wonderful driver who combined fearlessness with acute intelligence, and whenever she had a dangerous car journey to make, Laurent was the man with whom she liked to make it.

Fournier continued to be her most loyal supporter so that she found it easier every day to forgive him his short temper. Besides – his wife nagged him and Nancy always felt sorry for a man with a nagging wife.

161

Only Gaspard, although now quite friendly, remained passively uncooperative. Nancy had come to respect him as a man, but as a soldier in command of other soldiers he enraged her. Nevertheless, he was training his men hard, and in his group, as in them all, morale was superbly high. A formidable fighting force had thus been set up, high on the plateau above Chaudes-Aigues, at St Martial in the heart of Germany's Western Forces.

Then, on 5 June, she received a special message from London that 'Anselm' was being dropped that night and would have to be collected from Montluçon. Anselm, his code name, was being sent to her as a weapons instructor.

Montluçon was Maurice Southgate's area but Southgate had long since been arrested. From Nancy's point of view the arrest was doubly unfortunate. First because of poor Maurice himself, secondly because he had been supposed to give her the address of and password for his contact in Montluçon, and that contact was the person from whom Anselm was now to be collected. This he never had time to do. Nancy knew only the contact's name – Mme Renard – but had not the faintest idea of where she lived or what the password might be to which she would respond.

Therefore, she must now go into Montluçon, which was stiff with Germans, and find a Mme Renard, who might live anywhere and, having found her, then persuade her to deliver up Anselm. It sounded a highly improbable project, but orders were orders and Anselm could not be left in Montluçon for long or the Germans would find him and then her own men would never be adequately trained in the use of their newly acquired weapons.

Fournier gave her his best car and his best driver for the journey. Because of the risk of snap controls (both German and Maquis) the trip took all of that day rather than the two hours it merited, and at every farm and village Nancy had to get out and inquire about Germans.

'Just down there,' the villagers would point and warn. Or, 'They have gone. But the Maquis will stop you. I will come with you and tell them that you are of the Maquis d'Auvergne.' So it went on – until the outskirts of Montluçon.

They hid the car in the bush and the driver hid himself where he could see the car and anyone who might examine it. If, at any time, it were to become an object of German suspicion he would slip away and warn Nancy.

Nancy unstrapped a bicycle from the car's roof and cycled into town. First she called on the pregnant wife of one of her men. She delivered messages and gave the woman some money.

'Do you know any Madame Renard?' she asked.

'I don't think so,' the woman replied.

'Then I'm on a wild goose chase,' Nancy told her. 'All I know is that she probably lives on the outskirts of the town and that she was once a cook in the house of an ambassador.'

'I don't know,' the woman said dully.

'Heavens,' thought Nancy, 'you poor dear. I've never seen any-one as pregnant as you before.'

'But, if you are willing to risk it,' the woman suggested, 'you could go and see a friend of mine who might know your Madame Renard.'

'What's the address?' The woman gave it to her and Nancy pedalled off. The town was lousy with Germans, she noted. The new contact remembered Mme Renard only when Nancy explained that she had once been an ambassador's cook. Then, yes, she knew the address.

Again Nancy pedalled away and eventually found Mme Renard's house. She knocked at the door and it was opened by a pleasant-looking woman with white hair. Nancy asked was she Mme Renard and the white-haired woman nodded in assent.

'Madame Renard,' Nancy declared at once, 'my name is Andrée Joubert. You don't know me but I do know you. I believe you have a "packet" for me.'

Mme Renard simply stood very still and said nothing.

'You don't have to believe me,' Nancy continued. 'Frankly I wouldn't if I were you. Perhaps if I were to tell you how I found you?' She told the long story. Mme Renard still made no response. The two women, instinctively liking one another, nevertheless stood silent and divorced by suspicion. A faint sweet aroma of cooking floated to the door.

'Ooh,' Nancy murmured, sniffing blissfully. 'Lovely! I know all about your cakes.'

It was better than any password. Promptly Mme Renard stood to one side and said, 'Please come in.' She led the way into the kitchen and motioned to Nancy to stand still.

'It's all right, Anselm,' she called. Swiftly she flung open a cupboard door.

Anselm, white-faced and brandishing a .45 revolver, stood staring out at them. Then his face relaxed into a grin.

'Oh, it's you, Nancy,' he said in broad American tones.

'René!' she burst out. 'René Dusacq. What on earth are you doing here?'

'Like you said when I kissed you goodbye at Wimpole Street,' he told her. 'I was jealous! So I've come all this way to join you.'

Mme Renard prepared strong coffee from René's supplies and fed them with a delicious *baba à rhum* cooked by herself. René grinned hugely at the extravagant comforts of life in the Resistance.

'Where to from here?' he asked.

'Chaudes-Aigues' she told him. 'Fournier's headquarters.'

'Far?'

'Yes – but we've got a car!'

'You've what?'

'Got a car,' she repeated tranquilly. 'Don't worry, René – it's much the safest way. They do it all the time in this district.'

They said goodbye to Mme Renard and Nancy led the shaken American back to where she had left her car. The driver appeared from his hiding place in the bushes as they drew level.

'Anyone been snooping?' Nancy asked.

'No one,' he assured her.

'Good. Let's go.' With René sitting petrified in the back seat and Nancy, a Sten gun lying easily across her lap, in the front, they drove uneventfully back to Chaudes-Aigues. When they arrived there they were told that the Allies had just landed in Normandy and that the long-awaited D-Day had become a fact.

14 PITCHED BATTLE

Before they had left London Nancy and Hubert had been given a list of those demolitions to be effected by the Maquis d'Auvergne on D-Day – vital points to be attacked and destroyed the second the invasion started.

These were the plans that, along with money, Nancy had carried in her handbag in the early days of her meeting with Gaspard – the plans and the money the Maquis had hoped to steal from her.

The targets listed for destruction had been the underground cables which the Germans laid throughout the area and used – imagining them to be safe – instead of telephone lines; factories at Clermont-Ferrand and Montluçon; a synthetic petrol plant at St Hilaire and a railway junction at Moulins.

As soon as he had become amenable to reason, Nancy had passed on this list of D-Day targets to Gaspard and he, in turn, had delegated the various tasks to groups situated conveniently to those targets. In the ensuing weeks the Maquis had planned their various operations very carefully and they had even located all the underground cables which the Germans had imagined so secret and safe.

And so, whilst Nancy sought and found Dusacq, the Allies landed. By the time she had returned to her headquarters the underground cables had been cut, the steelworks at Clermont-Ferrand had been rendered useless, the factory at Montluçon had been destroyed and the Moulins railway junction was a madhouse of torn and tangled lines and shattered rolling stock. Only the petrol plant remained intact – and that, the Maquis had asked, since they themselves were stealing all its petrol, to be permitted to spare.

'Hell,' protested Nancy, 'we've missed all the fun.'

René Dusacq was very welcome because he had arrived as a weapons instructor and strange new weapons were now flooding down to the Maquis every night. Although he was an expert on every sort of gun, Dusacq's great passion in life was the bazooka. So fervently did he sing the praises of this deceptively harmless-looking stovepipe that the Maquis promptly dubbed him Bazooka. Thereafter he was never called anything else – although fate saw to it that no bazookas were ever dropped into the Auvergne in his time.

For the next ten days Bazooka instructed Maquisards frenziedly in the use of all the weapons that were dropped to them out of the heavens, the Maquis attacked everything they could, and Nancy and Denis were kept busy organising replacements of weapons and ammunition expended in these engagements.

The Germans did not accept these onslaughts lightly. On the contrary, they indulged in fearful reprisals against anyone who lived anywhere near the scene of any such attack.

Time after time Nancy drove past farmhouses that the Germans had doused with petrol and then fired. Outside sprawled the bodies of the farmer and his wife and children. Charred, mutilated bodies which the Nazis forbade to be buried. Corpses swung hideously from the branches of trees. Hostages were taken out and mercilessly shot. The whole country was blazed by the track of anti-terrorist reprisals in which the frightened Germans now indulged.

And no sector, on the whole, gave the Reich more cause for fury than Nancy's – the Auvergne, the Fortress of France. Methodically, the SS laid its plans and prepared to obliterate the group whose stronghold was the plateau above Chaudes-Aigues. Troops were massed in towns all around the plateau; artillery, mortars, aircraft and mobile guns were made available; then, steadily, secretly, an enormously powerful army began to close in – through the valleys and over the mountains – from all sides.

But of this Nancy and her mission were blissfully unaware. On 20 June 1944 they were advised that there would be a heavy parachutage that night and a massive daylight parachutage the following afternoon, both of them on the plateau. No less than a hundred and fifty Liberators were to take part in the daylight drop.

Cursing the fact that they must attend two drops within twenty-four hours, Nancy and her men went out to receive the night parachutage, little knowing that a force, whose object it was utterly to destroy them, was already close at hand and ready to pounce. It was very late when they returned to Chaudes-Aigues and they were all tired, dirty and cold. Invasion or no invasion, Nancy had to have a bath and a few hours' rest. For too many weeks on end now she had made do with two hours' sleep a day – usually after lunch – and now there was need of absolute strength and alertness.

Chaudes-Aigues boasts hot springs, so Nancy at once adjourned to the public bath centre and took a long, hot plunge. Then she retired to bed, clad elegantly as usual in her nightie. She had brought two handmade French nightdresses with her and from now on, until the end of the War, regardless of what the next day might seem to offer, she always went to bed in one of them. However masculine her garb might be whilst she walked or fought, she would sleep like a proper lady! Just before dawn she was rudely awakened by the sound of gunfire.

Flinging herself out of bed she dressed in slacks and shirt, grabbed her money, carbine, revolvers and Sten gun and joined the rest of a now thoroughly roused headquarters. The sound of heavy rifle fire reached them from up the valley.

Packing everything they could into their car, they rushed off to Fournier's house. Then, at a hot pace, they drove up to the plateau and joined the main body of the Maquis.

The seven thousand Maquis were being attacked, in a determined attempt to wipe them out, by a huge encircling force of twenty-two thousand SS troops. The Germans were being supported by artillery, mortars, spotter aircraft and dive bombers. Steadily they closed in from all sides and then began their crawling drive up towards the plateau itself. Confidently the Frenchmen awaited them.

Nancy, Hubert, Gaspard, Laurent and Fournier held a hurried conference at the village of Freydefont on the edge of the plateau. Nancy listened to the steady stream of battle orders that were dispatched to all points around the perimeter – listened to them and memorised them. Only Gaspard's orders displeased her. He and his men, he declared, would fight to the death.

Nancy knew that it was not the task of any of them to fight to the death. To fight, yes, but only fight to fight another day. There was a long war ahead of them yet and if all Gaspard's men died the group couldn't possibly execute all the future tasks that would be assigned to them by London to hamper the Germans *after* D-Day in the battles that had been planned to secure the liberation of both France and Europe.

'We'll get out tonight under cover of darkness,' each leader agreed, except Gaspard. Nothing Nancy could say would alter his decision. Furiously she went and found Denis.

'Got through to London yet, Den?'

'Yep, Gertie. They've given me a time to come back on the air. They'll be ready for me an hour from now.'

'Well, when you get through, tell them about this attack. Tell them we're going to try and get away tonight. Cancel today's parachutage and ask our people to *order* Gaspard to evacuate tonight. The idiot wants to stay here and fight it out.'

Carefully Denis began coding the long message. So far it had been a hellish morning. First of all, the dawn flight from Chaudes-Aigues; then tapping furiously at his set for over an hour trying to attract London's attention at a time when London, not expecting him, wouldn't listen to his unscheduled transmission; now, less than fifty minutes in which to prepare all his messages and start transmitting again. Shells began to crash down into the village. Nancy looked across at him and smiled.

'Gertie,' he muttered absently, 'I'm terrified.' But he kept on coding. Nancy kissed him affectionately from behind his chair. 'I'll go and collect last night's containers and see how the boys are doing,' she said.

First she drove alone to the scene of the previous night's parachutage. They had not had time to unpack any of the containers then. Now, with a battle on, all these supplies would be needed.

Single-handed she opened every container and loaded its contents on to a truck. For hours she worked, ignoring the occasional mortar bombs that exploded on the field, completely occupied with the physical effort of opening containers, lifting out their grease-packed arms, carrying them to her truck and loading them. But at last it was done.

She then drove to all the fortified vantage points on the plateau and at each one she found the Maquis blazing away happily and effectively. Wherever they were needed, she distributed more weapons or ammunition. For all their vast superiority in numbers and arms, she noted, the Germans were being pinned down and suffering heavy casualties among the mountainside's volcanic rocks.

171

Bazooka, when she met him, was furious that she travelled alone, but she told him to stay where he was.

'Keep an eye on their fire,' she told him. 'Make sure they aim low.'

'OK, OK,' he growled. 'But tonight, when we pull out, I'm gonna make sure there's someone to look after you.'

'Bazooka,' she mocked, though secretly touched by his chivalry, 'I didn't know you cared!'

'Bah,' he shouted after her. 'Scram!'

She continued her drive and noticed, a little absent-mindedly, that the shelling had become heavier. An observation plane circled maliciously round her car and directed artillery fire which pursued her into the village. The house trembled under a barrage of explosions as she entered it.

'Did you get through?' she asked Denis.

He nodded.

'Parachutage cancelled?'

'It's all done, Gertie. Don't like this shelling much.'

'Why don't you get outside?'

'Waiting for the message about Gaspard.'

'Oh, yes. The idiot still says he won't budge. Well, there's nothing we can do till London comes through. I think I'll have forty winks.'

'In *this* lot, Ducks?'

'I could sleep anywhere,' she replied. 'Anyway, there's nothing else I can do. I might as well rest.' Retiring to her bed, with shells pounding the whole village, she took off her revolvers and her boots, loosened the belt on her trousers and went to sleep.

A frantic Fournier woke her up a little later.

'Andrée,' he shouted, 'you must not lie here. Already the house has been hit.'

'The Germans are still being held, aren't they?' she demanded.

'Yes.'

'Then I can sleep.'

Again he shook her. 'You must not sleep here,' he persisted. Complaining bitterly, she got up, put on her boots, did up her belt, collected her carbine, Sten gun and revolvers and walked outside. A shell exploded in the street and splinters of stone smacked against the wall behind her.

'Much worse out here,' she grumbled and dashed across the road. She found a convenient patch of cool shade under a tree and lay down. It was a fine hot day on the plateau.

'I will be here if anyone wants me,' she told her companion. Then she went to sleep again.

She was woken next time with the news that London had sent through a personal message for Gaspard. It ordered peremptorily that he evacuate under cover of darkness with the rest of the Maquis and it was alleged to have been inspired by General König himself – König being the head of Free French Headquarters.

'London says König says Gaspard's got to withdraw with the rest of us,' Denis shouted.

'Thank God for that, then.'

'Do you believe König really said it, or do you reckon London made it up?'

'I don't even care, Den. Just you write that message out again and this time *sign* it König.'

Delighted at such an unscrupulous order, Denis obeyed it at once.

Straight away Nancy drove alone and under fire to Gaspard's position. She handed him the message. A grunt was the only indication he gave that it meant anything to him at all, but she now knew him well enough to be confident that this meant that he would do as he was told.

'See you later on,' she shouted in farewell. A small village about a hundred kilometres away, and close to Saint Santin, was their rendezvous when and if they escaped the German encirclement. Leaving Gaspard to repel a heavy attack, she drove off along the winding and exposed mountaintop road, heading back towards Fournier's group at Freydefont.

Five planes flew overhead and machine-gunned Gaspard's position. Nancy careered along the difficult road and flung an apprehensive glance back over her shoulder to see where exactly the hated Henschels were. To her horror two of the planes at once broke sharply out of formation and headed wickedly down the road towards her.

There was a vicious clattering behind her, a roar overhead and the dusty spurt of machine-gun bullets along the road in front – then both planes whipped away from her. In her rear-view mirror Nancy could see that the back of her car was riddled. She swore volubly in French and felt better.

But it was not yet over. Climbing sharply upwards the planes parted company. One whirled down towards Gaspard again, the second swung around sharply and then hurtled straight back at her car.

The car and the Henschel arrowed towards one another. For once the road was straight and there was no cover. Instinctively, in her terror, Nancy slowed down. The bullets spat like chain-stitching into the road ahead and the burst ended twenty feet from the car's radiator. Her sudden change in speed had spoilt the pilot's aim. As he thundered low above her Nancy caught sight of goggles and helmet and muttered to herself, 'Good God, Old Nick himself.'

Twice more he attacked and twice she slowed and swerved to save herself. And she was still more than two miles from Freydefont, with the Henschel preparing for yet another onslaught, when a young Maquisard flung himself into the roadway and signalled her to halt.

'The village has been evacuated,' he gasped. 'Quick, follow me.'

They flung themselves into a ditch as the plane, chattering unpleasantly, returned. As soon as it had passed the young Frenchman leapt to his feet and started running.

'Just a minute,' Nancy called after him. Puzzled, he halted. She dashed back to the car and wrenched the door open. Already she could hear the snarl of Old Nick's approach as she rummaged along the bullet-torn back seat. Finally she flung herself back into the ditch. Machine guns chattered, the car exploded in flames and, the second the plane had roared past her, she joined her companion behind a rock.

'Forgot these,' she explained. Proudly she displayed a small saucepan, a jar of face cream, a packet of tea and a red satin cushion. The Frenchman looked at her as if she were mad and then, shrugging, told her that Fournier's group were in the woods some distance away.

Whilst the German plane circled, they ran; whilst he machine-gunned them, they crouched behind rocks. And so, alternately galloping and crouching, they reached the woods. There they found their colleagues highly amused by the curious sight that Nancy (clutching cosmetic jars, saucepan, tea and red satin cushion) had presented as she hurtled downhill with the Luftwaffe in pursuit. After a moment's reflection she too decided that it had been funny and joined in their laughter. With gratitude she learnt that the youngster who had halted her car had volunteered for the job and had insisted on doing it alone.

Darkness was falling at last when the Germans began to force their way over the plateau's ledge. But they had left it too late. Already, along their previously selected lines of withdrawal, the elusive and destructive seven thousand Frenchmen were making good their escape. By obscure tracks and rocky descents, and even by road, they were picking their confident way through the oncoming circle of Germans. Anything they couldn't carry with them, they burnt. They left nothing behind them except corpses and the rocks of the mountains.

Fournier's group had devised a particularly ingenious method of escape. Weeks ago it had been decided that the one way that no one could get out would be across the deep and fast-running river Truyère. Therefore, they chose that as their route. In the ensuing weeks Fournier's men had worked hard and long, driving logs into the riverbed – logs that reached to within an inch of the swift-running water's surface. They had thus created an invisible footpath to safety.

The Germans, confident that the river could not be crossed in force without a bridge, and confident that there was no such bridge because their planes had not spotted one, guarded the Truyère only loosely that night, and at ten-thirty Nancy, escorted by Bazooka and four hundred of her men, slid quietly down the riverbanks.

Guides led them across, footstep by footstep. They were fired on but they crossed in safety. Then they began the long trek to Saint Santin. It was a hundred kilometres by road and they intended marching there by obscure tracks and valleys over a route probably half as long again as that.

They had walked an hour, silently and purposefully, when they met Gaspard's group. Gaspard himself at once joined Nancy. Then, arm in arm, Gaspard on one side, Bazooka on the other, in the utmost goodwill, Nancy and the two men plodded along together. Each had at last learnt the true worth of the other and was well satisfied with the day's action. They had cause to be satisfied. For the loss of under a hundred of their own men they had vitally engaged the attentions of twenty-two thousand crack German troops, of whom fourteen hundred now lay dead on the slopes that led to the plateau. And they themselves, in good order, were marching surely away to a rendezvous where they would live to fight many more battles for France and the cause and freedom.

On the principle of keeping one experienced officer with each of the small escaping parties, Denis, Hubert and Nancy had all left along different routes. An Alsatian officer led Nancy's group because he knew the area well. He had no teeth and no conversation but he was a good guide. Continually along the route the party would split up into smaller fragments as they reached districts familiar to others of its members.

Finally, Nancy and a hundred and twenty men marched together. They stumbled on for three days and nights, passing through villages only when they knew that those villages had no telephone lines, going ten miles out of their way, if necessary, to avoid civilisation. All the way they met with friendly peasants and constant news of other groups who had passed by.

The first night they halted by a prosperous-looking farm. One of the Maquis asked for water for his men and for 'the girl'. The farmer's wife refused the request except that she offered 'the girl' a glass of milk.

'If you haven't got water for your own countrymen,' Nancy vowed, 'you haven't got milk for me.' Raging with thirst they continued on their way. A little further on, at a very small farm, where poverty and hardship were written on every line of the family's faces, they were proudly offered food and coffee. The coffee was terrible, but the marchers enjoyed it as much because of the spirit in which it had been offered as because of their thirst.

On the second night they again received ready hospitality from a peasant couple. They had all adjourned to a barn to sleep when the wife called Nancy.

'You must not sleep out there with the men,' she said. 'You must sleep in my bed.' Gratefully Nancy accepted the offer and the Frenchwoman herself prepared to sleep on the floor. But when Nancy saw the filth of the sheets and of her hostess's feet, as the other woman removed her sabots, she suddenly lost her appetite for the bed, made her excuses and rejoined her men in the barn.

On the third day they had trouble with German spotter planes, but they made good time nevertheless. They marched all night as well and in the morning reached their destination – a little village near Aurillac.

The deputy mayor at once made them welcome and found them all billets. That day many others of the Maquis joined them – among them Denis and Mme Fournier.

Typically, Denis arrived in a flurry of extravagant dramatics.

'Gert,' he said, 'I found some of your eau-de-cologne when I left so I brought it out with me.'

She looked in wonder at him. The joy of pouring eau-de-cologne all over her tired body was almost too beautiful to contemplate.

'But,' he added, 'I've used it! I rubbed it on my feet on the way here! They were giving me hell.'

Nancy knew that Denis had bad feet and she understood the solace that eau-de-cologne would have brought him on the long march.

'That's all right, Den,' she told him. 'I'm glad you used it.'

Behind Denis she heard someone smothering his laughter and glanced towards him. Rake, when she looked at him again, had gone crimson. Then everyone began to laugh.

'Well, actually, Ducks, and probably you'll kill me for this, I didn't use it for my feet, I drank it!'

'Denis!' she shrieked. 'You fiend!'

'Sorry, Gert. But I just had to have a drink. No use trying to lie to you. All the way, for three days, I've reeked like a perfume bar. Everyone between here and Freydefont knows it!'

In the general amusement that followed, Denis drew Nancy aside.

'There's something serious I've got to tell you,' he said. She stopped laughing and looked at him intently because it was unlike Denis ever to be serious about anything.

'What is it?' she asked.

He drew a deep breath, straightened his shoulders, looked her squarely in the eyes and said, 'I burnt my codes on the way out. I was afraid the Germans might get me, so I burnt the codes. Hid my set too. That doesn't matter – easily get another set, they're hidden everywhere. But I haven't got any codes. Sorry, Gert.' His voice trailed off.

'That's all right, Den,' she told him gently.

'I had to do it,' he muttered miserably.

'Of course you did,' she reassured him. But even as she spoke her mind was working fast. She *had* to get in touch with London. There would probably be many orders to be received and certainly there was a vast amount of information to be given. Without these orders, without delivering her information, without fresh supplies from the air, the successfully withdrawn Maquis d'Auvergne would no longer be seven thousand fighting soldiers but simply a disorganised rabble. Yet she had no code with which to transmit her messages even when she did find a wireless set. Well, there was only one thing to do – get a message through to London through an operator in another group that had *not* lost its code.

She called on a banker and told him she needed a contact.

The banker, who could travel with impunity, went into Aurillac and saw a man called Valentin. Valentin called on Nancy and advised her that there was a French operator across the mountains.

She carried a bicycle across, having made arrangements to rejoin all her group at Saint Santin, to find the Frenchman.

It was a long, hot trek, pushing her cycle up endless miles of mountain road and she reached her destination tired and irritable only to find that the radio operator had fled the district the day before.

Wearily she wheeled her bicycle along to the nearest bistro. The patron rushed out in considerable agitation.

'You must not come in here, Madame Andrée.'

'Why not?'

'There's a Communist here. He says he will shoot you.'

Nancy was in no mood to be blackguarded out of a much-needed drink by the threats of a Communist. Angrily she strode into the bistro, head down like a young bull in a manner that had become almost characteristic, flung herself into a chair beside the Communist and slammed her revolver down on top of the table.

'I hear,' she announced disagreeably, 'that you are going to shoot me. Well . . . you'll need to be very quick on the draw! Patron, a cognac.'

Not for a second, whilst she drank her brandy, did her eyes leave those of the Communist. Then she left the bistro, mounted her bicycle and rode to her rendezvous at Saint Santin. The vital message to London had still not been transmitted.

When Denis heard of this disappointment he flung himself into a frenzy of concentration, tugging at his right ear, pinching the end of his nose, rolling his head back and slamming his forehead with the open palm of his left hand. These were his customary aids to a hilariously unprecise memory. Finally he announced to Nancy that when he had landed in France he had stayed in a 'safe house' en route to Lieutadès, at a town called Châteauroux, and in this house, he was sure of it, there was an SOE operator. Unfortunately Denis was always extremely vague about addresses. Often, in England, for example, he had addressed letters to friends simply by putting on the envelope their name and the town and then drawing the house in which they stayed. On another occasion he could only remember the number of the house across the road from the one he wanted – so he had addressed the letter 'opposite No 27'. These were now the kind of directions he gave Nancy.

One of the men who had looked after him was, as he had said, an operator. Didn't know his name, but he had a hunch shoulder. Couldn't remember the address, but the house looked like this. Wasn't sure of the contact, but it was the patron of a bistro in a tiny square that was unmistakable because it contained one scraggy tree and faced on to a rather squalid canal. Graphically he described the square, the tree and the canal.

Then and there Nancy decided to cycle the great distance to Châteauroux to look for the bistro, the house and the man whom Denis had described.

15 EMERGENCY MESSAGE

Clothing was her main problem because, having abandoned everything on the plateau, she possessed only the slacks and blouse that she had worn all the way from Freydefont – and she did not imagine that she would be very successful travelling by bicycle for two or three days through German-infested country clad in such unfeminine and battle-stained slacks.

She decided, however, to wash and patch them and then risk riding into Aurillac, where she knew a tailor who would make her a respectable-looking outfit. As she was doing these repairs, a car drew up outside the house. From it descended Laurent. He had driven contemptuously straight through the German encirclement on the plateau and so had made a leisurely trip all the way to Saint Santin.

For a while everyone alternately hugged him and cursed him, glad to see him, but furious that they themselves had walked whilst he (typically) drove. At once Nancy discussed with Laurent the possibility of her travelling by car to Châteauroux, but even he admitted that that was impossible. The Germans, he pointed out, furious at their failure to wipe out the Maquis on the plateau, had tightened all roads through the main towns almost to the point of strangulation. Nancy would be lucky to get through by bicycle; by car it was out of the question. Personally, Laurent objected to the idea of her going by any conveyance whatever.

'I've got to go,' she said, and that ended it. She had had the power of being the group's sole contact with London; now she had the consequent responsibility.

In her clean slacks she cycled into Aurillac and visited the tailor. He measured her quickly and told her to come back in two hours for a fitting. Although his shop was right alongside the Milice he seemed unperturbed and anxious to help. The suit, he declared, would be ready for her to wear the next day.

'All right,' she agreed, 'I'll be back in two hours. Now where can I buy some shoes?' He gave her the address of a shoemaker and so, still conspicuous in her slacks, she left him.

Idly she shopped for an hour, buying things that she thought would be useful for her men, then she went to the shoemaker.

'Get out of Aurillac,' he warned, the second she entered his shop. 'The tailor has sent a message that both the Germans and the Milice have been asking him who the woman was who came into his shop in trousers.'

Leaping on to her bicycle she sped out of the town, using back streets all the way, and returned to Saint Santin. So she still had no clothes in which to travel to Châteauroux and now she could not possibly return to Aurillac for her suit wearing slacks.

Instead she borrowed a dress from a very old lady in Saint Santin. This was an elegant peasant model, date about 1890, and Nancy felt far from happy in it – not because of the Germans but because of her own men!

She made arrangements that she should ride into Aurillac in the cart of the old lady's husband, travelling as his daughter. So that no one should see her in her terrible disguise, she agreed with the old man that he should pick her up with his cart at dawn.

But all her cunning was in vain. Just as she clambered into the cart, looking, as she frankly admitted to herself, like the complete 'farmer's dopey daughter', Denis came out into the road. Maliciously he surveyed her scrubbed and shining face, on which there was no trace of make-up, her hair, deliberately washed and combed so that it was lank and straggly, her incredible peasant's boots and her quaint white piqué dress. Then, doubled up with laughter, he raised the alarm.

'Hey,' he shouted. 'Quick, quick. Just come and see our Gertie!' Sitting in front of a mound of vegetables, a pair of torn trousers in her arms (her excuse to re-visit the tailor) and affectionately mocked from all sides, she rattled off towards Aurillac, her face deep red with embarrassment and laughter.

The old man's cart was halted a dozen times during the twenty-kilometre ride. The Germans questioned him and searched his vegetables, but they showed no interest at all in his revolting-looking daughter. Nancy didn't blame them.

When they arrived in Aurillac, she climbed awkwardly down from the cart and clomped into the tailor's shop. For thirty seconds he too failed to recognise his customer of the day before. Then, quite delighted, he gave her a fitting. All the time he tucked and pinned and marked with his chalk, he chuckled to himself.

'*Quelle type, quelle type,*' he kept on gurgling.

When he had finished he promised to send the completed suit over to Saint Santin the next day.

After she had done some more shopping and eaten a fragrant meal of bread and garlic, sitting straddle-legged on a bench in the public square, she got back into her 'father's' cart, helped him sell all his vegetables, repassed the endless German control points and finally returned to Saint Santin. The next day her suit arrived and she was ready to leave for Châteauroux and (she hoped) her radio contact with London.

As part of their security-tightening process the Germans had called in all identity cards issued in the Cantal. New cards were to be issued. Nancy's identity card purported to come from a Cantal source, but she did not now accept the German invitation to call on them and obtain a replacement. The only thing to do was to travel to Châteauroux without papers. Also, her men remarked, she would have to travel without a licence for her bicycle.

This added risk heightened the anxiety felt by the Maquis on Nancy's behalf. For every minute available before she set off they conferred and exchanged notes, so that finally they could give her a list of contacts and safe houses along the question-mark-like route that seemed most dangerous to them.

Armed with this information, looking smart in her new suit and riding a brand new bicycle, she set off. It was a fine morning and she felt full of confidence.

'Remember,' Laurent shouted after her, 'after the Puy-de-Dôme, go by Saint Amand, Bourges and Issoudun.' She waved gaily back and soon left her anxious men far behind her. The route they had mapped out for her meant a ride of three hundred kilometres to Châteauroux. Then, of course, she would have to ride back again. For the moment, though, she would worry only about getting there.

Her contacts along the route that first day were magnificent. Whenever the road was safe, they knew it and hastened her on her way. Wherever there was a risk of German control points, they scouted ahead and then waved her on when the danger was over. At each main-road junction a guide would escort her across – and through towns also. Thus she cycled through the mountainous Puy-de-Dôme in safety. She was making good time.

It was getting dark and she needed somewhere to sleep when she came to a country bistro, miles away from all other habitation. She bought a simple meal and a glass of wine and listened to the conversation of two other customers. From them she learnt that the Germans were very quiet in the area, which was all that she wanted to know.

She left the bistro, loudly announcing her intention of riding much further along the road, and then hid in the bistro barn. Unwilling to crush her suit, she took it off, hung it up on a nail and covered herself with straw. She was woken just before dawn by the sounds of an Allied air raid somewhere nearby.

She dressed quickly and rode to Saint Amand. There she bought herself a cup of coffee and once more sat down to eavesdrop on her neighbours' conversation. The coffee was filthy but, from the man behind her, she learnt that Bourges had been raided by the Germans the day before.

'If they were there yesterday, they won't come again today,' she told herself, and set off at once for Bourges. Her legs were aching but there was no time to lose. Alarmingly, Bourges was not what she had expected. It was deathly silent, all the shutters were up and the streets were being heavily patrolled by German soldiers. Pedalling as calmly as she could, she rode out of the town again. Finally, she learnt that a group of hostages had been taken by the Germans that same morning and shot. She rode faster than ever after that.

She carried on along the road to Issoudun until she reached a black-market restaurant where she ordered an excellent lunch. While it was being prepared she seized the opportunity to clean herself up, conscious as ever of the fact that she must not attract attention at any stage by looking like a woman who had cycled two hundred kilometres.

After the meal she ordered a bottle of brandy and invited the proprietor to join her in it. By the time half the bottle had gone the proprietor, who loathed everything German, had reached a stage of gloriously outspoken indiscretion so that, from him, Nancy learnt everything she needed to know – town gossip, local events of importance over the past few months and the nearest way to the markets. This was the kind of information that enabled a Resistance worker to travel through strange country without appearing to be a stranger – the kind of information that saved lives.

Blessing the proprietor for his drunkenness and his loose tongue, Nancy, sober as ever, set off on her bicycle for the Issoudun market. There, like any other good Issoudun housewife, she shopped briskly and stowed her purchases in a string bag which she slung from the handlebar of her bicycle. Then she rode out of the town, threw away her weighty groceries and headed boldly for Châteauroux, which she reached late that afternoon, thirty-nine hours after she had left Saint Santin. She had travelled two hundred kilometres, slept six hours, talked and eaten for three. Thirty hours' riding then. That meant an average of ten kilometres an hour and over mountains as well. No wonder her legs and backside were on fire.

She was delighted to find Châteauroux very peaceful. She rode round and round looking for the bistro Denis had described with such typical vagueness – the bistro where he had said she would find a contact who could give her the address of the hunch-shouldered district leader. Would a hunched shoulder be sufficient description? And would the contact in the bistro, if now she found it, give the man's address to a strange woman anyway?

On her third circuit of the town she was beginning to feel both conspicuous and worn out. She still had not found the bistro. Full of pessimism she started yet another circuit – and then, suddenly, she saw the place for which she had been searching, right under her nose, looking exactly as Denis had described it. She parked her bicycle and went inside.

She had to wait quite a time, and drink quite a few Pernods, before the patron allowed her to be included in the general conversation. Gradually then she won his confidence. Finally she asked if the man who had the hunched shoulder was still around. Expressionlessly the patron admitted that he was and later told her where he could be found.

As she was mounting her bicycle a young Frenchman passed her. He looked familiar. 'Hey,' she shouted, 'Bernard.'

He turned round. 'Andrée!' he exclaimed in delight. 'What are you doing here?' She had met him once in the Maquis of Corrèze – a good memory was a necessity in her calling.

She explained to him why she was there. He then told her that his group had also been attacked. Their wireless operator had been killed and he too was looking for an operator to send a message for him. He knew of a Free French operator in Châteauroux and planned to contact him now.

'Then we both want the same thing,' she said. 'Look, you come with me while I send my message, then I'll go with you while you send yours, then we'll ride back to the Creuse together. Agreed?' The Creuse was a department between Châteauroux and Saint Santin and she had now grown so weary that she wanted desperately not to be alone.

'Agreed,' he said, and escorted her to within two blocks of the address given to her in the bistro. This building also agreed with the graphic but unlocated description Denis had given of it.

Cautiously she climbed the staircase and approached the door of what she now knew must be the SOE man's flat. She heard voices inside but, when she knocked, the voices stopped and no one answered. After three attempts she gave up and rejoined her friend, who still waited for her two blocks down the road.

'No good,' she told him.

'Perhaps my friend would send your message also,' the Frenchman suggested. They cycled across Châteauroux and reached a bar that faced the flat in which, Bernard declared, the French operator lived. Nancy's companion left her looking after their two bicycles and went inside the bar, but when he gave the password he was at once warned to stay away from the house opposite. The Gestapo had raided it. The French team had escaped but they had had to abandon their radio, and two members of the Gestapo were still waiting in the flat, hoping that someone like Bernard would call.

Night was approaching fast by now and neither Nancy nor her comrade had anywhere in Châteauroux to sleep so they determined to try her contact again and once more rode through the town.

This time they approached the building together and found the front door firmly closed.

'Ring the bell,' the Frenchman suggested. Nancy pulled the *cordon de sonnette*, but not for her contact's flat: she rang for the flat below, remembering that the SOE agent had already refused to open his door to her once. The main front door opened and Nancy then explained to the lady who confronted her that she had made a mistake – that she actually wanted one of the neighbours.

Very obligingly the lady offered to call her neighbour and padded upstairs to knock at his door. He opened it just as Nancy and her companion arrived behind her. Cautiously – unable to do anything else – he invited them inside. He had a hunched shoulder.

Once again without any password or means of identification, Nancy laid her cards on the table, talking fast and authoritatively to the elderly man who stood before her.

'I don't expect you to introduce me to your friends,' she concluded, 'but I would appreciate it if you would take them a message to send to London for me. If you don't want to receive the answer on your set, a BBC message to me will be perfectly satisfactory.'

He questioned her closely and eventually convinced himself that she was not a Gestapo agent. Mention of Denis's name concluded the matter and he agreed to pass on her message. At that moment, a voice called him from the next room. Leaving Nancy and her friend, he withdrew. They heard a murmur of conversation. Then he returned.

He proceeded to deny everything he had said, told Nancy he didn't know what she was talking about and asked her to leave the flat. Obviously the people in the room beyond had decided that she was from the Gestapo.

'You idiots,' she blazed. 'If I *had* been Gestapo, I've got a witness here of everything you've said and you'd all be under arrest by now. God preserve me from ever having to work with fools like you again.'

She and Bernard then rode out of Châteauroux, heading for a Maquis group in the Creuse, forty kilometres away. They slept a few hours that night in a haystack and next day the Maquis leader told Nancy that she could, if she liked, visit his operator and, if this man agreed to send her message, he would not object.

He told Nancy where to contact the Free French operator and she then drove across to him in a borrowed Maquis car. She explained that her own countryman had not trusted her and that she must get a message through to London. 'I know there's a lot of friction between your headquarters in London and mine,' she admitted frankly, 'but will you do it?'

'Certainly,' the operator agreed at once. He sent off a message asking that his headquarters, in Algiers, should cable London to tell them that Nancy's group had no radio and no codes and needed replacements of both.

Straight away she drove back to Creuse, collected her bicycle and then set off alone again, through a series of completely German-controlled towns, on the shortest route back to Saint Santin. No detours now. She travelled direct.

She chose the shortest route, in spite of its dangers, because she was rapidly approaching that stage of exhaustion where not only did every mountain-choked mile count, but also she doubted that she could ever last the distance.

However strong she was physically, she had led an exhausting, near-sleepless life in the past three and a half months. In the last fortnight she had done a forced march of a hundred and fifty kilometres and now – unaccustomed to cycling – had ridden almost continuously for four hundred kilometres more. She still had another hundred to go before she reached Saint Santin.

Her legs were in agony and her seat was so sore that she no longer dared to dismount. She was distressfully aware that, if she did, she would never again get back into the saddle of this machine that had become nothing less to her than an instrument of torture. She ignored the torments of tiredness, thirst, cramp and all the calls of nature, rather than submit to the ordeal of re-mounting her cycle once she had given herself the exquisite pleasure of parting from it.

So, panting, and even occasionally moaning, she flogged herself on. Short distances became nightmares. The final goal of Saint Santin became a sort of lunatic obsession. Sometimes she cursed dully, sometimes her mind wandered and she returned to reality only just in time to avoid plunging off the road and into the gorge below, but most of the trip was just relentlessly determined slogging.

And then, at last, it ended. Her face greasy with sweat, her eyes deep in sockets drained white by sheer physical exertion, and every nerve in her body shrieking for the sort of comfort which nothing, except perhaps death, could have provided, she ground the cycle up to the headquarters in Saint Santin and clumsily tottered off it.

A roar of greeting surged down and around her from the veranda of the house where her men were eating their midday meal. Wild with excitement they swept towards her and gathered her to them. Whereupon, to their utter astonishment, Madame Andrée burst into tears.

She wept chokingly like an exhausted and terrified child and the men stood awkwardly round her, wanting only to comfort her but not knowing what to do.

They thrust her into a chair – at which kindness she emitted a shriek of pain and sobbed more loudly than before. Then her men looked so bewildered and distressed that she found herself hysterically laughing as well as sobbing.

'She must lie down,' ordered Fournier, convinced that her iron nerve had at last failed her and that she was suffering from a nervous emotional storm.

'No! No! No!' she bellowed.

They gave her a drink and she drained the brandy as if it were tap water and imperiously indicated that she needed more. Anxiously they gave her more – and slowly she began to regain her composure.

Soon she was sufficiently self-possessed to admit the main cause of her distress.

'I'm sorry,' she said, 'it's just that damned bicycle. I'm so saddlesore I could die.'

Everyone then explained to her how it was that there had been no one on the road to meet her. They hadn't expected her back for at least another twenty-four hours. Many had felt gloomily certain that she would never come back at all. It was incredible to them that, in less than seventy-two hours she should have completed her mission and cycled more than five hundred kilometres as well. It was almost as incredible, knowing the region she had traversed, that she was still alive.

Typically, it was Denis who restored her equanimity.

'What you need, Gerty dear' – and he gently massaged his rump as he spoke – 'is a good rub down with eau-de-cologne!'

'Denis, for that I could kill you,' Nancy told him emphatically. He took her arm and led her in the friendliest possible way to a chair.

'Try sitting on one side at a time,' he urged. Gingerly she let herself down. 'Now,' he continued, 'what happened? How did you do?'

With great gusto Nancy told them the story of her trip to Châteauroux and back to Saint Santin. She spoke particularly forcefully about radio operators.

'Don't ever,' she commanded, 'let anyone tell me again that the Free French won't cooperate with the British. Without the Free French I would never have got my message through. They were wonderful. Don't worry, Den-Den. Any day now London will be sending you more codes and another wireless set.'

Now they could think about fighting again.

16 AMBUSH

It took Nancy three days to recover from her ordeal by cycle and by that time it was clear that everyone had escaped the Nazi net at the plateau of Chaudes-Aigues. All they had to do was listen in every day to each of the BBC's special message periods and wait for the one that would mean that a new set of codes and more arms and money would be parachuted down to them.

Among the new arrivals at Saint Santin was a strange Frenchman who claimed that he was a colonel. As such he was certainly the most senior officer in the area, but that did not entitle him to speak the way he did. He was arrogant and dictatorial and Nancy encountered him for the first time one day at lunch. The colonel was busy telling Hubert that he was going to assume command of everyone in the area. Very quietly and very ominously Nancy interrupted him.

'*Mon colonel*,' she said, 'I don't know your name because no one has introduced us and because I've never seen you before in my life. But if you've finished giving us your orders, perhaps you would now explain to us just *how* exactly you are going to get arms and money when you have assumed command. You see,' she explained, 'I am the *chef du parachutage* for this Maquis and I can assure you that you will get nothing from me!'

Denis and Bazooka took no pains at all to conceal their joy at the colonel's consequent discomfiture, nor did the French. Everyone suspected that Monsieur le Colonel was a fake, anxious only to jump on the bandwagon now that the Allies were coming; but no one had so far dared to challenge a person of his alleged exalted rank. In cases such as these, however, Nancy always felt quite confident that a *chef du parachutage* could, if necessary, outrank even a field marshal.

She took Hubert, Denis and Bazooka for a long walk in the forest that afternoon. 'If this bloke is typical of the sort we're going to get down here,' she told them, 'then I've had enough. There's nothing but complications with these bloody politicians like our friend the colonel. We're not having any more of it.'

'What do you want us to do, Gert?' Bazooka asked. 'How about Denis and I shoot him?'

'I can only shoot people when I'm drunk, Bazooka,' Denis announced with dignity. 'And Gert hasn't got any more eau-de-cologne. Have to think of some other solution.'

'The Allier, that's the solution,' Nancy told them. 'Hubert, you and I will drive up there and see Tardivat. We'll find a new base and move our headquarters there. OK?'

'OK.'

'Bazooka, you'll have to take over while we're away. And, Den, probably your codes and radio will come then, too. If they do, you'll have to receive the parachutage yourself.' Their minds made up, they returned to their house in the village.

Publicly snubbing the colonel, Hubert then announced formally that he and Nancy were going to find a new headquarters in the Allier and that, in the meantime, Bazooka would be in command. Immediately after that, the two leaders left Saint Santin by car.

Tardivat welcomed them with open arms and was delighted that Nancy should have decided to move into his area. She was as delighted to be moving her group so near to him, and when he showed her a possible forest site for a camp, she at once accepted it. Tardivat also told her that a group of anti-Fascist refugees from Franco's administration formed a Spanish Maquis nearby in the forest. She was introduced to them and found them a most impressive body of men.

'We'll bring our people up here,' she announced decisively.

'Good,' said Tardivat. 'Then we can fight together.'

Hubert remained in the forest to make arrangements whilst she returned in the car to Saint Santin to collect her men.

There she found that the message warning her of the parachutage had already come through on the BBC and that Denis and Bazooka had gone out in her absence to receive the 'packets'. It turned out that as well as the arms and the radio and the codes she had requested, London had also sent her a radio operator – a young American Marine called Roger. He was about nineteen years old, fair, tall and good-looking, and he spoke very little French. Henceforth he was to be Nancy's personal operator. Denis, who had recovered his buried set, became personal operator to Hubert, using the same codes as Roger, and Bazooka was ordered to go to another Maquis near Clermont-Ferrand to instruct in weapons there.

They parted with Bazooka sadly and then, about two hundred strong, they set off for the Allier. Arriving there, the men camped in the forest whilst Roger, Hubert, Denis and a handful of others set up their headquarters in a farmhouse near Ygrande. Nancy commandeered a bus, had it converted into an office and living quarters for herself and parked it alongside the house. In a few days they became an efficient fighting unit once again.

July 1944 arrived and Tardivat, now regarding Nancy as an equal comrade-in-arms, took to inviting her to accompany him on ambushes laid against German convoys heading for the Normandy front.

They would prepare their plans and choose their position with scrupulous care. Also they would manufacture large numbers of home-made bombs – plastic explosive wrapped in socks or stockings. Then their party would drive to the chosen spot which was usually not closer than twenty miles from their camp. The drivers of their trucks and cars would wait in their vehicles on the far side of the vineyards, away from the road, whilst the Maquis lay in the drains immediately alongside the road.

Soon the convoy would rumble towards them. They always allowed the whole column of vehicles to enter the trap. Then they would destroy the first two or three armoured cars and the last two vehicles in the column.

Toss their bombs, fire from the hip as they withdrew across the vineyards, into their vehicles and away – leaving behind them twenty or thirty German dead and a mounting Nazi dread of the forest terrorists.

Half a dozen times Nancy and Tardivat fought together thus, so that she grew to admire him as she had seldom admired anyone and he, describing his regard for her to the Spanish Maquis colonel, said, 'She is the most feminine woman I know – until the fighting starts! Then' – and he kissed his fingers – 'she is like five men.'

On the other hand, Nancy, explaining her somewhat unladylike actions to Denis, declared, 'If I'm to keep the respect of these camps, Den, I've got to keep up with them. I mustn't panic and I must seem as game as they are. And when you're with a man like Tardivat, that isn't easy. After all, he *is* a man and I *am* a woman.'

◆　◆　◆

It was their lookout up on the hill who warned them of the coming German attack. Swiftly but calmly they collected all their gear and left in cars and trucks and on foot along the inevitably prepared line of withdrawal. Three thousand Germans attacked, and their fire was heavy, but the Maquis group had had plenty of warning and when the attackers finally closed in they captured only an empty farmhouse.

◆ ◆ ◆

London's recent orders had been that Nancy should concentrate her attentions primarily on those Maquis groups in the Allier, although she would still be at liberty to provide such help as was required by a few other groups in the Puy-de-Dôme, groups like Gaspard's and Laurent's. Therefore, she moved camp now only into another nearby forest.

Moreover, she had to stay in the area, Germans or no Germans, because the next night it had been agreed that two more weapons instructors were to be dropped to them – unfortunately in a field close to the scene of that day's attack at Ygrande. London advised that these instructors were Americans.

Late the following night she, Hubert and a few others prepared their field. Fires were stacked, torches were held ready, sentries watched anxiously for enemy patrols and about eighty men circled the clearing to fight off any attack.

In silence they waited and softly the dew wet the grass. For the hundredth time in her career the thought struck Nancy that nothing was more symbolic of the Resistance than this evening dew. When darkness fell, it would suddenly appear, wrapping the whole of France's mountains and fields and forests in its heavy, pallid hand. It was silent. It was everywhere. And then, as daylight dawned, it evaporated magically into thin air – until nightfall, when it would appear again. So it was with the Resistance. A force of the forests and of the night; silent, ubiquitous, mysterious. And yet, when the sun rose, gone; leaving only the ashes of a fire or the wreckage of a bridge to mark its furtive descent.

So it had been through the months and years of occupation and right up to the present time. Now, of course, its nature could change. With the Allies back in Europe, the Resistance movement could become less a heavy dew and more an avalanche, fearfully poised, unsuspected and yet ready at any moment of the day or night to crash on to the enemy who lay below.

It had been a long road that the spirit of France had trod. Nancy remembered the first milestone along that road. She had been standing in a crowded tram just as the Germans marched into Marseille. Two German officers crossed the road in front of the halted tram at the Boulevard de Gambetta. Their boots gleamed, their uniforms were brutally smart, their whole bearing was unshakably confident. Nancy had happened to glance at the tram driver behind whom she was standing. She saw two tears trickle down his cheeks. Just two. Then the Frenchman's eyes had grown hard and he had carried on with his work, his face grim but no longer grieving.

And the second signpost on the way to victory? What had that been? Undoubtedly Madame Sainson, her intelligent brown eyes gleaming with the joy of battle and laughing at the irony of being photographed in the joint company of three American evaders and three soldiers of the Axis.

The next milestones, it seemed to her, had been Judex's raid on the sports store, then the battle on the plateau, and now these final preparations – not just for small ambushes or for fighting their way frantically out of enemy encirclements – but for full-out Maquis attack. She glanced back at one of her devoted Spanish bodyguards, past him then towards a sentry, away from him to a crouching Maquisard – none of these were any longer mere hunted outlaws: they were all confident fighting men who were certain that they would win.

'*Advise whether the Maquis D'Auvergne is suitable to be financed, equipped and instructed for use on and after D-Day . . .*' That had been the initial reason for her visit to France.

Well, she had advised and they had been equipped, financed and instructed, and D-Day at last had come. She felt passionately proud of the France she saw today and of her own Britain that had never lost its confidence in the spirit of Frenchmen.

Hubert broke the trend of her thoughts: he could hear planes. They lit their fires, alerted all their men and flashed their torches. The cars and lorries on the field's perimeter, facing inwards, turned on their headlights. Then the planes roared overhead and the parachutes came tumbling down, out of the moon-drenched sky into the flaring field.

The first instructor landed on the wrong side of the hedge and was appalled to see the area now seething with running men, vehicles of all types, three bonfires and flashing torches. Then he heard hoarse shouts of '*où sont les americains?*' so he shouted back across the hedge.

He saw (vaguely, because he had jumped without his thick glasses) a young woman running confidently towards him. She had black hair and a cheeky, white-toothed grin. With one hand she dragged along a laughing man, in the other she held a bottle of champagne. Reaching him, Nancy and Hubert introduced themselves, using their pseudonyms, as Hubert and Madame Andrée. The American's name was Reeve Schley.

'Call me Gerty,' Nancy said. 'Everyone does. Here . . . have a drink and welcome to France.' Whilst Schley gulped good, dry champagne out of her proffered bottle, Hubert asked the vital question.

'Do you speak French?'

'No.'

'Jesus Christ,' replied Hubert. 'Does your friend?'

'Only a little.'

'God Almighty,' quoth Hubert. He now had a mission in the centre of France in which his American wireless operator and his two American instructors spoke either very little or no French at all. It was a trifle perplexing. Nancy, on the other hand, seemed to find the tall American cavalry officer a perfect recruit to their organisation. Quite apart from the fact that she approved of the guts of anyone who would risk parachuting into France when he could speak no French, she was delighted to observe that Schley was in uniform. Very shrewdly she realised just what a magnificent boost to morale it would be for all her men at last to see an Allied officer boldly wearing his proper uniform instead of skulking round in civilian clothing. Such boldness could only mean, to anyone who observed it, that the day of Liberation was close at hand.

On the other side of the field the second American officer, also in uniform, had been located and identified by two of Nancy's men. His name was John Alsop and he had spent the last twenty minutes searching for Schley's bag which contained his glasses, because without his glasses, Schley was quite blind. Alsop was led to the middle of the field where, already, much of the gear that had been dropped, including bazookas, was being loaded on to trucks. There he met Nancy and Hubert, was offered a drink, and exchanged glances of consternation with Schley. Never had they seen so much chaos. But the woman, Gertie, seemed self-possessed and confident, so they left themselves in her hands.

They were bundled into cars and driven away, and to the mechanically minded Americans their convoy of assorted French automobiles and trucks was the most ludicrous collection of vehicles they had ever seen.

Surprisingly soon they arrived at the Maquis' new forest-shrouded headquarters and there promptly adjourned with Nancy and Hubert to her converted bus to eat and talk and drink several bottles of excellent wine. Vastly relieved, Schley found his spare glasses in the one suitcase that had been brought back with their convoy from the field. He put them on at once and examined his hosts with new-found interest. He found that his hosts were examining himself and Alsop just as shrewdly.

The two British pumped them first for news of England. Wittily and amusingly, for both were cultured men, the Americans filled in the gaps left by the BBC's excellent news service.

The Americans inquired searchingly about their duties for the future and the attitude of the Germans at the moment.

'No need to worry about them,' Nancy stated.

'Don't they ever try to round you up?'

'Oh, yes! They attacked yesterday. But we always have a way out.' The Americans gulped at this casual assessment of what, to them, sounded highly dangerous – and then carried on with their questioning.

'How many Maquis are attached to your mission?' Schley asked, surveying Nancy curiously as he spoke. He observed a young woman who slouched a little to identify herself with her men and to disguise her own quite unmasculine charms, who coped with the roughness of endless male conversation by assuming a mask of amiable vagueness, whose eyes gazed at him with unfailing politeness but also with an occasional blankness which perhaps indicated that mentally she had withdrawn to a gentler mental environment and whose lips were constantly parted in a cheerful and slightly crooked grin. Here, unmistakably, was one who lived fully and equally the life of her fighting men but who remained always a woman.

'Difficult to say exactly,' Nancy replied, 'but it would be more than seven thousand.' (Actually it was 7,490). This information impressed the Americans profoundly. Gradually Nancy then dug out the story of how they themselves had come to land in Europe as agents of the Allies.

Reeve Schley, a lawyer on the outbreak of America's war, had volunteered for the Navy. They rejected him because of his eyesight. Always an enthusiastic equestrian, he had then enlisted with the Horse Cavalry as a private. Eventually he got his commission – whereupon the powers-that-were took away the Cavalry's horses and scattered the cavalrymen all over.

Schley then pulled strings and was shipped to America's saboteur group in London – the OSS. There, after the past two years of what he himself described as 'intensive training, creeping and crawling, etcetera', he found himself doing a 'twelve-dollar-a-week job as a clerk in the city of London'.

'Found all sorts of folk, who'd only been my juniors in the legal profession, were now majors and colonels in OSS – and I was a mere lieutenant.'

Meantime Alsop had had similar experiences. Both the Army and the Navy rejected him for service as a volunteer and eventually he was drafted into the Military Police. 'Not exactly the thing I wanted to do,' he explained wryly to Nancy.

He was later transferred to England as a second lieutenant in the Police Corps. On leave in London one day, he met his brother Stewart, who had for a long time been a member of the British Army. 'Stewart suggested we should go and jump into France,' he related. 'This seemed a novel sort of idea so I went round to OSS and suggested that they might like to put it into effect.'

Apparently OSS approved of the suggestion that they might employ Alsop and accordingly they secured his transfer to the office of their Western Europe Section. There he met Schley.

'And then,' Schley explained, 'instead of one twelve-dollar-a-week clerk doing a desk job, there were two!'

They had nothing to do in their respective jobs, except sit with their feet on the desk and smoke cigars. Eventually they made themselves so persistently troublesome to authority that they were shipped off to Scotland, trained and parachuted, in late July 1944, into the Allier.

'Talking of cigars,' Schley said. 'I've got a boxful with me in this suitcase. My father sent them to me in London. But I don't seem to be able to find my other bag and that's got my best pair of glasses and most of my personal kit in it.'

'Don't worry,' Hubert urged. 'It's probably still down on the landing field. I'll have a look for it for you in the morning. As it's nearly four o'clock now – how about some sleep?'

They were shown to a farm outhouse which Nancy had had scrubbed clean for them. There were two mattresses on the floor and these Nancy had herself made into neat beds. Between them, also on the floor, was a jar of forest flowers. Not much of a welcome, Nancy had reflected when she had finished preparing it for her guests, but better than nothing.

As they crawled into their beds and felt the soft smoothness of parachute-nylon sheets, and remembered the night's good conversation and superb wine, Alsop turned toward Schley.

'Hey, Reeve,' he whispered. 'After all those buzz-bombs and what else in London, these silk sheets will do me. G'night.'

◆　◆　◆

At about eight that morning the peace of the sleeping camp was rudely shattered by long bursts of machine-gun fire.

Schley woke under the violent shaking of Alsop's hand. 'Listen, listen,' Alsop said.

'Go back to bed,' Schley urged, 'it'll only be the Maquis practising.'

Out in her bus Nancy heard Denis's voice come startled to her from his tent.

'Gert, what's that?'

'The Germans, you twerp,' his Gert snapped back, shedding her pink nightie with the embroidered neckline and donning slacks and revolvers instead as she spoke.

The camp burst into furious life, men deploying in all directions to meet the attack. In the farm shed, Schley and Alsop dressed frantically. Schley jammed on his beautiful cavalry boots first and then couldn't get his equally beautiful trousers over the top of them, so he hacked off the narrow bottoms and emerged from the shed curiously clad in ragged shorts.

Nancy called Denis to her. 'Where's Hubert?' she asked.

'Don't know, Gert.'

'Well, no use worrying. Look, find young Roger and put him in a truck with all our records and the codes. Send him out to wait for us in the forest.' It was essential that wireless operators be protected and the codes saved. Without them, cut off from London, a Maquis was crippled. 'You go with him,' Nancy ordered.

'No,' Denis refused. 'One operator is all you'll need. I'll stay here with you.'

Some wounded were brought back to the headquarters, many of them seeming to be only children, mostly with abdominal wounds. Schley and Alsop rushed over, horrified at the fate of these eighteen-year-old forest fighters.

'Here,' they said, 'use this for the kids,' and offered their brandy flasks. Nancy found some pure alcohol and then again spoke to Rake.

'Den, darling, will you look after the wounded?'

'Me?' he exclaimed in horror. 'Why me?'

''Cos I'll only faint and there's no one else.'

He muttered mutinously but he agreed.

'Den,' she called back again, 'look after the bus and Roger first, will you?'

Rake straight away took command of the evacuation. He was pushing a bicycle up on to the bus roof when Schley appeared in his raggedly chopped-off shorts.

'Very fetching indeed,' Denis murmured . . . and the next second was shrieking with terror. The local electricity wires hung low over the bus and, in passing up the bicycle, he had placed the metal frame in contact with the cables. A stream of current was charging through him.

Yelling and jerking, Rake gave every indication of being electrocuted. In the middle of the battle the whole headquarters group gathered round to help – and then, realising that the wireless operator would not die, began to laugh. Whilst Schley and Nancy held a conference to try to work out the interesting electrical problems of disentangling Denis from his high-voltage bicycle, the rest of the Maquis rolled round the ground in helpless mirth.

Eventually Rake freed himself and joined in the general hilarity. He succeeded in stowing the bicycle on top of the bus without further hitches and then Roger, enigmatic as ever, although furious that he was not allowed to join in the fighting, drove out of the area along a woodcutter's track which, although the enemy did not know it, led to safety.

A runner arrived to tell Nancy that the Germans were entrenched at the junction of the main road and the road that led down to the camp and that they had armoured cars there as well. At once a Maquis captain, whose knowledge of things military was as small as his courage was high, suggested that a party of twenty men should go up to the crossroads with *les deux américains* and there, simultaneously, be instructed in how to use the bazookas that had arrived the previous night, and, with bazookas, attack the German armoured cars and machine guns, thus relieving the group of its most immediate danger.

Nancy translated to Schley and Alsop, who first registered immediate dismay and then quickly agreed. For a second she wondered what was wrong. Neither Schley nor Alsop were the type to be afraid, so why the dismay? But, of course! Pitched battle is hardly the time to give weapon instruction to men whose language one can't speak. On the other hand, the Frenchmen were now clamouring to go, and the Americans would not consider backing down.

'I'll go with you,' she told them, seeing the quick gratitude that spread over their faces as soon as she spoke. She looked very matter-of-fact about it all and they decided that probably the battle was not as serious as it sounded.

Actually the battle was just as serious as it sounded. Reports that had reached Nancy indicated that they were being attacked by between six and seven thousand Germans, and with her there were only two hundred Maquis. Still, this was no time to show any panic and there was a job to be done.

Leaving Denis to command the headquarters and look after the wounded (however reluctantly) she chose twenty men and they then set off up the curving road towards the crossroads. Each man carried a Bren gun or a Sten; Nancy and the Americans carried carbines, revolvers and grenades; also they had four bazookas and an ample supply of rockets.

Several hundred yards up the road Schley suggested tentatively that their progress might perhaps be more militarily correct if they were to deploy into the cover of the forest. Nancy gave this order and thirteen of the men at once obeyed her but seven of them deplored this cowardly technique and continued to walk brashly along the road.

No sooner had Nancy and the rest reached cover than there was the sound of fierce machine-gun fire. All seven men on the road toppled to the ground and stayed there.

The thirteen other Frenchmen were only seventeen- or eighteen-year-olds and their nerves failed them when they saw the gruesome fate suffered by their friends. So they dropped their arms and ran.

Nancy sprang to her feet at once, infuriated by this display of cowardice, and bellowed after them. Rage had an extraordinary effect upon her. The customary vague amiability of expression, the slightly crooked grin, the slouch with which she had for months camouflaged her own femininity all vanished from her. Except for her cheekbones, her complexion paled whilst her eyes flared with green fury, her features tautened into porcelain smoothness and her body straightened until she achieved a posture of statuesque fury. Anger and danger seemed to stimulate her. There was no fear in her face nor in her mind. Rather her brain worked with the speed and smoothness of skates on ice and her casual acceptance of authority crystallised into a full-blooded instinct to command and to lead. Wholly feminine, transformed by the catalyst of her own anger into an astonishingly erect and fine-drawn beauty, she stood there, feet apart, hands on hips, head flung back and surveyed her fleeing men. Then, like a whip, lashing them through the forest trees and ringing out savagely even above the sound of machine-gun fire, her voice pursued them.

'My God,' exclaimed Alsop, 'who'd have thought it? You could hear her across the Rhine. Wonder what she's saying?'

'Whatever it is, doesn't sound like it'll ever be quoted in a drawing room,' observed Schley laconically.

Schley was right. Nancy was using every foul oath she had ever heard in the days of her black marketing in Marseille, the days when Henri had taught her the correct responses to the vile abuse of the market traders.

Some of the fleeing men were only speeded on their way by this fearful blast of language, but some, after a particularly ripe reference to a lavatory brush and what each of them might do to himself with it, halted and returned, shamefaced, to the fray. Fiercely then she ordered them to provide cover for her own attack.

Alone, she and the Americans advanced, leaving the others to guard their rear, to within firing distance of the crossroads and delivered a sharp volley of bazooka rockets at both armoured cars and the machine-gun posts. With devastating violence, the rockets burst – first in front of the crossroads trench from which the Germans fired straight down into the heart of the Maquis camp and then, with awful finality, in the trench itself. Abruptly life in that enemy trench died. Next the armoured cars were destroyed. Nancy peered for a long minute towards what had been, seconds before, a group of living men firing machine guns. Then, certain that the threat to her camp had been obliterated, she allowed her eyes to drop and shrugged a little at the ugliness of what had happened. The two Americans saluted her ironically and instantly she grinned mischievously, allowed her body to sag into its customary slouch and started walking back to the camp. As Shakespeare might have said, Nancy was herself again. She rounded up the few Frenchmen who had returned to support her and ordered them to collect all the weapons abandoned by the fleeing men. Then, in good order, they withdrew a quarter of a mile back to their headquarters.

There they found Denis attending to the wounded. His head averted, he was deliberately swabbing their wounds with a pad soaked in pure alcohol. In between swabs he took a regular sip of the alcohol for himself. He was very drunk and armed to the teeth. From his belt hung a terrifying array of grenades, suspended only by their rings, over his shoulder was a carbine, in his holster was a .32 Colt with a bullet up the spout and the safety catch off! He was certainly the most hostile-looking medical orderly the Americans had ever seen.

'Can't stand all this mess,' he explained as he dabbed gently but blindly at a stomach wound. 'How's it going?'

'Not too well,' Nancy replied. 'I must get word through to Tardivat. If he could counter-attack from the rear for a while, we could get out. Otherwise we've had it.'

'Anything I can do?'

'No, you stay here with the wounded.' Rake groaned but stayed on the job. Now that he was drunk he would much rather fight.

Nancy called over Schley and Alsop and told them, a little untruthfully, that everything was under control. Then she ordered a scout to accompany her and set off towards the Spaniard's camp. It was two miles away on her flank. Tardivat, on the other hand, was well away from the area under attack and at its rear.

For much of the way she was under fire and for the final stretch she had to crawl the entire distance through long grass on her stomach. But eventually she found an outpost of the Spanish camp.

'Tell your colonel I'm in trouble,' she ordered him urgently. 'Ask him to contact Tardivat for me and see if he can counter-attack from the rear.' The Spaniard repeated the message and then Nancy and her scout returned to their besieged headquarters.

'We hold out till Tardivat relieves us,' she explained to the Americans. So a tight perimeter was formed round their position and Schley (deciding that there seemed to be very little chance of his ever using them in the future, and determined that they should not fall into the hands of the Germans) distributed his boxful of cigars. Cheerfully smoking a fine Havana, Nancy now blazed away in the direction of their attackers.

There was a slight interruption when some of the Spanish Maquisards entered the camp and delivered the bodies of the seven men killed on the road. Each man had, whether dead or still living, been shot again by the Germans, very deliberately, in the middle of the forehead and all the faces had been cold-bloodedly mutilated.

'Put them in there,' Nancy said, indicating the shed in which Schley and Alsop had slept. 'I'll come back for them tomorrow.'

At that moment sounds of a terrific onslaught against the Germans' rear were heard.

'Tardivat,' said Nancy. 'Quick – let's get out.'

The Germans, unsure of the extent of the attack on their flanks and rear, turned to fight off this new enemy. After a short time the attack subsided and then ceased. Turning round to resume their battle against the first group, the Germans found that Nancy and her men, in cars and trucks, had vanished. At the same time Tardivat's force melted away from behind them.

At their agreed rendezvous all her men met again. Roger was there as arranged. Soon Tardivat, grinning hugely, a vital, athletic figure, also joined them.

'I got your message,' he said, 'when we were having lunch. I just shouted to my men, "Come quickly, Madame Andrée is in trouble", and so they all stopped eating and we fought the Germans.'

'Frenchmen stopped eating?' she queried.

'For you, yes,' Tardivat laughed. 'A special exception.'

17 SABOTAGE AND COGNAC

When Schley and Alsop had accustomed themselves to this sudden atmosphere of war, they went to find Nancy and inquire if there was anything they could do to help set up the new camp. They were told that she had left the camp to go back and look for Hubert.

'You know,' Alsop remarked to Schley, 'that girl would cheerfully risk her own life to save any one of the men here. She's gone straight back to where we've just come from to look for a guy who should be looking after her.'

'Don't forget,' Schley reminded him quietly, 'that only this morning she was looking after us! Remarkable girl.'

'Remarkable temper too. Hope she never gives me a tongue-lashing like that.'

A car drove into the camp; in it were Nancy and Hubert.

'He was looking for your lost bag,' Nancy shouted to Schley. 'Got cut off from us by the attack. Too bad. He missed all the fun – *and* the cigars.'

'Any Germans down there now?' Schley asked curiously.

'No. All gone home.' She walked quickly away to give Roger a message for London. Placidly he coded it, then balanced his wireless on the wheel of a truck and tapped the signal out. Nothing ever bothered Roger. He could send messages from any place in any circumstances. Nancy felt positively maternal towards him.

'Well that,' summed up Schley, talking of their recent foray at the crossroads, 'must have been one of the most unsuccessful missions in the history of war. But why do you imagine the Germans broke off the action so early?'

'Union hours,' Alsop informed him. 'It was four o'clock. I guess we're free for the evening!'

◆ ◆ ◆

Next morning Nancy took a truck back to the outhouse in which the Americans had slept on their arrival, to collect the bodies of the seven dead Frenchmen. There she met Gaspard and Laurent. They had driven up to see her the afternoon before, had heard the fighting and lain low. Now they helped her load up the corpses.

Back in camp she washed the bodies carefully, particularly the hideously torn faces, and then shrouded them in parachute silk – this, the same woman who only two years earlier had nearly fainted when her hand was placed against the cheek of a dead woman. Gaspard watched her respectfully. '*Formidable*,' he murmured.

Nancy then held a conference at which she suggested that the least they could do was to give the bodies a decent burial and, when everyone agreed, the whole group got into their transport and drove to a nearby cemetery. The cemetery was surrounded by a high wall and had only one exit and into it poured the executive of the entire Maquis, plus all their foreign assistants, to conduct a forty-five-minute burial service. Outside, just so that no passing Germans could possibly fail to see them (or so the alarmed Americans felt) was posted a Maquisard with a machine gun.

Eventually it was over. 'Did that feel like forty-five minutes to you?' queried Alsop. 'More like five days,' responded Schley.

And since Nancy and her followers had seemed perfectly at home throughout the ceremony, the Americans wondered, as they drove back to their camp, whether they would ever get used to the strangeness of it all.

They stayed for several days in the forest near the Spaniards and then moved on to the forest of Troncet, to a much more elaborate camp. Here the routine hard work really began.

For the men, in between attacks on convoys, bridges and rail-way lines, there were the regular chores of camp life – cleaning, doing sentry duty, cooking and fetching water – and, in this respect, only a recent batch of gendarme recruits failed to fall into the spirit of the place. Full of the dignity of their social position as police-men, they refused to do their stint of water carrying. The matter was reported to Nancy.

'You don't want to collect water, I hear?' she asked, marching up to them. They were all sitting on a tree trunk and they indicated that this was so.

'Well, then, of course you mustn't,' she said sweetly. 'You are gendarmes. Water carrying is not for you. Now you just stay there comfortably in the sun and I'll get the water for you.'

'This,' remarked Denis, 'I must watch.'

She put the buckets in her car, drove to the nearby lake, filled them up and drove back to the headquarters. Then, grim-faced, she opened the door of her car, took out one bucket of water, marched across to the first gendarme and deposited it violently upside down over his head.

'Don't move!' she bellowed at his startled companions. Petrified, they sat where they were. And so, one after another, she helmeted every one of them with a pailful of water.

'That's our Gertie,' commented Denis placidly.

'In future,' rapped out a very cold Mme Andrée, 'whether you're gendarmes or not, you'll do your share of all the work. Now – go and get me ten buckets of water.'

Sadly, the ten gendarmes disappeared with their buckets down towards the lake.

For the Americans work was endless. They started with squads of trainees at dawn and they switched from squad to squad, right through until dark. They instructed on Brens, Stens, mortars, piats, bazookas, grenades and carbines. Stripping, loading, aiming, cleaning – everything had to be taught. Especially the cleaning. Nancy, whose own weapons were always immaculate, was fanatical in her insistence on that. But she had only the profoundest admiration for the way the two Americans persisted in their task of instructing anyone who needed instructing in a group that numbered nearly seven and a half thousand.

Hubert and Rake were kept occupied with reporting to London on the purely military aspects of the situation and now that it had become less fluid and more orthodox, Hubert had found his feet and was working very efficiently.

Nancy herself, as *chef du parachutage*, had almost insurmountable difficulties to overcome. Every single day there were engagements of some kind or another with the Germans. Most of the time she was too busy to join in them, but always she had to replenish the ammunition used by them, replace any weapons lost in them, pay out the subsistence allowances for her 7,490 men, make allowance to their dependants, wait in the dew-drenched fields for parachutages that occurred four times or more a week and inspect the various groups to see that they both needed the weapons for which they asked and correctly maintained those she had already procured for them.

All of these inspection journeys were done now with the protection of a personal bodyguard. Several times recently Nancy had had to shoot her way out of attempts by the Germans to halt her car. Once, even, a drink-crazed Communist had attempted her assassination. He had aimed for her car with a bomb. It had exploded too early and he had been pulped against a wall whilst Nancy herself escaped unhurt. Hubert thereupon asked for volunteers to travel with her as an escort on any subsequent expeditions.

The colonel in charge of the Spanish Maquisards at once begged her to allow his men the exclusive privilege of protecting her, and Tardivat, who knew the Spaniards well, urged her to accept their offer. Gratefully she did so.

For a while the Spaniards always drove in the car ahead of hers and in the vehicle which followed Roger's car. They had removed half the windscreen of each car and filled the empty space with Bren guns. Whenever they met trouble, the plan was, the front and rear cars would fight; Nancy and Roger, in the two middle cars, must run. But after only two trips she declared her intention thereafter of travelling in the leading car.

'Very brave of you, Gert, but why?' inquired Roger.

'Not brave at all, Roger,' she assured him. 'It's just that I can't stand any more dust!'

Their skirmishes were numerous but always ended up safely – except once. Then, having shot their way out of a road check and careered away, they continued along the road at hair-raising speed and swerving wildly.

'Don't swerve so much,' Nancy instructed firmly. Her driver gave her a furious glare and then jerked self-righteously at the steering-wheel, which promptly fell off the column and into his lap. Abruptly, they were precipitated, car and all, into the ditch.

The devotion of the Spaniards to their British leader was a touching one. Whilst regarding her as their complete equal as a soldier, they nevertheless protected her with the utmost gallantry because she was a woman.

In the course of journey upon journey, and fracas after fracas, they never lost patience and never failed in their enthusiasm. Riding along the dusty roads Nancy would suddenly order a halt.

It would be time to listen for the special messages on the BBC or it would be the scheduled moment for Roger's transmission of his coded phrases to London. Whilst she listened attentively at her tiny set, or whilst the fair-haired American tapped casually on a wireless that he balanced on his knee, the escorting Spaniards would wait silently and patiently, smoking cigarettes, watching alertly for the enemy.

But it was when a long journey made it necessary for them to eat away from their headquarters that the bodyguard were at their fiercest and gentlest with her.

They would stop at what seemed a safe restaurant and at once all the Spaniards would pour into the building. They would check everyone's identity – motioning savagely with their Stens – examine each room and interrogate the proprietor. Only when they were convinced that all was entirely safe would they allow their dust-stained Andrée to leave her car and enter the restaurant.

They would seat her alone at the best table, order the establishment's best food and wine and then stand menacingly around her whilst she ate in solitary splendour, guarding her throughout. Then, replete, she would get back into her car and they would continue their dangerous journey.

She grew to feel that she was never out of her car with its faithful escort of Spaniards. She and Roger seemed eternally either to be sending the message: *Hélène to London*, or listening for the emergency BBC call: *Special for Hélène*, or waiting for the code phrases that came after the news that would mean *the planes will be over tonight*. All the time, using only the weapons of her own personality and her ability to grant or withhold supplies, she controlled, moderated, changed or cancelled action by the Maquis so that it conformed with her instructions from London.

July and the beginning of August were fabulous months for France's Maquisards. They attacked, sabotaged, killed and raided all over the country. Only occasionally could Nancy spare the time to go out with them. She joined in a few more cheerful ambushes with Tardivat, she led one attack on a railway line and participated in two others and she and a Spanish bodyguard shot her way unhesitatingly out of any German attempt to check her car. But mainly, at this time, she was a *chef du parachutage* and a leader.

Until the War ended – or she was captured and tortured to death – she would always have to have fields ready, for ten days before the full moon and ten days after it, every month. Twenty days a month her seventeen chosen fields must be manned by a skeleton staff who would hide in trees and watch the area continuously so that, if ever anyone should start snooping, she would be warned at once.

Then, when her message came over, she must have a full reception committee ready, with trucks to carry the containers away and herself in readiness to supervise every detail of the actual parachutage.

And if there was an emergency drop, she would have to make snap preparations – or, if the drop came in a non-moon period, she must go to the field with her Eureka radio set (which was attuned to a sister set in the plane, called a Rebecca, and which would guide the blind navigator to her tiny field that lay invisible in the blackness of all of France below him) and operate the delicate instrument until the plane roared overhead, when fires and torch flashes would indicate their position quite definitely.

The task was unending and remorseless. Yet London showed her repeatedly that she was not unappreciated. Regularly, once a month, amid containers full of grenades, explosives and deadly weapons, there would be personal parcels containing such pleasant surprises as face cream, sweets, lipstick and little notes (often rude but always delightedly received) from her various friends back in the headquarters of SOE in Wimpole Street.

Twenty nights a month, as long as life or the War should last, she had to be ready. Hers was the sole responsibility, but hers also was all the power and authority attached to that responsibility.

The forest of Tronçais is a large forest and it comfortably accommodated many, many groups of the Maquis. In other, rosier days for the Germans, the great Goering himself had once hunted wild pig there. Now Goering was gone and the Maquis hunted instead. But they lived a harsh open-air life because, although these forests provided safety, it was the experience of people who lived in them that they were also the welcoming refuge of every stray thunderstorm in Europe. It was always raining in Tronçais.

There were no houses available, so Nancy lived in her bus, beside which, with a corrugated-iron roof and lean-to walls, there was an officer's 'shower room'. The others lived in tents manufactured out of different-coloured parachutes.

Their furniture was logs on which to sit, packing-cases off which to eat. Their recreation was swimming in the lake, submerging whenever enemy planes flew overhead. Their home comforts were, in the beginning, nil.

But this was not allowed to last. Nancy, appreciating the value of good food and good living, soon had supplies of meat, milk, vegetables, wine and tobacco coming in. If her men couldn't drink wine with their meals, or smoke after them, then neither would she nor any of her officers – until she had acquired a sufficient stock to make possible a general distribution. Usually though, and it was something of which she was proud, her housewifely instincts prevailed to such an extent that cigarette and wine rations were a daily event. She would buy them, or steal them, but she would rarely allow her men to go without.

Swimming alone was not sufficient amusement for men like Schley and Roger – so she bought them a horse. Thereafter the cavalryman (expertly) and the marine (enthusiastically) were, in turn, regularly to be seen galloping off into the woods.

She also encouraged the Americans to use their cameras. Time after time they sneaked off to a main road and then – from ten feet away – took photographs of German convoys or staff conferences, amusing themselves with the thought that they held the lives of these gentlemen in their hands if they chose to throw a grenade instead of clicking a shutter and refraining from doing so only because they were too close to home. Often, on these expeditions, Nancy liked to go with them. They were not so violent as ambushes, though the technique was the same, and she had always hated violence, but they were exciting, and she loved excitement.

It had been intended by the Maquis to welcome the first Americans to land in their midst with a huge banquet as soon as they arrived. The German attack at that time had changed their plans. But now it was put into effect.

Tardivat went into the nearest town and there kidnapped the chef of the leading hotel. Complete with tall white cap, this chef then prepared a magnificent outdoor meal with a menu that ran to eight courses. Hundreds of men sat down to it on planks and logs, and the Americans were toasted in every sort of wine. Right through until one in the morning this party raged and then, inevitably, it began to rain.

The storm was one of fierce tropical intensity and it broke up the celebrations completely. Nancy retired precipitately back to her bus. The men withdrew to their tents.

Soon, though, Nancy began to feel very sorry for Schley's horse. Not even a horse, she considered, a little alcoholically, should be out in such a downpour. So she ran out into the rain and led the horse into the 'bathroom' beside her bus.

The horse, however, was not accustomed to bathrooms, still less to a galvanised-iron bathroom roof which, a foot above its head, was thundering under the rain. It became extremely unhappy and started neighing and kicking, so Nancy opened the bus window to inquire after its health. 'How are you, Horse?' she said. Promptly the horse poked its agitated head through the window and into the bus.

Nancy now felt very sad for the horse. She had had a great deal to drink and she was exactly in the mood to feel sad for somebody – the horse was nearest at hand! She spent most of what was left of the night talking to the horse, feeding it an entire month's supply of sugar and trying to look into both its eyes at once whilst she spoke to it. Because horses' eyes are so wide apart, and because she was so close, she found this impossible. Also it was dark. Very politely, then, she would light match after match and change from side to side, whilst they had their long conversation, so that she could look into each of her guest's eyes in turn. Finally, just before dawn, she said good night to her equine friend and went to sleep.

The horse then became most agitated and kicked the bathroom to pieces, but everyone was so tired and the rain was so loud that no one heard him doing it, or came to console him, so eventually he bolted frenziedly out and vanished into the forest.

When Schley and Alsop had gone to bed hours previously, Alsop, who always died the second he hit the pillow, fell asleep with his head hanging under the eaves of their coloured parachute-silk tent. In the morning, when Schley woke him up, Alsop's face was stained a brilliant yellow – the night's torrential rain having stripped even the dye out of their tent's fabric and then dropped continuously on to the heedless head below.

Having at last got the jaundiced Alsop out of bed, Schley wandered across to the bathroom. There he found an indescribable scene of devastation. Shaving cream, toothbrushes, razors, horse manure, cartons, soap and towels had all been mashed together under the terrified hoofs of Nancy's guest. Schley woke Nancy and invited her to survey the wreckage.

'Ah, that poor darling horse,' she said at once. 'He was so lonely and frightened. Somebody should've come and talked to him when I went to sleep.'

Denis wandered over, took one look at the chaos and withdrew again, quoting loudly from his theatrical digs' days, 'Please leave this bathroom as you would wish to find it.' Alsop arrived two minutes later, looking quite transformed since the previous evening.

'Well,' he commented, summing up the events of the banqueting night, 'at least we got through it all without any loss of life.'

Rake returned. He looked at Alsop's dyed face, moaned gently to himself and clasped his head in his hands.

'Gertie, I'm ill,' he declared.

'Are you, Den? What's wrong?'

'My eyes,' he informed them. 'You wouldn't believe it, m'dear, but to me Alsop looks bright yellow! I think I'll go and lie down again.'

Such was the social life of the Maquis in 1944. They sent out search parties to retrieve their errant steed and they searched all day. But they never found him again – he had obviously had a bellyful of service in the Maquis.

That night, when Roger asked her what phrase she wished him to transmit to London (as the code message they would hear back from the BBC to warn them of their next parachutage) Nancy looked at him with a dead-pan face and said, 'Tell them to send the message *"Andrée has a horse in the bathroom"*.'

18 OPERATION GESTAPO

Before Nancy had finished dressing, the early morning atmosphere of comedy was cruelly dispelled. A report was brought to her which alleged that three women, one of whom had some time earlier been captured and convicted of espionage against the Maquis, were being held captive in shocking conditions and were being continuously and viciously used for the satisfaction of the group that held them.

Nancy made prompt inquiries. She found out that two of them had been arrested simply because they had not been able to give the Maquis a satisfactory explanation of why they were in the area, and that the third had, as reported, confessed defiantly to espionage and was a German.

She knew that there was no alternative to the sentence imposed on this woman. She must be shot. The Maquis had no convenient jails in which to keep spies; and, if the woman should escape, the information she could carry back to the Germans would be unthinkably dangerous. So, militarily, the verdict did not worry Nancy.

Nor, as an individual, did she any longer have any great revulsion against the thought of a firing squad. It was the penalty that had hung over her own head for four years and it was the fair rule of war for people who played the game she and this woman had played.

She had long since decided that what she hoped for most, if ever she were trapped, was a swift and certain execution before a firing squad. She had also long since appreciated that such a mercy would be, for her, a most improbable one. Much more likely, months of torture and then the ovens of an extermination camp – unless she could get at the button on her sleeve first. In that she carried a tablet that would kill her.

Therefore, she had no argument of any kind against the sentence imposed on this convicted woman. On the contrary, in all humanity, she thought it should be promptly put into effect. First, though, she determined to interview the woman and see for herself that the sentence had been just. She gave orders that the prisoner should be brought to her and then sat down in her office in the bus, smoking a little distractedly as she waited.

When the woman arrived, Nancy was horrified by what she saw. For a moment all thoughts of the military considerations involved vanished – she was simply one woman overcome with distress at the condition of another.

The German was practically naked, wild-eyed and filthy dirty. She had quite obviously been savagely misused. At once Nancy passed her some of her own clothing and said simply, 'Here, put them on.'

Sullenly she dressed.

'How long has this been going on?' Nancy demanded.

'All the time.'

'You were not willing?'

'Never.'

'Where are you kept prisoner?'

'In a pig pen.'

'Is it clean?'

'No.'

'Are you being fed?'

'No.'

Nancy paused to crush back her own instincts of pity and revulsion. She had a soldier's duty to perform – this was not a woman before her, it was a spy; an active enemy spy.

'You know you've been convicted of espionage?'

'Yes.'

'And you know the penalty? It would be the same if your people had caught me.'

'Yes.'

'Are you a spy?'

'Yes.'

'Then you must pay the penalty. But I promise you,' she said earnestly, 'that this torture will stop. Is there anything you want to say? Any message I can send to anyone for you when France is free?'

'Nothing.'

She was defiant, sullen and unafraid. Nancy called the escorting guard.

'Tell your leader,' she instructed, 'that either the sentence on this woman must be put into immediate effect or I personally shall come over and set her free. I will not allow women to be tortured by the Maquis.' The man nodded. 'You must go,' she said gently to the other woman. 'I'm sorry.'

She spat and tore off the clothes that Nancy had so recently given her. Flinging them on to the floor of the bus, she stepped, half-naked and contemptuous, out into the wet morning air of the forest. Nancy watched her as she was marched away, but she didn't look back; and, in a group twenty yards distant, the British and American officers watched their leader anxiously, knowing the torment she was enduring.

She sat down and soon her breakfast was brought to her. Mechanically she began to eat, knowing that she must give no sign of weakness. A volley of shots rang out in the distant shade of the forest. Only for a second did her eyes flicker up from her plate, then she continued eating stolidly until all the meal was gone.

After breakfast she summoned the other two captives to her. One, she discovered, had told an unsatisfactory story because she was having an illicit love affair with a married Frenchman in Montluçon and wished to protect him. She was innocent of any cause for detention. The other, a very beautiful nineteen-year-old, was equally innocent and had been seized and held only because some of the Maquis had wanted her body – and had taken it.

Savagely Nancy ordered the immediate release of both and restored to them all the money that had been stolen from them when they were caught. The nineteen-year-old wept with gratitude and asked could she remain to look after her rescuer. Thereafter she slept on the floor of the bus and became Nancy's personal maid. Chivalry was not entirely dead in the Maquis.

◆ ◆ ◆

The targets assigned to the Maquis d'Auvergne for D-Day had all long since been destroyed – except one. This was the small synthetic petrol plant at St Hilaire.

The plant had not been destroyed for the very good reasons that its entire output of fuel at the end of May had been seized and used by Tardivat's group of Maquisards and that there would not be another consignment ready till early August.

Nancy had contacted London, advised them of Tardivat's most profitable coup before D-Day and obtained permission to leave the factory intact, rather than destroy it, so that the coup could be repeated. The plant would be an invaluable asset to the Maquis, whose cars now ran mainly on alcohol – a fact which hurt the feelings of the cars and the Maquis equally, and now there was another stock of synthetic petrol ready. It had been decided that the Germans should not take delivery of the fuel. On the contrary, the Maquis would seize it and would themselves even take over the administration of the factory!

Nancy, Schley, Alsop, Hubert, Denis, Roger, Tardivat and a powerful force of men therefore called on the home of the plant manager. To his great consternation and terror, they informed him that henceforth *they* were in control.

'But how,' he moaned, 'shall I ever explain to the Germans that I have given my petrol to the Maquis?'

'How, if you don't,' Nancy retorted threateningly, 'will you ever explain to us that you have given your petrol to the Germans? Now – enough. We, in the future, shall run your plant.'

Then, to give effect to their words, they drove him over to the distillery and demanded that he should lead them at once to the boardroom. There, armed to the teeth, they held the most extraordinary executive meeting ever inspired by the thirsty throat of the internal combustion engine.

Employing Schley's legal knowledge, Alsop's business technique, Tardivat's commercial training, Hubert's military experience and Nancy's unholy delight at a situation both logistically valuable and humanly comic, they solemnly prepared production schedules, delivery dates, pick-up centres and ways and means and instructed the unfortunate manager to adhere strictly to all their formal resolutions.

As they drove back to the forest Nancy started to laugh.

'Guess we looked kind of peculiar directors.' Schley grinned.

'Just to think of it,' cooed Nancy. 'Me, an oil king!'

For a long time the presence of a Gestapo headquarters in Montluçon had irritated Tardivat. He discussed the matter with

Nancy and they decided that life would be pleasanter if the Gestapo were to vanish.

The town was very thoroughly reconnoitred and the movements of its large German garrison carefully noted. Similar attention was paid to the habits of the officers in the Gestapo headquarters.

Finally it was agreed that the best time to deal with the problem was at twenty-five minutes past midday. At that time, invariably (for they were systematic creatures) all the Gestapo gentlemen would be sipping aperitifs, just prior to taking their lunch at half past twelve.

At noon, in four cars, Nancy and fourteen others, all dressed in makeshift uniform, drove into the town, a covering party having preceded them into Montluçon and scattered into various 'safe houses', where they had collected an impressive array of Bren and Sten guns.

Precisely at 12.25, it had been planned, Nancy, Tardivat and their small band of attackers would rush up to the Gestapo headquarters in cars. At the same moment their cover party would arrive, to provide any support necessary to their withdrawal after the attack.

The plan worked perfectly. To the second, the entire force was punctual, halting violently at the unguarded rear door of the building.

Nancy leapt out of her car, dashed through the back entrance, ran up the staircase, flung open the first door, deposited her hand grenade inside it and was halfway down the stairs again as it exploded. Every room in the building was similarly treated. Half a minute later they were into their cars and roaring away down the street, their cover party following in their own vehicles.

Roused by a series of shattering explosions in the middle of the town, the locals came rushing out into the street. And, seeing a convoy of semi-uniformed Allies, they began to cheer and shout, '*Les Alliés sont arrivés.*'

'My God,' screamed Nancy, 'stop them or soon they'll all be waving Union Jacks! They think we're liberating them!'

Frantically they persuaded the excited inhabitants to return indoors. Then they quit the town. Behind them they left a destroyed headquarters and, in it, thirty-eight dead Germans.

Cosne-d'Allier was their next port of call – a semi-social, semi-official call. They wished to see exactly what was happening in the town and they also wished to demonstrate to its inhabitants the growing power of the Maquis.

In convoy, heavily armed, therefore, they drove into the town centre. Everyone turned out to greet them, throwing flowers and cheering, and their progress became a triumph. A restauranteur, who claimed that he had been chef on the *Ile de France*, even insisted that they should dine as his guests at his establishment, and so they had a superb meal as well.

Just as they were taking their coffee, a train was heard entering the town. By mutual consent the two Americans, the Maquis and Nancy abandoned their proposed liqueurs and marched spectacularly to the station. There, in the best German tradition, they thoroughly 'checked' the train.

Every passenger on board was required to show his identity card; many were questioned severely as to why they travelled and where; and only after the Maquis had completely demonstrated their ability to 'control' traffic in that area did Nancy give the signal which permitted the train to proceed on its way into German-dominated territory.

'Let the Gestapo think over that one,' she gloated. With Frenchmen now stopping and checking trains in what was still officially Occupied France, the war of the Underground had made vast strides. The inhabitants of Cosne-d'Allier, not to mention the passengers on the train that had just passed through it, were all profoundly impressed. Nancy's gesture may have been a mischievous and frivolous one, but it had certainly had the desired effect.

◆ ◆ ◆

London advised that the long-overdue landing on the southern shores of France was imminent. Arms were to be lavished on those groups in the lower part of Nancy's area of control so that maximum destruction of roadworks, railways and installations might be effected in that zone.

In two Citroëns of pre-war vintage, machine guns poking through their windscreens, Nancy, Hubert, Schley and Alsop drove down to the extreme southerly group below Clermont-Ferrand. They drove through territory teeming with German garrisons and troop movements – and yet both Nancy and Hubert, to the unaccustomed eyes of their American colleagues, seemed utterly unconcerned.

'Fascinating,' commented Schley.

'The way those two travel about the French countryside, you'd think they owned it. They drive,' Alsop concluded, 'as if they were going from London to Plymouth.'

Schley and Alsop were quite justified in their concern. Though Nancy chose secondary roads which the Germans usually avoided, these were not usual times. Also, they frequently had to cross primary roads, and anywhere on the approaches to such main routes they might be observed by an enemy patrol. Then, with whole armies of the enemy in the area, their lives would be short.

On the other hand, Nancy herself was justified in driving as she did. She *had* to get to almost every one of the southern groups to organise parachutages and, if she had to, then there was no use being timid. She took a calculated war risk and she was successful. She brought Schley and Alsop with her to train her men in the use of the new weapons they would soon be receiving.

At each group headquarters they were welcomed with open arms and a night of celebrations. The Maquis sensed victory on the wind and was anxious to show its gratitude to those who had armed and trained them.

In woods, in fields, in farmhouses and in villages these celebrations took place. There would be feasting and drinking and toasting – and finally the national anthems.

The Maquis would roar 'The Marseillaise', Nancy and Hubert would sing 'God Save the King', and then everyone would look expectantly at Schley and Alsop. But they, excessively embarrassed, simply could not sing 'The Star-Spangled Banner' – because they didn't know the words.

After two of these dismal failures they put their heads together.

'You know, Reeve,' ruminated Alsop, 'I guess we ought to do something at these functions on behalf of poor old Uncle Sam.'

'Sure, but how can we when we don't know the words?'

'Well what *do* you know the words of?'

Each went through the short list of songs all the words of which were familiar to him. They found that only one was common to them both. One, however, was all they wanted. They went at once to see Nancy.

'Gert,' Schley said, 'Alsop and I've been thinking we should do something about this anthem business. It's getting kind of embarrassing the way everyone stands and looks at us so expectantly and then we don't have anything to say.' Nancy stared at them intently and waited for what might follow. Knowing Schley and Alsop, she felt that anything might follow.

'Well,' Alsop continued the tale, 'the only song Schley and I know isn't exactly "The Star-Spangled Banner". So we thought next time it's necessary, you might announce that we are going to sing a *new* anthem. Not the American anthem but the specially composed "Entente Cordiale United Nations Anthem".'

'What *is* this new anthem?' Nancy inquired suspiciously.

'It goes to the tune of "Hark the Herald Angels Sing",' Alsop replied evasively. 'We both of us had a church education so we know the tune well.'

'OK,' Nancy agreed, 'I'll do it. What was it you called it again?'

'"The Entente Cordiale International Anthem",' Schley told her unctuously. 'Explain that it is a new international anthem of goodwill, signalising the unity of our people.'

'You know, when you two talk like that,' she replied, 'I don't trust you at all.'

At the very next celebration, Nancy, the toasts concluded and the national anthems about to be sung, made the agreed announcement. It was greeted with widespread murmurs of approval and it fired the other groups to an even more fervent than usual rendition of their own anthems. The French thundered 'The Marseillaise', Nancy and Hubert delivered a confidently fortissimo 'God Save the King', and then the Americans burst into their anthem of the United States, of the Entente Cordiale and of international goodwill. Their faces glowing with zeal, they sang:

> Uncle George and Aunty Mabel
> Fainted at the breakfast table.
> Wasn't that sufficient warning not to do it in
>   the morning?
> But Ovaltine has put them right:
> Now they do it morn and night.
> Uncle George is hoping soon
> To do it in the afternoon.

Their success was instant and riotous. The men saluted and stood quivering to attention, women wept, flowers were thrown all over them, bouquets were pressed on them from every direction. And throughout, as the ditty rolled sonorously through the tune of 'Hark the Herald Angels Sing', Nancy and Hubert also stood at attention, also quivering, also with tears in their eyes – but through an emotion entirely different from that of the French.

'You devils!' Nancy hissed as they finished.

'Gertie,' reproached Schley, 'how could you? I thought we scored a tremendous success!' From then on, at each celebration, the two Americans sang their new anthem continuously – and the British joined them in the singing of it!

South of Clermont-Ferrand they picked up Bazooka and Alsop gave him a new uniform they had brought over specially for him from England. He at once put it on and attached to it his recently awarded insignia of captain. Then they pressed on to their southernmost group.

Crossing the region south of Clermont-Ferrand was a ticklish business because they had to drive over one of the main bridges. They had halted well short of the bridge, in a side road, and were just preparing to reconnoitre the main road, when an armoured car suddenly appeared in front of them.

With Clermont-Ferrand and its garrison of twelve thousand Germans less than eight miles away, and a job to do further south, anyhow, there was no sense in doing anything except lie low. They couldn't possibly damage or cripple an armoured car and to fire on it would only be to rouse hordes of the enemy from all sides. Nevertheless, a shot did ring out. Turning furiously round they saw Bazooka aiming for a second time.

They knocked his carbine to the ground and then prayed that the Germans had not heard the shot. Unconcernedly the armoured car carried on its way and vanished. Alsop and Schley were furious with Bazooka, but they were mere lieutenants and therefore out-ranked by him, so they could say nothing. Nancy, to their astonishment, seemed unperturbed. Privately she had decided that, since the Germans had taken no action, the incident no longer mattered. It had angered her momentarily, but she was too fond of Bazooka to show her anger publicly – anyway, she excused him, everyone made slips some time or other.

'Well,' muttered Bazooka defiantly, 'we're here to kill Germans, aren't we?'

'Kill maybe one or two,' Alsop whispered to Schley, 'when there are a whole twelve thousand just over the way! You know, I don't see why the Yankee part of this mission hasn't driven Gertie crazy.'

They completed their five-hundred-kilometre journey, did their work with the southern group and then drove casually back to the forest of Tronçais. Safe again in their yellow tent, Alsop summed up his emotions on the long trip to Schley.

'If those British hadn't been so calm about everything at the time, I reckon I'd be ready now for the nut-house.' In fact, the compliment should have been reversed. The British knew the territory perfectly – were well aware of when they needed to worry and when they could travel in calm confidence. But the two Americans possessed none of this reassuring local knowledge, and yet constantly, without showing any fear, they drove long distances through districts that must, to them, have seemed nightmares of danger. It had become one of the strengths of the mission that each of the Allied officers had at last learnt to trust implicitly the specialised knowledge of the others. Thus Nancy could admire the Americans' superb skill with weapons, they her generalship, or their wireless operator's devotion, and they could all admire together the results they were achieving, because, at last, they had brought it about that the tired and retreating German had nowhere any longer where he could rest even his head in peace.

19 SILENT KILLING

Their biggest day in the forest of Tronçais was undoubtedly 15 August 1944. On that day the Allies landed (rather belatedly) in the South of France and Germany's fate was sealed. The Maquis were not now merely *asked* to sabotage and disrupt, they were honour-bound to attack whenever and wherever they could. Not a day passed without a violent skirmish of some kind.

Naturally there were casualties and Nancy, busier than ever with messages to London and parachutages, was delighted to accept the services of a Resistance doctor called Pierre Bellay.

Bellay set up a hospital for wounded Maquisards in a small Maquis-controlled village and thereafter all the group's casualties went to him. It was a weight off the minds of both Nancy and Denis, particularly Denis, that this duty no longer rested on their squeamish shoulders.

On the night of the fifteenth Hubert received his uniform from England. Determined also to show the flag, Nancy then displayed her pips too. She carried the rank of captain and her neat collar, khaki tie, her purposeful-looking army slacks and her obvious pride in at last being able to assume her true identity filled the Maquisards with delight. Wherever she went after that she was accorded all the privileges of her rank, salutes being not the least of them.

She celebrated by attending the demolition of two bridges, one rail, one road, in Cosne-d'Allier.

Enthusiastically the whole town turned out to watch the Maquis blow up their main means of communication with the outside world, chattering among themselves about how only a few weeks ago this same group, led by the same woman, had 'controlled' one of their trains.

'This,' declared Alsop, 'must be the most popularly attended demolition ever!'

The Spanish Maquisards, who had learnt their destructive trade in the war against Franco in 1938, industriously dug holes and laid their wads of TNT and plastic. Numerous other warriors were busy keeping guard . . . at any moment German convoys might approach. But Nancy's task turned out to be solely to try to persuade the locals *not* to stand gaping at the Spaniards on the edge of a bridge that was about to be blown to eternity.

As fast as she drove one lot off one end, another lot would wander on from the other. Children and old men were the worst offenders. Finally she carried all the children off, one at a time, and then delivered the old men a fearful blast of dirty Marseille-ese. Abruptly the roadway and approaches were cleared and, to the resounding applause of their large audience, the Maquis blew the bridge.

◆ ◆ ◆

Attacked from both west and south, the Germans were at last desperately trying to withdraw a large part of their garrison forces back into Germany, through the Belfort Gap. Tardivat decided to prod them on their way by seizing Montluçon, whose depleted German garrison now numbered only about three thousand.

Nancy and Hubert went into conference with him and quickly, with about three hundred Maquisards, the attack was launched from several divergent points.

Whilst Schley and Alsop led a group of men with bazookas (which they used like mortars, lobbing rockets into the old fortified areas of the town) Nancy charged round the perimeter, from one vantage point to another, in her Citroën car.

A message was given to her at one of them that Tardivat had managed to seize half the barracks occupied by the Germans and that, 'if she wanted some amusement, she should join him with a bazooka and help him fight the other half'.

'How do I get to him?' she asked. They indicated on their map a bridge that crossed a canal. 'He is just beyond that,' they told her.

With her driver she raced to the bridge they had pointed out. There was a roadblock at the far side of it, behind which she knew would be Tardivat's men. Halting her car on the bridge itself she got out and walked towards the roadblock. Bullets sang out around her head.

'Hey,' she shouted indignantly, 'it's me!'

More bullets, whining off the parapet and stinging the cobbled road. Only then did she realise that she had been directed to the wrong bridge and that she was, in fact, on German soil.

Her driver had already whirled the little Citroën round in its tracks and as she careered towards him he started to move. The instant she flung herself in through the door he held open for her, he roared off, machine-gun fire now flailing round them. Miraculously they were not killed. They got fresh instructions, and more accurate ones, and then found that Tardivat held the bridge and the area *adjacent* to the one she had actually crossed. This time, circumspectly, she went to his position on foot, carrying the bazooka he had requested.

'*Quelles andouilles*,' he bellowed at her as she walked towards him. 'You stupid sausage. Only an *Anglaise* would do anything as silly as that!'

'Sausage yourself,' she told him good-humouredly. 'What do you want the bazooka for?'

'Come on, I'll show you.'

He took her into that half of the barracks held by his own men. Rifle shots pinged wickedly down at them all the time.

'Snipers,' he said, 'in that room up there, we haven't been able to get near them.' As he spoke he lined up the bazooka. He fired; there was a deafening roar and a cloud of dust and shattered stone. Tardivat looked up and grinned. 'No more room,' he said simply. 'No more snipers.'

'Anything else I can do for you?' Nancy asked.

'No, thank you.'

'Then I'll leave you.'

They held Montluçon for several days and then the Germans, stung by the insolence of the Maquis' onslaught, sent across a heavy counter-attacking force from Moulins. Cheerfully the Maquis withdrew again into the depths of the forest of Tronçais – where, to greet them, it rained.

Nancy then sent Schley and Alsop to another area where, rumour had it, a whole army of Americans had appeared. They were to ask that this army should come and capture Montluçon, complete with its now swollen body of defenders. Instead of the 'army', Schley and Alsop found only a small, four-man OSS mission whose sole claim to fame was that it was headed by a prince. Since not even a mission led by a prince could capture a large German garrison, the two Americans returned empty-handed to the forest.

Here the Maquis were now in so commanding a position that they could at last move out of the wet cover of the woods and into the open. Nancy gave orders that her headquarters were to be transferred at once into surroundings that were both more congenial and more civilised.

She and her men spent almost all of one rainy night trying to drag her bus out of the mud into which it had sunk so securely in the past hectic three weeks. The bus and the mud resisted them with all the stubborn strength of the inanimate and when, at dawn, they eventually had it clear, they were utterly exhausted.

They then drove to within six miles of Montluçon and installed themselves in the huge Château de Fragne that had been empty (except for caretakers in a cottage at the main gate) since 1914. There Nancy allocated rooms for herself and most of her men.

'Aren't we a bit close to the Germans, Ducks?' Denis inquired tentatively.

'Don't worry about them,' she retorted. 'They've got too many worries of their own just now to give a hoot about us!'

Nancy, the guerrilla chieftain, the second they entered their new abode, suddenly became Nancy, the house-proud hostess of the château. She set everyone, officers and all, to polishing the brass, sweeping out the dust of thirty years, scrubbing the floors and preparing the rooms. The château emerged, out of a cloud of cobwebs and bad language, as a place transformed.

The entire Allied mission, plus their bodyguards, plus a large number of Maquisards, were then installed in the château in greater comfort than they had known for years. Compared to the eternal damp of the forest of Tronçais, they lived in paradise – for all that there was no water or electricity laid on.

The Germans obliged them next by evacuating Montluçon and Moulins. Rather unfeelingly they did not advise anyone of their intention to do this, so that the first thing the group knew about it was when Alsop suddenly rushed inside and shouted, 'Gertie, quick. The entire German army's coming up our drive!'

'Shut all the windows and keep inside,' she ordered crisply. She was confident that the Germans would not have guessed that anyone had occupied the château in the past few days. As far as they knew, it was deserted and she saw no need to disillusion them. So, with every window and shutter closed and the whole group waiting tensely inside, the huge German convoy approached them.

The road wound up one side of the château and down the other. His ear glued to the shutters, Alsop therefore heard the whole convoy grind slowly past them in two directions – and then vanish into silence. He heaved a sigh of relief and turned to congratulate Nancy on the calm accuracy of her judgement, but she had grown bored with the rumbling of so many German trucks tiresomely heading back towards the Reich and had gone down to the cellar to look for a bottle of something suitable with which to celebrate the liberation of Montluçon.

The cellar, in spite of the fact that the château had been empty for thirty years, held quite a large stock of wines. Unfortunately, the thirty years had done them no good at all and, though they were quite palatable, they had lost all their alcoholic content. Having sampled various bottles, Nancy decided that she was wasting her time and returned upstairs.

'Have they all gone?' she asked, referring to the Germans.

'All gone,' Alsop told her.

'Good. Now I can get on with organising my new field for parachutages.'

The last few parachutages she had supervised had been irritating affairs. The containers had landed all over the countryside, the planes had arrived late and kept her waiting hours in the wet grass, and a great deal of energy had been expended getting the arms and supplies dropped to them back into the château.

Nancy therefore decided to shortcut all this wasted effort. She ordered Roger to send a message to London advising them that her new field for the future would be the main front grounds of the château itself!

Also she installed numerous labour- and time-saving devices. 'I want floodlights I can switch on. Much better than bonfires. Den – you're good with electricity! How about fixing it up for me?'

They all laughed at the recollection of the unfortunate Rake clamped to his bicycle by the full force of the current that ran through the overhead forest wires at the time of the German ambush.

'I'm an actor, Gertie,' he demurred, 'not electrics. The union'd go mad if I touched a floodlight. What're you trying to do – start a strike?'

Nevertheless, the idea appealed to everyone. By the time a rather startled London sent out its next airlift the château was equipped with a series of buttons and switches which enabled everyone to stay comfortably in bed until the sound of plane engines was actually heard. Then the alarm rattled throughout the whole building, floodlights switched on and bathed the field in a bright glow (power being supplied by a phalanx of batteries) and all they had to do was watch the containers thud down on to their own front lawn.

'If only you Americans would mechanise your war effort like our Gert has,' announced Rake, 'we'd all be home a lot quicker.'

Across the Channel in London, a group of Canadians about to be dropped behind the lines in France were being briefed.

'You'll drop here,' they were told and given a map reference. One of them looked it up on his Michelin map and then uttered a howl of disbelief.

'But that bearing is clearly marked on the map as a château.' A brief nod was his answer. 'Well, who fixed that crazy field?' demanded the irate Canadian. They told him.

'Oh,' he said, 'Nancy! Well that explains everything!' He had trained with Nancy and nothing she could do would surprise him any longer. On the other hand, knowing her, he accepted her judgement and prepared himself cheerfully for his flight and the drop into France.

◆ ◆ ◆

The Maquis held a small group of German prisoners in the forest of Tronçais. Now that the enemy had withdrawn from the area and the Allied armies were about to replace them, there was no longer any need to shoot such captives – in fact, Nancy went to considerable pains to ensure that they were handed over safely into American custody.

Also in the forest was a notorious collaborationist – an old woman whose record was a shameful one of betrayals and vicious hostility towards her own countrymen. The Maquis tracked her down and were a little disconcerted when she finally took refuge, of all places, up a tree. Nothing they could do would persuade her to come down. They were frightened to climb up after her because she had reached the highest branch already and she was too old, much as they hated her, to hound to her death.

Eventually, with the old dame still roosting up in her lofty nest, the Maquisards asked Nancy's advice. Shrieking with laughter she gave it.

The Maquisards did what she said. They returned to the tree and, very deliberately, began to saw through the trunk. Spitting with rage the old lady came scurrying down to captivity.

A large group of the Milice had defected to the Maquis in the last days of their stay in the forest of Tronçais. These, with the addition of some other specially selected Maquisards who had volunteered for the job, were now being trained by Schley and Alsop as a crack force of demolition and small-arms experts. With their police backbone, this group turned out to be extremely smart in their formal military drilling, which is not a charge that could ever justifiably be levelled at the Maquis as a whole.

Whilst the Americans were thus occupied, Hubert and Denis were kept happily busy dealing with the purely military aspects of the cracking German occupation, which left Nancy more free to relax than she had ever been since 1939.

Relaxation was no longer an art which she possessed, however. Instead she seized the time available to her to visit Gaspard and Fournier and Laurent and was soon involved in one of their escapades.

There was a factory producing machine parts vital to the Germans in Gaspard's area. Rather than allow it to contribute even one more ball-bearing to Hitler's war effort, the Maquis decided to destroy it.

Contacts on the factory staff gave them all the details of vital installations and working shifts; reconnaissance revealed the enemy system of guarding the plant.

There were four gates into the factory – gates in a high wall. Each gate was guarded continuously by two German sentries who patrolled up a short stretch of the wall, each in an opposite direction, and then marched back again to the entrance.

The surrounding country was flat, with low scrub that reached to within ten yards of the wall. That ten yards had been completely cleared.

It was decided that the attack should be made in two waves against each entrance. The first wave was to silence all eight of the German sentries, the second was to immediately enter the factory through the unguarded gates, set the charges and then withdraw. Nancy was put in command of one of the groups in the first wave.

In the darkest part of the night they left their transport and crawled into the scrub. On their bellies they wormed their way forward. In half an hour, undetected, they had reached the cleared strip round the wall. Silently they edged their way down until they lay opposite their gate.

At this stage they must wait till the sentries met, about-turned and had taken their first few steps apart. Then they must run between them, overpower and silence both Germans simultaneously and then wave on the second team.

Quite still, Nancy and her three men lay and watched. Twice the Germans walked past on their beat, met, turned and walked it again. On the third occasion, four or five paces after they had parted, Nancy gave the signal. Four dark figures sprang across the cleared strip towards the backs of the unsuspecting sentries. They must do their job swiftly, surely and silently. There must be no shots and no shouts to disturb the other gates.

Nancy and her companions were within six feet of their victim and still he seemed unaware of their presence. She was glad of this because it meant that they need only knock him unconscious and he would suffer no more than a headache for his misfortune. But then he turned and saw her.

There was no time to think or to hesitate. Like a tiger she sprang and, as his mouth opened to shout, her forearm clamped under his jaw and snapped backwards. The dirty work she had always loathed in her training days had at last become not training but fact. There was a sharp click and the German slumped limply against her. Utterly revolted, she allowed the dead man to slide to the ground. At the same time she heard his colleague thud down. She waved on the demolition team and watched them sprint through the gateway, herself standing sickly against the wall.

She and her men guarded the gate against a surprise attack by the Germans whilst the others laid their bombs and explosives inside. Time after time she found herself wiping her hands on the side of her trousers, trying to remove the taint of violence. Her teeth were clenched so hard that they ached and her throat was dry. Then the demolition squad emerged and the whole party faded off into the night. They were halfway home to their camp when the factory blew up. Gaspard's men were triumphant, but Nancy could still feel only the suddenly lifeless weight of the sentry's body against hers, so that she was glad when she could leave them and return to her room at the château.

◆　◆　◆

On 30 August 1944 it was Nancy's twenty-seventh birthday, and for weeks the entire Maquis had been preparing to make it a historic event. Also, on 25 August, Paris had been liberated and this added passionate zeal to their plans for a celebration.

Food was brought in from all sides, and so was wine. A guest list was drawn up, added to, argued over and amended. Finally, invitations were issued for a midday banquet to be held on the thirtieth in the great hall of the château itself.

On the day, Nancy was escorted by all her officers to the steps of the château and there, in the courtyard, the Schley-Alsop crack force, augmented by hundreds of other Maquis enthusiasts, marched past her in the most exemplary manner.

She stood on the steps, bouquets in her arms, flanked by her officer colleagues, and took the salute from her Maquis. As soon as they emerged from the courtyard, they doubled around the other side and rejoined the rear of the column they had previously led. Apparently tens of thousands of men marched proudly past their Madame Andrée. Theirs was a most impressive display of military might. Bareheaded, clutching her flowers, smiling broadly, she accepted the tribute that was being paid her.

There were presents too. The Maquisards gave her a dozen silver ice-cream spoons. Schley and Alsop gave her six etchings. Denis gave her a large bottle of perfume.

'Too strong to drink, Ducks.' He grinned. 'Many happies.'

From Tardivat there was linen, from Hubert a ring, from the Spaniards (who had no money at all) flowers, and from Mme Renard of Montluçon (the agent who had sheltered Bazooka) there were *babas à rhum* and *Pavé de Venise* – a deliciously rich pastry with cream – and eclairs.

She was very happy on that day – happy for France, for the victory that was now inevitable, for the tribute Frenchmen were paying a Briton, for the warm and generous camaraderie that, in the past months, had made life seem so wholesome and worthwhile to her. All the irritations and agonies of the past four years were expunged in the glowing companionship of that moment.

But better things were to come. Their display of martial might concluded, the entire group, plus their many guests, adjourned to the great hall. Tables had been set up, filling the entire chamber and so, with everyone seated, the banquet began.

After the meal there were toasts and, after the toasts, speeches. Everyone made speeches. It was *Vive la France, Vive les Allies* and *Vive Madame Andrée* – who, as far as the guests were concerned, was the epitome of all three. Then a little man who sat, almost ignored, at the end of the furthest table stood up and announced that he was glad everyone was having such a good time because he, in fact, was the owner of the château! After that everyone was very polite indeed to the little man.

Such was the happiest and most satisfying day of Nancy's entire war.

◆　◆　◆

News reached them that the Germans were about to evacuate Vichy.

Vichy was doubly significant to the Maquis. It represented both German Occupation and French collaboration by traitors like Laval, Petain and Darlan. At once Nancy led her group southwards to link up with Gaspard at Clermont-Ferrand and then to formally liberate the symbolic town.

At Clermont-Ferrand they discovered that Gaspard had already marched on Vichy. Post-haste they pursued him. And so they made their triumphant entry into the traitor capital.

Their reception was rapturous. 'Not surprised,' was Nancy's sardonic comment. 'Nine out of ten of them, to have lived here all this time, must be *collaborateurs*. They're just delighted to see Allied officers in uniform 'cos they hope we'll protect them from their own French boys.'

Whatever their motive, the inhabitants of Vichy certainly went mad. The roadway was flanked with cheering Frenchmen, flowers filled the Maquis cars, everyone was presented with garlands and bouquets and, when Nancy finally stopped, a thousand locals swarmed around her.

'In here, Duckie,' said Denis, with great presence of mind, and led her into a café. Five hundred shrieking Vichyites followed the party inside. Drinks were ordered, toasts were drunk.

They were just unloading their cars when a man, very tall and distinguished, approached them and introduced himself as the Swiss Ambassador.

'I am giving a cocktail party tonight, Mme Andrée,' he said. 'I want you to come, you and your friends.'

Nancy looked uncomfortably down at her crumpled khaki slacks and her army boots. 'Your Excellency,' she stammered, 'thank you very much but I can't possibly. I've got no clothes. Look' – she pointed at her boots – 'these are all I've got.'

'My dear, you must come,' the Ambassador insisted, 'the party is being given especially in your honour.'

'But I couldn't possibly. Well . . . just look at me, Excellency . . .'

'Don't worry,' he urged. 'Come as you are. What you wear will become chic in Vichy. Please, Mme Andrée. This party is for you. Tomorrow I leave for Switzerland. I have been recalled.'

All her colleagues joined the Ambassador in his urgings so that eventually, reluctantly, she agreed. No sooner had the Ambassador departed than two elegantly dressed women walked by. They looked at Nancy, from her boots to her dishevelled hair, and then spoke loudly. 'If *that's* what women look like in uniform . . . Well, really!'

Hubert was furious. With difficulty Nancy persuaded him not to knock them down. 'Hubert,' she said, 'I can't go tonight. They're quite right.'

'You bloody well will go,' he raged. 'They're quite wrong.'

She went to a hotel and sent her slacks to be cleaned and pressed. Then she wrapped herself in a blanket and went to the hairdressers where she had a shampoo and a facial. There was no power in Vichy so the Maquis rigged up batteries to work the electric dryer for her hair. She bought a new shirt and a pair of tan walking shoes. Finally, clean, smart, carefully made-up and wearing flowers bought for her by Denis, she marched with her brother officers to the Ambassador's cocktail party in honour of herself. And at the reception one of the first people to whom his Excellency introduced her was the elegant woman who had been so outraged by her uniform earlier in the afternoon.

Nancy, who had already told the Ambassador this irritating story, now jolted him with her elbow.

'That's her, that's her,' she hissed. The Ambassador was markedly distant with the elegant woman, who excused herself in considerable embarrassment as soon as she could. Thereafter the guest of honour enjoyed herself all night.

The next afternoon there was a big ceremony at the Cenotaph at which Nancy and the others were to lay wreaths. Again crowds packed the square. Steadily the atmosphere grew more excited. The Mayor began to make a speech.

Whilst he spoke, a woman edged her way steadily through the press of the crowd. Shoulder by shoulder she inched her way towards Nancy, until at last she stood by her side. She tugged at Nancy's sleeve and shouted – but her words were lost in the uproar of the seething square. Nancy, laughing, bent her head towards the woman and the woman shouted in her ear.

Nancy froze, the laughter died on her face, her eyes dulled and then, almost collapsing, she burst into tears. Denis, the Americans and Hubert leapt to her side.

'Gertie, Gertie, what is it?' Denis begged. The most sentimental being in the world, he couldn't bear to see his indomitable 'Ducks' in tears. Helplessly, bitterly, she wept on. 'Come on, poppet,' he urged, 'tell me what it is. *Please*, Gert.'

'Den, Den,' was all she could choke out, 'get me away from here.'

They took her to a hotel, away from the frantic crowd, and as they buffeted their passage through the mob she told them, in three stark phrases, what had made her cry.

'It's Henri,' she said. 'The Gestapo picked him up in our flat. He's dead.'

20 RETURN TO MARSEILLE

Nancy slowly regained her composure and, cold-faced, rejoined her people some time later. 'I want to go to Marseille,' she told them.

They didn't question her. They knew that she hoped to find out who had been responsible for Henri's death and then to track him down. They just mumbled their agreement and led her to a car.

The car was a big, red Talbot and into it piled Hubert, Alsop, Nancy and Denis. They drove fast towards Marseille and stopped for the first time for dinner at an inn which was famous, its proprietor told them, for the number of people who, in the past, had been murdered there. Nancy greeted this information with distaste and soon they were on their way again.

They reached the River Rhône and found, every bridge having been blown, that they could not cross it. Nancy hurled herself into an impassioned argument with all the available authorities, and with an old ferryman as well, and eventually persuaded the latter to transport them to the other side.

They ran out of petrol and refuelled the unfortunate Talbot with alcohol instead. And so, in remarkably good time, they entered Marseille, which they found still in a state of siege and teeming with what seemed to be at least half the American troops in Europe.

For their part, the American troops were decidedly puzzled by the sudden appearance in the city of four allegedly Allied desperadoes in a large red Talbot. The party stayed with some friends of Nancy's, whose warm welcome to their long-lost comrade almost compensated for the angry whine of snipers' bullets in the street outside.

◆ ◆ ◆

O'Leary had been arrested in March of 1943. In the course of his various interrogations certain facts emerged which he realised should, at all costs, be passed on to the Resistance. Accordingly, in late April, he managed to persuade a man, who was about to be released, to take a message to Henri. O'Leary gave the man the password by which he could identify himself to Henri, and the response which he might expect in reply.

Thus, early in May, a stranger knocked on Henri's door. Henri opened it and was greeted with O'Leary's password. He gave the response and invited the stranger inside. Seconds later he was being driven away to Gestapo headquarters in the Rue Paradis. Henri had admitted into his flat a German counter-agent.

He was imprisoned and treated with merciless brutality. Months passed and then the Gestapo sent his father to see him, to deliver him a message in his cell.

'All the Gestapo want,' the old man told him, 'is that you tell them where Nancy is. Tell them and they will let you go.'

Henri looked at his father for a long time before he replied. Then he said quietly, only, 'Papa – leave me in peace.' Weeping, the old man quit the cell.

They took Henri to their headquarters again and there they tortured him to make him tell them about Nancy. He told them nothing and returned to his prison cell with his kidneys exposed through the mangled flesh of his back. Again his father was shown into his cell. Again Henri refused to say anything about his wife's plans.

'Leave me,' he begged the old man, 'and Papa – please look after Nancy.'

On 16 October 1943, the night of Nancy's strange dream about the death of Dédée's husband, Henri was taken out of his cell and executed.

After this there was only one other thing to do in Marseille – look for Picon. Nancy inquired of all her old friends, but no one knew where Picon had gone after Henri had been arrested. No one had dared go near the Fiocca flat for fear of being observed and implicated. The dog, they thought, must have starved to death, or perhaps been eaten.

But Nancy had her own theories as to Picon's whereabouts. Head thrust forward, long-striding like a man, she marched confidently towards the quarter where her good friends the Ficetoles lived, but when she reached their address, she lost her confidence – the Ficetoles' house was just bombed-out rubble.

For a moment she could not think where to go next. The whole street had been destroyed and there were not even neighbours from whom she could inquire where the Ficetoles now lived or whether, in fact, they lived at all. Then she remembered her butcher. For years she had been his best customer and he had known Ficetole well.

The butcher's shop was closed but she went round to the back door and knocked. Through the glass panel, she saw him mouth the words, 'My God, it's Madame Fiocca.'

He opened the door to her and he and his wife stood there, awkward and silent, as she came inside. Immediately Nancy sensed that they were terrified by the thought that they would have to tell her about Henri's death.

'It's all right,' she said quickly, 'I know.' They talked for several minutes and then Nancy came to the point.

'I'm looking for Picon,' she said.

'He's with Ficetole.'

'Where?' They told her and, as soon as she could, she left them to walk through the blasted city to Ficetole's new home. She found the district first and then the wretched street itself – Marseille had suffered badly in the battle of liberation. Two blocks away a small battle against holed-up Germans was still raging.

'Do you know where the Ficetoles live?' she asked one of the men standing on the corner. He shook his head.

Tired and disappointed she walked away. An old lady who had looked at her as she passed, looked again when she heard Nancy's question and then trotted back after her.

'Surely,' she said, 'you must be Madame Fiocca?'

'I am.'

'Then you will want to see your little dog again. It's in a house down here.' And so she led the way to what she declared was now the home of the one-time tram conductor Ficetole.

'There is no one at home,' the old lady said, 'but I will go and find Madame Ficetole, if you will wait.'

'All right, I'll wait for you here,' Nancy told her. And at once, at the sound of her words, there came from inside a hysterically urgent barking – Picon had recognised his mistress's voice after an absence of twenty months. Frantically he yelped and howled and clawed at the door. Nancy tried to talk to him soothingly, but his desire to get out and be with her only grew more frenzied each second. As she knelt on one side of the door she heard his desperate scratchings and whimperings on the other.

At last Mme Ficetole arrived, running down the road and fol-lowed by all her friends. She unlocked the door and opened it and out hurtled a ball of white fur which flew into Nancy's arms.

Picon licked her and nuzzled her, pressed himself close to her and howled with pent-up emotion. He trembled and whimpered and, as the minutes passed, grew more, not less, hysterical. They

256

became genuinely alarmed at his condition and eventually a doctor was fetched. He gave the terrier a sedative and, a little while later, Picon fell exhaustedly asleep in Nancy's arms.

She went to the bank to check up on her deposit box, with its fortune inside of £60,000. It was empty. So was Henri's. She had no money at all – just debts for things like rent that had accrued since Henri's death, his tailor's bills and the shoemaker's bill. Before she had entered the bank she had thought herself a wealthy woman. Now she knew that all that remained of her one-time life in Marseille was Picon.

Denis fell ill with what seemed a form of epilepsy and swiftly Nancy enlisted the services of the leading psychiatrist in the American forces and asked what should be done.

'Get him home as soon as you can,' was the advice she received.

In the shattered, wreck-strewn, mine-laced harbour she found a British Landing Ship, Tank (LST) captain and that night entertained him liberally at her favourite restaurant, after which he agreed to take Denis back to England on his ship. Then Denis recovered and they decided that there was no need for him to go home after all.

'You know something,' Alsop remarked. 'That girl would have pinched a boat and rowed him home if she couldn't've gotten anything else.'

'You're right,' Hubert admitted. 'Typical of her, though, that she should tame the captains of half the British LSTs in harbour instead.'

On their second afternoon in Marseille she went out and bought herself a black dress, high-heeled shoes and a small flowered hat. She had arranged to meet the men in the bar at Basso's that evening and now decided to do so dressed in her new clothes.

She changed at a friend's home and then walked down to Basso's, her high-heeled shoes feeling strangely light and insecure after so long in boots, her body crisply cool and delighted to be, at last, out of coarse slacks and rough-dried shirt.

Her skirt swirled and her heels clicked elegantly as she swept into Basso's. Hubert, Schley and Alsop stood at the far end of the bar, talking to three women.

'Hullo there,' Nancy called down to them. They looked up casually and saw a smartly dressed woman with a curious little hat and fine ankles. They nodded to her politely and turned back to their own companions.

The barman gave Nancy a second look – a long one. 'Madame Fiocca,' he exclaimed, at last recognising her, 'you do look smart!' The heads of her three colleagues jolted towards her.

'Good God,' said Hubert, 'it's Gert!' For six months they had lived and fought with a bare-headed girl in shapeless slacks and heavy boots. This woman with the fashionably covered head and the slender silken ankles and neat waist had no bearing on the comrade they had been expecting.

'Nancy,' Alsop said admiringly, 'you look marvellous. Allow me to escort you to dinner.'

The dinner was a large party specially organised to celebrate the victory of the Resistance as represented by their group and it was a very jolly effort indeed, in spite of the starvation rations prevailing in the city at that time. Alsop even made a brilliant after-dinner speech in Russian, which entranced all the guests although they understood not a word of it.

'I didn't know you could speak Russian,' Nancy said to him later in the evening.

'I can't,' he confessed to her. 'Seemed a good idea, though, and it did sound like Russian, didn't it?' They decided not to admit the fact to anyone else.

One of Nancy's friends called her over.

'I want to tell you something about Henri,' she said. 'No! Don't stop me. After you left Marseille he would come to our house sometimes, other times he would just stay at home. But all the time, at our home or his, every night, he just sat and played patience. He wouldn't go out or meet people. Not anyone. All the time – just patience. And whenever we tried to shake him out of it, he would look at us and say, "I'm all right. I just want to wait till Nancy gets home." I thought you would like to know.'

◆　◆　◆

Finally, complete with Picon, they all got back into their big, red Talbot and drove north again because France was not yet completely free and there was still fighting to be done.

Characteristically, Nancy did not grieve over Henri for long – for three reasons. First, her husband was dead and grief would neither bring him back nor please him; second, intuitively she had known he was dead for almost a year and, a year ago, on the day of the dream itself, she had begun to mourn him; finally, there was still plenty of work to be done and she now had more reason than ever for doing it.

So they drove back from Marseille to the château. Everywhere they went they were feted as heroes. The Allies still had not driven their armies into the regions through which the Talbot now nosed its way, so that often the uniforms worn by Nancy and her colleagues were the first British and American uniforms the local

French had seen. To these people the Talbot was as good as a unit of Allied tanks; its passengers were not just passing travellers but the Liberators themselves.

Just outside a small town, in the middle of a storm, the hard-pressed car registered its extreme indignation at the treatment meted out to it by bursting into flames. Everyone except Alsop seemed supremely unconcerned at this disaster and laughed feck-lessly at the growing conflagration. They simply stood on the road-side in the pouring rain and watched and laughed. The American, however, had no taste for walking, and walking was obviously to be their fate unless something was done, and quickly. So he dashed to a puddle, scooped up water in his cap and flung it into the flaming engine. Hilariously his companions followed his example – where-upon, to their surprise, the fire was quickly extinguished. A loose nut was found in the carburettor, its leak was sealed when the nut was tightened, the tank was filled with *eau-de-vie* (there being no petrol) and once again they were on their way.

Once back in the château invitations poured in upon them from every village and town for fifty kilometres around. The local may-ors and Maquis captains *all* wanted to offer their hospitality and express their appreciation to the Anglo-American mission.

Night after night they would pile into their cars, drive light-heartedly through country once haunted by Germans and so reach their destination. There they would be wined and dined; the French would sing 'The Marseillaise'; the mission – thunderously – would render 'Uncle George and Auntie Mabel' and presentations would be made; finally, as they drove off, they would be pelted with flowers. As soon as they were on the open road again, they would ungratefully toss all these floral tributes out into the fields, mount their machine guns and thus career noisily home.

◆ ◆ ◆

Six men were dropped by parachute on to Nancy's front lawn. They were all heartbroken when they landed to find out that the shooting war was virtually over – especially one of them, who was an American marine.

'I tell you what,' Nancy suggested to him, 'if there *is* any excitement going, Tardivat will be in it! Would you like me to send you over to him?'

The marine was delighted at the idea and was accordingly transferred to Tardivat's group. A few days later he returned. He had not seen much excitement but he did have a problem, and this problem he duly expounded to the council of officers at whose head Nancy was then sitting.

It seemed that all agents, when dropped into France, were supplied with two tablets. They were tablets to be used only in the direst emergency. One of them was designed to kill the agent instantly, the other would knock him into a profound state of unconsciousness which, it was hoped, the Germans might even mistake for death. But if they did not so mistake it, the 'patient' would still be 'out' for at least six hours, so that he could not – even under torture – reveal anything he knew of his group or circuit for that time. (Time enough, with luck, for his colleagues to escape.)

The fatal tablet, the Marine hastened to point out, did not come into his picture at all because he had thrown it away the instant he hit France! It was the knock-out drops that were his problem.

'Y'see,' he informed the council earnestly, 'two of Tardivat's lieutenants have gotten themselves girlfriends in town. Sisters, they are. Real nice girls. And, well, the girls are willing but, um, Momma . . . ain't! If you get me.'

Nancy replied that she didn't get him.

'Well, y'see, these guys want to borrow my tablet because, well, because Momma always chaperones the girls. She won't move more'n six feet from her daughters all the time the guys are there. And they thought,' he tailed off rather lamely, 'that if Momma was to have a real good sleep, everyone'd enjoy themselves more!'

The Council deliberated solemnly. The Marine was given permission to donate his knock-out tablet to Tardivat's men, in the interests of Allied unity. Momma's coffee was doctored and Momma slept very soundly, six feet away, all night and two lieutenants returned to their group next morning much, much happier men.

'War,' Denis declared portentously, 'requires us all to make great sacrifices and awesome decisions – don't it, Ducks?'

'It does indeed, Den,' she sighed. 'So how about you make a great sacrifice and decide to take Picon for a walk while I get on with my messages?'

Amiably Denis did as he was asked. He was glad to see his Gertie getting so rapidly back to normal.

21 THE ENEMY DEPART

By mid-September the War had ended for the Maquis. About a quarter of a million of them had been actively engaged in subversive activities for over a year. Many others, less ardent, had been fighting only since D-Day. But their joint effort had been a massive and heroic one. Now the enemy were no longer before and around them, but behind them, bolting for the Rhine and their last few gangplanks into Germany. So the Maquis had done their job and were now free to go home.

Or, if they were officers of established units of the pre-1940 days, they could fight again as uniformed soldiers.

Tardivat was one of those who accepted this offer. Ever since he had escaped south from Belgium, in 1940, he had fought the Germans boldly and implacably and he would not stop until Hitlerism had vanished utterly from Europe. He rejoined the French Army which was then fighting at the Belfort Gap.

There he was so badly wounded in the leg that the limb, unskilfully treated in the first place, was eventually removed high up against the hip. Tardivat, the active, vital, Rugby-playing Resistance leader, suddenly became a cripple.

Schley and Alsop were recalled to London. They took an affectionate farewell of Nancy, Denis and Hubert, and then flew to Britain. There Schley met a friend who worked in OSS and who wanted, unofficially, to take a week off. Schley agreed to hold down his desk job for him whilst he did so.

'Typical of the way these organisations are run,' he commented a few days later to Alsop. 'Nobody's even noticed the difference!'

It turned out that the job his friend had been doing was the writing up of official citations for the various heroes of OSS. Schley, noting a familiar name on the list, spent a pleasant and sincere hour's work revising a citation for his recent leader, Captain Nancy Wake. In the best official language, he mentioned that Captain Wake had on several occasions saved the lives of two American officers ('Yours and mine,' he explained to Alsop, who nodded emphatic agreement) and that she deserved recognition from the US government. Apparently the US agreed. Some months later Nancy was decorated with the American Medal of Freedom, with a Bronze Palm.

Back in the château Nancy could not rid herself of the memory of the siege conditions of hunger and discomfort she had seen on her last visit to Marseille, so she mentioned the subject to Laurent, Fournier and Gaspard. That was all she had to do.

A short time later she was able to collect from these two Maquis leaders a huge load of beef, mutton, eggs, cheeses and chickens. They had scoured the countryside to find these emergency rations. With Denis, Hubert and Picon as company she then drove to the succour of starving Marseille.

All her friends were fed and her butcher was given a complete shopful of meat to distribute to his customers. Nor did Nancy forget the captains of the LSTs whom she had met at the time when it had seemed vital that she should trick one of them into taking Denis home. To their tiny fleet she delivered dozens of the most beautiful French chickens.

They asked her to dine with them, of course, and the chicken arrived, apparently having been stewed in diesel oil, cooked as only wartime service cooks can manage. Rather than eat food prepared like that, she decided, it was better, much better, to starve.

From Marseille they drove to Paris – drove back through all their old groups, saying goodbye and thank you. No, not goodbye . . . *au revoir*. These Resistance folk were never really parted. Then, after two days in Paris, they flew back home to London.

Nancy glanced across at Denis and Hubert and grinned as they circled over the airport.

'Shall we go down with it,' she asked, 'or shall we jump – just for old time's sake?' Already their days together were becoming treasured memories.

'We'll go down with it, Ducks,' Denis told her firmly. 'We've had more than our share of luck already. I'm not tempting it any further.'

Nancy knew exactly what he meant. When she had made her last preparations for parachuting into France, a will had figured prominently in the list.

'After two and a half years of it in Marseille, I didn't ever think I could come out of a second lot,' she explained.

'You, Ducks?' remonstrated Denis. 'You're indestructible. Besides, what do you want with the Pearly Gates?'

'No use my wanting anything, Den. People like you and I just don't get in.'

So – perhaps not surprisingly, after all – Nancy returned to London for the second time since 1939.

◆ ◆ ◆

She, Denis and Hubert soon flew back to France – this time *not* with Buckmaster farewelling them with his gentle '*Merde*', but with Buckmaster in person. He wanted to meet all the French Resistance leaders, and Nancy and her two colleagues were to introduce him to their particular group.

Once again she met Laurent, Fournier and Gaspard. Also she heard the shocking news of Tardivat's amputation and for the rest of their grand tour was sad at this sudden misfortune that had befallen her especial friend. Then she left the others and travelled on alone to Marseille. There was time now to think and she had many urgent things to put in order in the city that had once been her home. She stayed in Marseille until May of 1945.

Her flat, after Henri's arrest, had been commandeered by the female branch of the local Gestapo. Three women agents had lived there for months. Until the last possible moment these women had stayed in Marseille. Then they had ordered three lorries to come to the building and they removed every stick of furniture and furnishings from the flat except a crystal chandelier in the drawing room and a large stove in the kitchen.

Louis Burdet, head of the Resistance in Southern France, met Nancy and advised her what to do. A short man, full of humour and vigour, looking every inch an athlete, for all his forty-one years, Nancy liked him enormously.

He told her that it had been agreed that anyone in the Resistance who had had property, and had insured it until or after 1939, and had subsequently lost it to the Nazis, would be entitled to claim from Germany, when she would be defeated, ten times the value for which such property had originally been insured.

This was neither greed nor victimisation. Ten times 1939 values and currency rates only just equalled 1945 costs of living in terms of French francs.

Nancy's furniture and household effects had been valued at 500,000 francs in 1939 and insured for that amount. She would be entitled, then, on Germany's defeat, to 5,000,000 francs reparations.

For the moment, however, there was no question of monies to be received: it was all a matter of debts due. She examined all Henri's books, called in all his outstanding accounts and then, out of her accrued officers' allowance, paid off all the money ever owed by him or by his estate, including the cost of flowers sent on her behalf to her husband's funeral.

After that, she and Burdet met often. She liked him because he made her laugh. 'When I was going to leave London, to drop into France,' he told her, 'my headquarters warned me about the tortures, if the Gestapo ever caught me. I did not like this very much, Nancy. But then I decided not to worry. With my grey hair' – he stroked his elegant silver head – 'I look too old. I do not look like a terrorist!'

'What are you going to do now?' she asked.

'Go back to London,' he replied promptly. 'To a hotel. That is my job. I have had enough of playing at soldiers. I was only an amateur after all.'

Amateur or not, he had been brilliantly successful and extraordinarily daring. Soldier or not, he had the old soldier's passion for the good things that had happened in his war. So he and Nancy swapped stories of their respective careers.

'There is one story, I think,' he told her, 'that shows us the best that there was in the men of France. It is the story of Hâche and Pioche.'

Hâche and Pioche were both young men, inseparable friends and colleagues in their Resistance work under the leadership of Burdet. Their pseudonyms meant, respectively, Axe and Pick.

They performed many bold deeds together – like attacking a factory and then, when the demolition was not complete, attacking it again the following night, even though every German in the district was alerted; like executing two Gestapo agents on the pavements of the Old Port itself. But it was their last action that touched their leader most.

A rendezvous for the Resistance had been seized by the Germans, who had then laid an ambush outside it for anyone who should later, unfortunately, call there. Burdet heard of this trap and determined to ambush the ambushers. He, Hâche and Pioche stole up on the house.

It was in a winding street off the main road of Aix-en-Provence. They attacked and killed the Gestapo men who lurked outside, and then hurriedly withdrew. It was some minutes later, when they met, that Burdet and Pioche noticed that Hâche was missing.

Hâche had been mortally wounded and, so as not to delay his friends, had hidden himself inside the door of a house in the street where the fierce little battle had been fought. Twenty-four years old, he died alone behind that door.

Word eventually reached Burdet that Hâche had not survived, though where his body was, no one knew.

'It will be in the morgue,' he declared. And so, boldly, the group, that same night, raided the morgue. There they found Hâche and removed his body.

Later, when Marseille was free, Burdet gave the funeral oration at his ceremonial burial.

'I was his friend,' he said. 'I want you to know this boy and to talk of him. He possessed treasures for his country more priceless than money. He was the personification of the intelligence, devotion and industry which are the richest qualities of France and French devotion.'

Then he turned to Hâche's mother – Mme Olive, for Olive was his proper name – and said, 'Nothing, Madame, can soften your sorrow. You have lost your son. But may we' – and here he looked round at his fellow soldiers – 'hope that when our time comes to leave this earth, we may see *you* again, Roger Olive.'

There were tears in his eyes as he told Nancy the story. Remembering the boys she had herself seen wounded and dying, or whom, dead, she had buried, Nancy knew why he spoke as he did and felt no need to reply.

'Hâche was a well-brought-up boy, Nancy,' Burdet said. 'When he trained in England he was made very happy by the people of your country, who always made him one of their own family. If he had lived, he would never have forgotten to go back there and thank them. Now . . . I can only thank you.'

'Louis,' she responded gently, 'don't you think that I've a lot to be grateful for too, to France?'

Looking at her sharply, remembering that her home, her marriage and her wealth had all been destroyed in France, he nevertheless suddenly knew she meant what she said. For all her tragic losses, he could understand that Nancy now felt grateful to the country that had become hers by virtue of her marriage and the War.

◆　◆　◆

Soon after VE Day, Nancy heard that O'Leary was alive and would soon be coming to Paris, so she took a train to the capital at once.

O'Leary, just out of Dachau, looked terrifyingly thin and ill. He had endured every torture the Gestapo could inflict without actually killing him, and he had survived for two years. But released prisoners of war recover quickly and O'Leary, in Nancy, had a devoted companion and nurse. After three weeks he was well enough to be left on his own, so once again Nancy returned to Marseille.

She stayed there till August of 1945 and, in that time, saw her award against the German government declared at 5,000,000 francs.

After that the city had nothing left to hold her any longer – even Picon seemed happier elsewhere – so she returned to Paris.

The last days of the Second World War, and Victory Night, she spent in the British Officers' Club. There was wild singing, screaming and celebrating. But Nancy found herself thinking of Tardivat's leg, of the dead boys in the forest of Tronçais, of the silly destruction of it all . . . and of Henri; abruptly she felt lonely and miserable. Victory Night – and all the people who *weren't* there.

For three months she worked for O'Leary in the Awards Bureau for repatriated political prisoners. Then O'Leary told her that he had started investigations to find Roger, the Gestapo agent who had caused his arrest.

'Roger?' she exploded.

He nodded.

'Well, you're wasting your time, Pat. He's six feet under.'

'What do you mean?'

'He was tortured by Judex and shot. They buried him outside the château at Mont Mouchet.'

'No,' O'Leary protested, 'you've made a mistake.'

'OK, Pat,' she replied earnestly. 'If you want to look for him, you look for him. But *I* know he's dead. I was there when they were questioning him.' As if, she thought to herself, she could ever forget that smell of burning flesh. 'He's buried at Mont Mouchet, somewhere near St Flour.' And with that their discussion ended.

After a short stay in London Nancy found herself back in Paris. Denis had got himself a job as Passport Control Officer with the Foreign Office and, irrepressible as ever, urged her to do likewise. So they found themselves together again in France.

Life now was good and seemed always to be full of laughter, probably because wherever Denis went there was laughter.

One of their favourite haunts for an evening aperitif was the V-Bar in the Avenue Franklin Roosevelt. The V-Bar was owned by their mutual friend Miracca from Cannes.

On their first visit there Miracca had been talking to Nancy when suddenly his barman had rushed round from behind his bar, flung his arms round Nancy's neck, kissed her resoundingly and asked, 'How are you, Madame Andrée?'

'What the devil you kiss my clients for,' shouted Miracca furiously, '*and* call them by their wrong name?'

'This lady was in the Resistance with me,' the bartender explained.

'Nonsense.'

'It is true. She liberated Vichy!'

'Is this so?' Miracca asked her wonderingly.

She nodded and laughed.

'And this,' he moaned, 'is the first I hear of it. When my barman calls you by the wrong name and kisses you. Why,' he besought her, 'do you all always call one another by the wrong name?'

'Security,' Nancy laughed.

'Security? Security?' he repeated. 'This word I do not understand.'

'And that,' Denis declared, 'even if he is an Italian, proves just how French our Miracca is.'

The three friends toasted one another and for the rest of the evening were scrupulously careful to use only their correct names.

The faithful little terrier, Picon, suddenly became ill. Nancy called in a vet and listened anxiously to his diagnosis.

'Dropsy,' he told her.

'Can you cure it?'

'No.'

'Then what do we do? Does it hurt him?'

'Yes. I am afraid so.'

'Then . . . ?'

'The only kind thing to do is to put him to sleep.'

After the vet had gone Nancy tried hard to convince herself that Picon was not really ill, not really in pain . . . that perhaps he did not have dropsy after all. But Picon himself defeated all her arguments. He was a sick, miserable dog.

Denis called round to see her and she told him what the vet had said.

'Do you think he's right, Ducks?'

She nodded miserably. 'Yes, Den, I'm afraid so . . . He's bringing a sleeping powder and a needle tonight,' she said. 'And later the crematorium people will come to . . . Oh, Den, I don't think I can face that bit. Handing Picon over in a box and paying them and . . .'

'Don't you worry, Gert,' Denis said firmly. 'I'll do that for you.'

Nancy rang Chez Phillippe, a luxury restaurant, told them she was ill and asked them to send her a steak chateaubriand, cooked rare. It arrived on a silver platter, beautifully garnished. The vet came at the same time. Carefully he sprinkled the sleeping powder over the steak. Then, silver platter and all, they presented it to Picon.

Wriggling with delight he gnawed and slupped his way through his last delicious meal. 'I wonder if you're remembering other days while you eat?' Nancy thought. 'The day Henri was taken and you were left all alone in our flat. The months you were with the Ficetoles and there wasn't enough for anyone to eat, not even them.' And later . . . 'I feel like a murderess.'

When he had finished the steak she gave him a bowl of ice cream. Delicately he licked it – and drowsily. It was only half finished when he stopped eating and lay sleepily on the carpet, his head on his paws. Nancy, her eyes full of tears, picked him up and put him on her lap. The short tail thumped devotedly a few seconds – and then Picon was asleep.

She could feel his flanks moving gently as he breathed.

'Dear God,' she said to the vet, 'this is awful. Now!'

He took the dog from her, carefully forced the hypodermic needle into the furry body and pressed the plunger. Seconds later, painlessly, Picon was dead. Quickly the vet placed the body in the animal crematorium's box and left the room.

Tears streamed down Nancy's cheeks as she looked across at Denis. She saw that tears streamed equally freely down his.

'Gert,' he choked, 'I'm sorry – but I can't face the crematorium people either.'

So they rang the Embassy and the Welfare Officer, understanding everything, came to Nancy's hotel, handed the small, heavy box to the man who called for it and paid the final fee.

And when it was done, Nancy wept. She wept as she had when France fell, when she had dreamed about Dédée and Paul, when she had heard, in Vichy, of Henri's death. She wept with every grief she had known, for every moment of joy she had lost, in all of the past six years. For days she was unable to recover from the blow – unable until, finally, she faced up to the truth, and, gulping hard, explained,

'You see, when Picon died, the last of my youth died too.'

Thus she confronted the difficult truth that comes, sooner or later, to every woman who has once been a girl and beautiful, and having confronted it, she could then leave the extraordinary story of her war behind her and turn confidently to face the peace.

22 THE LOOSE ENDS

She stayed in Paris until 1947, seeing a lot of Tardivat and Denis, then she was transferred for some months to the Embassy in Prague.

There she liked the Czechs and grew, through first-hand experience of it, to loathe Communism.

'I'd rather be killed by an atom bomb than accept the life these people have to live,' she growled.

Most vividly of all she remembered the occasion when a British friend decided to hold a dinner party and asked her to bring to it two once-wealthy Czech women. Nancy rang them up and arranged to collect them in an Embassy car.

The first woman, when she called, scurried swiftly across the pavement in her evening gown and leapt into the car. Then they drove to the house of the second woman.

She appeared at her door dressed in the drabbest of day clothes and carrying a large brown paper parcel under her arm. She also got into the car, not looking at all as if she were going to a party.

'I'm sorry,' she apologised, 'but nowadays one dares not appear in the street dressed in a gown. People would inform on you, say you were a capitalist.' So she changed her clothes at her host's home . . . and changed back again just before Nancy drove her back to her own apartment.

'I just couldn't live that way,' Nancy said – and was not sorry, shortly afterwards, to be posted back to Paris.

There, life was normal – a gay life in a city she loved with the people she loved. But nevertheless there was a restlessness in her heart because, after ten years abroad, Nancy Wake, the Australian, wanted to go home.

She resigned from the Foreign Office and wangled a passage to Sydney on a Norwegian vessel, on which she was to serve, of all things, as ship's nurse! Denis laughed till he was helpless at the thought of Nancy nursing a crew of Norwegians. Nevertheless, she did very well and was, before the end of the trip, even elevated to the rank of 'Sister' by the men she managed very successfully not at any time, on the whole voyage, to treat for anything. She merely looked coolly confident whenever they were well and vanished whenever they reported to the surgery with cuts and sprains. Being a good Resistance worker she always had a perfect excuse for these absences, so the doctor happily did her first aid for her and her reputation as a sort of nautical Florence Nightingale was left intact.

In January of 1949 she disembarked at Sydney. She had been a nurse (of a sort) when she left there; she returned a nurse (of a sort). That much had happened in the intervening years, we all now know. There are, however, a few loose ends that might interestingly be knit together.

The most remarkable feature of Nancy Wake's story is the way fate ordained that anyone who once entered her life should always return to it again later on – usually dramatically.

Thus Micheline Digard left England with her in 1939 and returned there from Gibraltar with her in 1943. Garrow, whom she met by chance in Marseille and helped to escape from imprisonment was later to be largely responsible for the fact that, early on the morning of 1 March 1944, she parachuted back into France. O'Leary was introduced to her by Garrow and was to return to the scene in 1945, looking for Roger, Gestapo agent Number 47. And through O'Leary, directly or indirectly, Nancy had been released from jail, fled to Spain and lost her husband. Roger himself, having once nearly brought her circuit to disaster, was to return to another circuit of hers, a year later, and die at its hands.

So it was with all her friends and all her enemies. Mme Sainson was highly decorated after the War by all the Allied governments. She continued to run her late husband's garage and was proud of the fact that, in memory of him, Nice named one of its streets Rue Sainson. Marseille paid the same compliment to the memory of Henri Fiocca.

Monsieur Comboult, the Macaroni Man, stayed in Nice after the War and became editor of the *Nice Matin*. He too received many well-deserved decorations.

Miracca went back to his role as General Catering Manager of the Palm Beach Casino at Cannes. Briefly he had once told Denis and Nancy his own wartime story.

'In 1941 this one,' he'd said, pointing at Rake, 'would come to my house late in the night and knock on my door. "Miracca, let me in," he would say. I would let him in and know nothing! I not know what he did, you understand? Not my business.' His eyes twinkled as he spoke because he had known quite well that Rake was a British agent working against Germany. For him, an Italian subject in Vichy France, the situation had been a curious one.

Eventually he was warned that to stay at Cannes any longer was too dangerous. Although wholly sympathetic to France and the British, he was nevertheless a loyal Italian supporter of his king, and the Resistance were beginning to look at him askance.

So he decided to move north to Paris which, with a certificate of protection from Senator Dreyfus, he did. 'It was very uncomfortable then,' he told Nancy. 'The French were after me and the Germans were after me. But I am still here.'

Françoise Dissard, after Nancy escaped from France, reopened the escape circuit and took command in O'Leary's place. Bossy and argumentative as ever, she ran the circuit till the War ended.

Then the British government offered to reward her with a very lowly decoration. Her eyes glinting behind her steel-rimmed glasses, a cigarette clamped into its bamboo holder between her broken old teeth, she refused it.

'My friend de Gaulle always said that the British were mean,' she declared. 'This would prove it.'

Eventually Britain gave her an OBE which she graciously accepted. 'Now,' she said, 'I can tell de Gaulle that the British aren't as mean as he thought.'

Commander Busch, who introduced Nancy to his Resistance group in Toulon, was deported, with his son, by the Germans and died in a slave camp. Louis Burdet, who told Nancy the story of Hâche and Pioche, ran the Stafford Hotel in St James's, London – an elegant man, full of vitality and humour, one of whose pleasures in life was to entertain Mme Fiocca to lunch.

Denis Rake remained a friend, and occasionally, if he could recall her address, he wrote to her. If he couldn't recall the address, he drew her house on the envelope and hoped that his note would reach her nevertheless.

Reeve Schley and John Alsop, when I wrote to them and asked for their recollections of Nancy, replied not by letter but by Dictaphone. They sat down together, with a bottle of Scotch, and talked into a microphone for almost two hours, then they sent five red plastic 'belts' and made arrangements for me to play them back at the head office of the Dictaphone Company in London. They completed their recording by singing, for Nancy especially, the 'Entente Cordiale International Anthem'! She replied to them, also on a Dictaphone 'belt', and started her message, 'Hullo, you two darlings . . .' Both Americans married and had families – but Schley dropped Law and became a gentleman farmer.

Tardivat married a woman called Susan and had extensive business interests on the Gold Coast – cocoa beans. His daughter was christened Nancy and was Mme Fiocca's godchild. He had some glasses in his Paris flat, each of which held a complete bottle of brandy, and it was his custom, when visitors arrived, to give them a full glass.

When I visited him he told me to call at 6.30. At 7.30 he arrived and found me sitting on the staircase outside his apartment on the third floor. 'Ah,' he greeted me cheerfully, 'I am late, yes?' and laughed. He took me in, presented me with the inevitable tumblerful of brandy and began to talk about Nancy. I poured the brandy into an elegant bowl of flowers (which was sacrilege and killed the flowers, but kept me sober enough to remember what he told me) and later we drove at terrifying speed to one of his favourite restaurants for dinner.

'Here there is no speed limit,' he'd shouted gleefully, 'and the brakes are good! Besides, during the War I drive much faster.'

Bazooka (René Dusacq) returned to America and was not heard of again by his friends except in two respects. They learnt that the captain's bars he wore (when he fired that single perilous shot at the German armoured car near Clermont-Ferrand) were just a hoax. In fact, he was a lieutenant. And both Schley and Alsop at the time, although they didn't know it, had already been promoted; so actually they outranked Bazooka, and not the other way round, and they *could* have abused him for his rashness with impunity.

Fournier returned to the business of hotels. Mme Fournier, after the War, revisited Freydefont, on the once embattled plateau, and there dug up a suitcase full of Nancy's clothes which she had found and buried in June 1944, just before the Maquis had withdrawn at night. (It was at the same time as Denis had discovered

Nancy's short-lived eau-de-cologne.) Mme Fournier sent the suitcase to Nancy in Marseille in 1945. After an interment of almost a year, the clothes were still in perfect condition.

Laurent, whose true name was Antoine Llorca, returned to his occupation as a mechanic. He always loved cars and could miraculously bring to life again even those vehicles which the Maquis seemed to have murdered.

Frank Arnal, whose information, after he was released from imprisonment in Fort St Nicholas, led Nancy to plan Garrow's rescue from Meauzac, became a deputy in the French Parliament, representing the department of Var.

Toni, the woman in the Mad House who discussed with Nancy the craziness of the psychiatrist's blots, married one of the Canadians with whom they both trained and lived in Quebec.

And Nancy herself? Well . . . first of all she was a fiend to interview. Her approach to the subject of her wartime exploits was matter-of-fact to the point of despair.

'What did you do next?' I would ask.

'Oh,' she would answer vaguely, 'blew up a bridge, I think.' And that would be all! Then the inquisition would start – for a chapter that reads merely '*Next she blew up a bridge*' is hardly satisfactory.

'What month?' I would ask.

'Can't remember.'

'What were you wearing?'

'Just slacks and shirt. Must've been summer, otherwise I'd have been cold.' So, a little later, we would arrive at the exact month.

'Anything happen?'

'What do you mean?'

'Any Germans?'

'Oh, yes.'

'Well, what did you do about them?'

'Shot our way out, of course.'

'How'd you get there?'

'By car.'

'Where'd you get the cars?'

'Stole them!' Thus, painfully and modestly, the chapters grew. She had to recall all of six years crammed with action – and yet she had no notes or diaries. She had to explain (and it must have been most tedious to her) every detail of an agent's life so that I could understand it and live it with her.

To her (for the hundreds of hours she made available to me with my silly questions); to Colonel Buckmaster, who introduced me to her; to Tardivat, who saw me in Paris; and Mme Sainson, who saw me in Nice and also introduced me to Monsieur Comboult; and to Louis Burdet in the Stafford Hotel; and Miracca in the Palm Beach Casino; and Schley and Alsop in the States; and Scavino in Marseille and Dissard in Cannes and Bill Sellars in London – to all of these, who pieced together her story for me and brought back for me what they had known of her, go my thanks for this book.

But particularly my thanks must go again to Nancy. Imagine the difficulty of explaining to *you*, my reader, the difference between an 'evader' and an 'escaper' . . . or why 'Time Schedules' had nothing to do with wireless 'codes' . . . or the distinction between a gendarme and a Milicien . . . or how a coming parachutage was evidenced by such a bald and extraordinary statement over the BBC as '*the cow jumped over the moon*' or '*Andrée has a horse in the bathroom*'.

You might think yourself silly about these things. Believe me, I was much sillier. And yet, step by step, Nancy made everything clear. She worked as hard on this book as I have, and all the time, as with everything she did, the task was full of laughter.

'Don't you dare,' she commanded me, 'write me one of those miserable war books full of horror. *My* war was full of laughter and people I loved.'

Now, to conclude her story, here is the balance of her life between 1949 and today[5].

It has already been stated that she was awarded heavy compensation from the German government, but after two small instalments of thirty-five pounds each, the payments stopped and the balance was never received. Seventy pounds . . . in exchange for a fortune, a home and a marriage.

After she returned home to Australia she was persuaded, in 1949, to enter politics, representing the Commonwealth Liberal Party. Her opponent was Doctor Herbert de Vere Evatt, who at that time held his seat by a majority of 23,000 votes. He was the leader of the Australian Labour Party and his was the safest seat in the land.

Knowing nothing of politics, Nancy applied the same rules of common sense and initiative to electioneering as she had to Resistance work. Dr Evatt's majority of 23,000 was shattered. He eventually limped back into Parliament in 1951, with a hollow victory over his inexperienced woman opponent of a mere 127 votes.

After that Nancy returned to Britain. She was unaffected by her high military awards and it was actually about the French Resistance Medal that she spoke most proudly.

'That means,' she said, 'that I was *officially* in the Resistance. That's all . . . that I was there in France. That's what's most important to me.'

She paused to give you that extraordinarily candid and perceptive stare of hers, and then went on – and whilst she talked, one

---

5   1956, the year of original publication.

remembered that, of 560 SOE agents who were sent to Europe, 133 failed to return.

'You see, I was lucky. I was in France at the beginning, when the Germans were right on top. And I was still in France at the end when we saw the Germans on the run. I know how Frenchmen felt all that time. I'd been part of their existence for a long while. I love France – people just don't realise how much she suffered. *Six hundred thousand French people died because of World War II*: two hundred and forty thousand of them in prisons and concentration camps. And yet there were always escape routes and "safe houses" for our men shot down over there and trying to get away. There was always a Resistance movement. Churchill says it shortened the War by six months. I know how they fought. And, because I know, I'm proud of them and love them, just the same as I'm proud of what we did and love my own country.

'I'm glad I was there. I'm glad I did what I did. I hate wars and violence but, if they come, then I don't see why we women should just wave our men a proud goodbye and then knit them balaclavas.

'And if I had to choose now whether I'd have my wealth, or the four years that caused me to lose it, all over again, I know what I'd say. I'd want the four years all over again. You see, in those days we knew what we were fighting and we had a job to do. We did it. I may have lost a lot during the War, especially Henri, but I made a lot of friends and I did what I felt I had to do. And plenty of other people lost more, or did more, than ever I did.'

Those were Nancy Wake's last words to me on the subject of her war. It is only right that they should conclude this book.

APPENDIX I

At the time when Captain Nancy Wake was to have been invested with the George Medal, His Late Majesty King George VI was ill. Consequently, the British Ambassador in Paris made the presentation instead.

The French government awarded her two Croix de Guerre with Palm and a third Croix de Guerre with Star. Also they gave her the Resistance Medal – an honour granted sparingly even to Frenchmen and practically never to foreigners.

The United States government sent her an invitation to attend a ceremony at which she was to be invested with the Medal of Freedom with a Bronze Palm. She had no idea what the merit of this decoration might be until she found that, in order of precedence, she was to follow immediately after the awards made to eight generals. As with the French Resistance Medal, she was one of the very few foreigners to hold this decoration.

Here below, for those who like their facts cloaked in the vaguest officialese, are Nancy Wake's American and British citations. The French give no citations but allow three Croix de Guerre and the Resistance Medal to speak for themselves.

Ensign Nancy Grace Augusta Wake, FANY
George Medal
Citation

This officer was parachuted into France on March 1st, 1944, as assistant to an organiser who was taking over the direction of an important circuit in Central France. The day after their arrival she and her chief found themselves stranded and without directions, through the arrest of their contact, but ultimately reached their rendezvous by their own initiative.

Ensign Wake worked for several months helping to train and instruct Maquis groups. She took part in several engagements with the enemy, and showed the utmost bravery under fire. During a German attack, due to the arrival by parachute of two American officers to help in the Maquis, Ensign Wake personally took command of a section of ten men whose leader was demoralised. She led them to within point-blank range of the enemy, directed their fire, rescued the two American officers and withdrew in good order. She showed exceptional courage and coolness in the face of enemy fire.

When the Maquis group with which she was working was broken up by large-scale German attacks, and W/T contact was lost, Ensign Wake went alone to find a wireless operator through whom she could contact London. She covered some 200 kms on foot, and by remarkable steadfastness and perseverance succeeded in getting a message through to London, giving the particulars of a ground where a new W/T plan and further stores could be dropped. It was largely due to these efforts that the circuit was able to start work again.

Ensign Wake's organising ability, endurance, courage and complete disregard for her own safety earned her the respect and admiration of all with whom she came in contact. The Maquis troop, most of them rough and difficult to handle, accepted orders from her, and treated her as one of their own male officers. Ensign Wake contributed in a large degree to the success of the groups with which she worked, and it is strongly recommended that she be awarded the George Medal.

Citation for the Medal of Freedom
With Bronze Palm

Ensign Nancy Wake, British National, FANY, for exceptionally meritorious achievement which aided the United States in the prosecution of the war against the enemy in Continental Europe, from March 1944 to October 1944. After having been parachuted into the Allier department of France for the purpose of coordinating Resistance activities, she immediately assumed her duties as second-in-command to the organiser of the circuit. Despite numerous difficulties and personal danger she, through her remarkable courage, initiative and coolness succeeded in accomplishing her objective. Her daring conduct in the course of an enemy engagement safeguarded the lives of two American officers under her command. Her inspiring leadership, bravery and exemplary devotion to duty contributed materially to the success of the war effort and merit the praise and recognition of the United States.

GO 3. Hq USFET, 9 January 1947

APPENDIX 2

Complement of Maquis Groups for which Nancy Wake was Chef du Parachutage

Group	Number of men in Group
Commander Fabre	300
Corps France. Issoire	150
ALLIER	
Chazemais	440
Cérilly	440
St Plaisir	450
Montmarault	800
Moulins (Cdt. Barbaroux)	360
Lapalisse	850
Montluçon	650
Ambert (MUR)	700
Ambert (FTPF)	800
Pontgibaud	400
St Gervais	300

Resin	300
Aigueperse	300
Sauxillanges	250
Ambert	600
Thiers	150

ABOUT THE AUTHOR

Russell Braddon was born in Sydney in 1921. In addition to *The Naked Island*, his bestselling memoir of four years spent as a prisoner of war during the Second World War, he also wrote a number of biographies, novels, histories and TV scripts. He lived in Britain from 1949 until 1993, and died in New South Wales in 1995.